no one was killed

John Schultz, whose many works include *The Tongues of Men, No One Was Killed, The Chicago Conspiracy Trial,* and *Writing From Start to Finish,* was for many years chair of the Fiction Writing Department at Columbia College in Chicago. Originator of the Story Workshop method of teaching writing, Mr. Schultz is the editor of *F Magazine* and a number of anthologies of writing, including *The Best of Hair Trigger.*

no one was killed
the democratic national convention august 1968

JOHN SCHULTZ

With a new foreword by Todd Gitlin
and a new afterword by the author

The University of Chicago Press   *Chicago & London*

For Tim and Susu

The University of Chicago Press, Chicago, 60637
Copyright © 1969 by John Schultz
Foreword copyright © 2009 by The University of Chicago
Afterword copyright © 2009 by John Schultz
All rights reserved
Originally published in 1969 by Big Table Publishing
University of Chicago Press edition 2009

Portions of chapter 1 were originally published in a different version in *Evergreen Review* vol. 12, no. 60. Copyright © 1968 by Evergreen Review, Inc.

Printed in the United States of America

18 17 16 15 14 13 12 11 10 09   1 2 3 4 5

ISBN-13: 978-0-226-74078-2 (paper)
ISBN-10: 0-226-74078-1 (paper)

Library of Congress Cataloging-in-Publication Data

Schultz, John, 1932–
    No one was killed : the Democratic National Convention, August 1968 / John Schultz ; with a new foreword by Todd Gitlin and a new afterword by the author.
        p.   cm.
    Originally published: Chicago : Big Table Pub. Co., 1969.
    ISBN-13: 978-0-226-74078-2 (pbk. : alk. paper)
    ISBN-10: 0-226-74078-1 (pbk. : alk. paper)   1. Chicago (Ill.)—History—20th century.   2. Chicago (Ill.)—Social conditions—20th century.   3. Democratic National Convention (1968 : Chicago, Ill.)   4. Riots—Illinois—Chicago—History—20th century.   5. Radicals—Illinois—Chicago—History—20th century.   6. Vietnam War, 1961–1975—Protest movements—Illinois—Chicago.   7. Democratic Party (U.S.)—History—20th century.   8. United States—Politics and government—1963–1969.   9. United States—Social conditions—1960–1980.   I. Title.
    F548.52.S3 2009
    977.3′11043—dc22   2008040821

contents

foreword

No One Was Killed is high on my short list of true, lasting, inspired evocations of those whacked-out days when the country was fighting a phantasmagorical war (with real corpses), and police under orders were beating up demonstrators who looked at them funny, and reality went squishy under the feet, and millions of non-stupid people weren't sure whether what they would find the day after tomorrow was revolution or fascism.

First-rate journalism, "news that stays news" (Ezra Pound's description of literature), is not only alert to living details but honors the texture of revelatory moments and never forgets what John Schultz calls "the terrible dignity of human motive and decision." It builds up a scene with small strokes but is unafraid to pull back for the bigger picture. Within this rare company are the still fewer books that place the writer amid the action—Norman Mailer in *The Armies of the Night,* George Orwell in *Homage to Catalonia. No One Was Killed* belongs in this select company. All of them bear the marks—the scars—of a writer striving to be honest about what he is doing in unaccustomed settings witnessing strange and remarkable things. None of them pretends to be in every part of the forest at once, omniscient and detached. None mistakes a surface for a depth or thinks that a depth can dispense with surfaces. Each marvels at the human capacity for self-deception. Each is self-aware and aware of the writer's limits as well. Each knows in his bones that in the world as it is, "everyone," as Jean Renoir's character says in *The Rules of the Game*, "has his reasons." Renoir said that this was an "awful thing," and the journalism that lasts—and deserves to last—knows it too.

Schultz promises "documentation and meditation" on the convulsive events of August 1968 in Chicago. Dwell on these demanding words for a moment, for they promise no small or routine achievement. A book of this sort must be true to fact—fact as best the reporter can know at the time—and must be true, at the same time, to the writer's inner life, an inner life that exists in some rich relation to the great sea of other inner lives at the time. In the case of Chicago that August, a book must relay something huge, the full depth and intensity of the psychic storms that enveloped any reasonable thoughtful and sentient person in the year of our ordeal 1968.

It would be monumentally pretentious to purport to tell "the whole story" of what happened in Chicago forty years ago. Leave such claims to the shallows of "in depth" journalism and textbooks. What Schultz does claim to do—and accomplishes beautifully—is to narrate the world as he finds it on the streets. Schultz is not the kind of gonzo journalist who revels in making things up for the sheer hell of it. Relentlessly, sometimes raggedly, sometimes with long pans and sometimes with zooms and montage, he reports what you might call a gonzo reality—a lived, kaleidoscopic experience of extremity, wildness, audacity, longing, and myopia.

Here, for example, a question he poses early on: "What kind of escalation, what fear, what satisfaction, could we expect tonight?" This is exactly right—fear and satisfaction belong in the same sentence. They locked arms on the streets and in the parks of Chicago that week, perhaps in affinity with the rush of armed combat. "There was nothing compelling about the Convention," Schultz writes at another point. "All reality was out in the streets, anger on all sides, *exhilarating* anger." He observes the "magnetic attraction of provocation between cops and Yippies and demonstrators." He is dead right to dwell on the exhilarating and reinforcing quality of anger—anger on all sides, from the screaming rage of napalm on Vietnamese villages to the how-dare-they rage of Mayor Daley and the police under his command to the fuck-it-all giddy rage of demonstrators in the streets—for this is the bedrock, emotional truth of that fiery, polarized time.

Schultz pays attention. He observes how the cops' "nonchalance . . . could change on the instant into white-faced fury." (Note: not the cliché "red-faced" but "white-faced.") He adds that "often the cops were provoked by [the demonstrators'] presence of mind, and other times they were most provoked by helplessness." How many descriptions of police clubbing have been written, but how few have exercised such subtlety. Schultz notes that the dullness of the Platform Committee hearings revealed the iron grip in which Mayor Daley held the convention. He notes Julian Bond's "tie pulled neatly loose." He hears the Viet Cong-flag-carrying fourteen-year-old boy from an Italian American "greaser" neighborhood say, "I'll probably never get to be 21." He punctures the bland pieties of the official Walker Report, which coined the phrase "police riot" but missed the method in the police provocations, which were far too orderly to be designated a "riot."

Many a compilation video has showed the kids on the statue of Civil War General Logan in Grant Park, some even showing the cop clubbing one boy, but leave it to Schultz to report this: "When the cops had first ordered the boy to get off the statue, he had been reluctant to come down because he was terrified of the way the cops were treating people around the foot of the statue." Schultz finds out that the kid, seventeen, gets busted for felony aggravated assault, and that he lost the nerve to his thumb and ended up with a metal plate in his arm.

Schultz rightly reports with devastating accuracy how greatly the street kids, doing their own things, outdistanced —in fact, rebelled against—the demonstrations' official leaders; how foolish was the assumption that the rebels were organized like an army. The kids' actions were "mythological ones, school-book heroics, theatrics, such as carrying a flag to turn a retreat into confrontation or riding an equestrian statue shouting protest slogans." Dead right to grasp the theatrical element, and not least the weird glow of the cameras—not only "hungry for news" but "helping the news to happen." Schultz knows "it is only because the media are incapable of thinking or perceiving outside of celebrity consciousness" that they couldn't figure out what was going on. He reports editors disbelieving their own reporters, censoring them, mangling their words.

Wandering between the front lines of a culture coming apart, tracing the force fields of energy, delusion, and wild hope that radiated from park to park, from confrontation to confrontation, across Chicago, Schultz remarks the peculiar way in which time collapsed as the present and the next apprehension kept erasing the recent past: "Throughout Convention Week you could come upon the scene of an action a few minutes after the action ended and no one would be saying anything about it, as if everyone hovered moment to

moment without immediate memory, waiting for the next
thing to happen, with eerie readiness in time."

Schultz is deft with portraiture: the famous (Jean Genet
"with those eyes that could see three inches into stone") and
unfamous (hippies with "ruined faces, about to disappear
behind the everlasting soft smile of acid"); group portraiture
too, as with the demonstrators who swarm out of Hierony-
mus Bosch against cops who step "off the pages of science
fiction comic books, invaders from an insect planet." When
he reports that his five-year-old son is worried that the cops
are going to beat his hippie teacher and "beat the little children too," he rams us back into what it felt like when "the
war came home," and succeeds in skirting the temptation
of mawkishness. He also has the knack of aphoristic gen-
eralization: the curious middle-aged men who show up in
the park are "World War II veteran[s], who had made it
economically in some way," come to converse with "kids
who were all born after that War was over. . . . The World
War II veterans had been intellectually disabled by the
idea that they had fought an honorable war. . . . Their
minds were not capable of coping with the fact that the
cops *were* unconscionable bullies, and that the kids *did* provoke them." There is a whole social diagnosis crammed into
these lines.

Schultz is frequently brilliant on the mentality of the
radicals, liberals, and freaks in that moment—the way in
which, for example, "some New Leftists, who had just
proven themselves in the past few days to be strong by the
impact of their actions, still felt themselves to be so weak
that they could only conceive that [Eugene McCarthy, in
deigning to speak in Grant Park] had crossed the line to put
them in his pocket." How they, we, for several years had
found "much comfort and nurture . . . in living before the
mirror of weakness and alienation." Schultz has the wit to

perceive that "New Left thought, which had been the most promising thought in this country in the past several years, had undergone a sea-change, a change without changing, becoming in some aspects a static fantasy, while the country itself was on the move." "The mind of the revolt," he knows, "is always in danger of succumbing to the burning comfort of being smothered by its 'authentic' clichés." And at the same time, in the respectable middle-class part of the forest, among "the eternally surprised," this: "In some places on this earth, people stand in line to buy things. In the United States, people stand in line to be arrested."

The world having come unstuck, Schultz is confident that, still, something constructive is aborning. Here and there he plunges into blade-running paranoia, or interjects a quirky anthropology, a whiff of prehistoric fantasy imposed upon twentieth-century apocalypse. Some hazy intimations of hallucinatory politics waft through his account like tear gas. Evocation has this peril—echoing the confusions of the time. But for the most part Schultz is content, and courageous, to let questions dangle unanswered when the answers of the moment could only be glib. An intelligent, observant, and deeply sensitive man wrestles with immensities and, time after time, pins them.

I reread the book—this is my third or fourth time straight through—with no little awe, jolted by one shock after another of recognition, appreciation, and memory.

Todd Gitlin

Todd Gitlin, the author of many books including *The Whole World Is Watching, The Sixties: Years of Hope, Days of Rage,* and *Letters to a Young Activist,* is professor of journalism and sociology and chair of the PhD Program in Communications at Columbia University.

introduction to confrontation

Blocked

Past fright, past exhilaration, past terror, past awe, past exhaustion, everything that happened that week in Chicago had a rightness about it. It came and went so fast and hard that we who shared and witnessed may lose that sense of it.

Every night when I went to sleep, I saw lines and lines of sky blue helmets and sky blue shirts, and, later in the week, Guardsmen in fatigue uniforms with gas masks on and M-1s at the ready. They were just standing there in my head, and they turned slowly and looked at me, facing me as I went to sleep. They were not clubbing, not charging, not tear-gassing, not wildly beating anyone, not jerking the wounded out of hospitals and shoving them into paddy wagons, not breaking into private homes and dragging kids into the street for beating. They were just standing there, blocking the startling and vivid rush of imagery that begins when the waking mind lets go and I am not yet fully asleep. They were

1

standing in a sourceless surreal light at night under trees
or along streets. They were not facing demonstrators or
Yippies, these cops and soldiers in my mind. They were
facing me. If there was a stir in their lines, it was not a
violent stir, it was the stir of underwater slow motion
or of a beast sleeping. They were not threatening me in
any overt way, they were not preventing me from going
to sleep. They were not the obsessive squirrel-cage rush
of cards or highway signs after a long night of poker or
a hard day's driving, or the elements of any obsessive
task. They simply stood there and blocked my dreams.

It is guilty, this power that lets these cops and soldiers
be there in the mind and in the parks and streets, blocking dreams, and it must die. It is guilty—and slouching
heavy with its guilt—of blocking off and attacking to
drive away that which will not be driven away, of blocking access, of blocking movement and anticipation in
soul and time and history, in the relations of people.

More than half of the demonstrators and Yippies came
from Chicago and nearby areas, and the rest from all
points in the country. The main stimulus for their coming, at source, was that they felt the War in Vietnam to
be nationally self-destructive, in every sense. They came
to call the Democratic Party to account for its betrayal
of the great popular mandate given it for peace and
domestic reconstruction in 1964. They came to groove
on anything that might happen, or that they could make
happen, festively, politically, theatrically, in a celebra-
tory wake of New Life in opposition to the funeral of
the Democratic National Convention. They came here
to unify themselves in the discovery of the common

enemy and the common cause. They came here at the call of the ancient excitement to go on the hunt for the beast. They were blocked because the Democratic Party was in a double bind, between the Vietnam War that it wishes would go away and the domestic economic and social problems that it also wishes would go away, and it knows its commitment to the Vietnam War prevents it from dealing with the massive domestic problems that insist on getting still worse the longer the War continues. The protest in Chicago was blocked by the rage of men who could not accept being held responsible for this bind. It was blocked by the decision of Mayor Richard J. Daley, presumably in consultation with the Democratic National Committee and its chairman John Bailey and the Secret Service. The Chicago cops obeyed their orders, night after night. The protest was blocked not only because it represented a mythic nightmare for those who control large material intentions and directions of this country, but because they know the protest-revolt to be a real and future threat to them. The Democrats might have chosen to handle the protest in different ways, but the protestors must finally be given the honor of being conceived as a true and growing threat by many who hold political power. In the way that history works so grossly and yet so subtly, the Vietnam War may prove to be one of the best things that ever happened to this country.

The violence by the Conrad Hilton Hotel—the Michigan and Balbo massacre—on Wednesday evening August 28, 1968, that got such a spectacular play on TV, occurred because a series of events during the afternoon (that was up for grabs from moment to moment with no one knowing what would or could happen next), resulted in a non-violent march that was blocked but

wouldn't go away. If blocking off does not cause people
and intentions to go away, then the next response is
attack. If attack does not do the job, then the next response is more attack, pitching higher each time, until
the cops were wrecked by their own rage.

The Yippies were blocked from getting a permit to
sleep in Lincoln Park, but they didn't go away, and so
they were attacked, again and again, night after night,
in Lincoln Park and in the streets of Old Town and other
nearby areas.* The police attack in Lincoln Park for

* Initially, the Youth International Party, the Yippies,
sought a permit from the City to use the park facilities day
and night in Grant Park, then changed their request to Lincoln Park, in wonderful obedience to the wisdom in which
all people and events of Convention Week, in the words of
the prayer, lived and moved and had their being. They were
hassled for months by the City, as was the National Mobilization to End the War in Vietnam, and finally, at the last
minute in the week before Convention Week, the City refused to give the permits, and so the aggrieved parties went
to court. On August 22, Thursday of the week prior to Convention Week, Judge William Lynch, former law partner of
Mayor Daley, gave the decision in Federal District Court
that withheld permits for marches and for sleeping in the
parks after 11 PM curfew, denying the suit of the National
Mobilization to End the War in Vietnam in the joint hearing in which the Yippies were denied too. This "teasing" by
the City aroused almost suicidal, kamikaze rage in some of
the kids. They felt, correctly, that the City deliberately withheld the permit decision until the last minute to lessen the
numbers of demonstrators coming to Chicago. They also felt
that the City deliberately threatened a bloodbath in the
streets of Chicago to put fear into all potential travelers who
might want to come to Chicago to demonstrate. So be it. This
gambit of the City's was so successful, so few people turned
up from out-of-town, that the City of Chicago, on that crucial
Sunday night August 25, the day before the Convention
opened, must have felt that one big burst of head-cracking
would clear the situation for good and all. Oh, the temptation of it.

four nights—Sunday through Wednesday—was at or near the level of the violence in front of the Hilton Hotel during the 17 minutes on Wednesday evening, at times worse.

The National Mobilization to End the War in Vietnam (hereafter called the Mobe) was blocked by the City and the Federal Court from getting a permit to march to the International Amphitheater, where the Democratic Party would hold its Convention; but the marchers didn't go away, so they were attacked, again and again. Inside the Convention, the McCarthy and other peace people were blocked—defeated by the regulars who were appointed or caucus-elected and never had to stand for primary election—on the peace plank issue, despite the will of the popular vote in the great primary battles in the months prior to the Convention; and then the peace people were harassed by Daley-control and the security apparatus in the Amphitheatre: but they would not keep quiet and would not go away, so they were attacked. The McCarthy kids, blocked from their main intention of ending the Vietnam War, would not go away because they went over to the demonstrators' side, and they were attacked. Senator Eugene McCarthy himself, that strange man, would not go away, though blocked from greater effect (perhaps all too willingly) by New Jersey Governor Richard Hughes and the decisions of the Credentials Committee of which Hughes was Chairman. McCarthy workers were also blocked by the finagling of timing on the main Convention vote on the minority report of the Rules Committee (in which the unit-rule, whereby a majority vote commits all of the delegation's votes, was abolished, down to the precinct level; thus ended a clever form of control by established party figures, but it was not abolished in time to affect crucial votes on credentials challenges before the Convention). That strange man was further blocked from greater effect by accepting (perhaps knowingly) cowardly advice to drop the credentials challenges of the Pennsylvania and New York delegations—states in which McCarthy won clear popular preference in the primaries, but the state party-machine figures would not let the delegations be constituted to reflect the popular will. McCarthy would not go away. On Thursday afternoon, August 29, he crossed the lines of troops and cops to speak uneasily to the demonstrators in Grant Park, legitimizing them for his thousands of followers; and within a few hours, his headquarters in the Hilton was attacked by Chicago police. There is the wisdom of God in the stupidity of tyrants.

I Am Here in Lincoln Park/Wednesday Midnight

Some minutes after Wednesday midnight, I drove my car from the Conrad Hilton Hotel south of the Loop north to Lincoln Park, a few miles away, and was told that there was no one in the Park because a rumor was out that a cop had been killed downtown, beaten to death by Yippies, and next to party disloyalty, the major crime all over the world is killing a cop. They might as well have said that a Yippie had killed a cop by stuffing his horrible, filthy long hair down a cop's throat, or sucked the blood, vampire-style, from a cop's body. The image that pops into the minds of all those who have sharp sentimentality about method, heroism and death in their professions, which feeds rocket-fire feeling into their rage, is that of the widow sitting on the edge of the sofa by the coffee-table weeping, while the slain officer's commander stands there holding his cap a touch awkwardly. But the right of revenge that the human soul feels is not the preserve of the police alone.

How did I get here, Wednesday midnight, in the numb but exhilarated world of a turning point in history (whether turning back, forward, or to the side is a speculative matter)—numb as a strong high when all senses are awake, clear, certain, with icy warm sexiness sliding back and forth in the soul? I had been inside the Convention proceedings at the Hilton and the Amphitheatre, but mainly on the streets and in the parks day and night since Tuesday a week ago. I had been hit on the head once, gassed several times, chased by cops, threatened, and in general made once again aware of the fragility of all individual and specie life. Yes, I chose to be here, I actively sought to be one of the first to leave my footprints on the sands of the new continent swelling up between the Veils of Death and Life, of Time Past and Time to Come, in between which all living things move, now and forever. Years ago, in Time to Come, in 1960 when I returned from a long stay in Mexico where my mind is always visited by images of Life That Can Be— I am now approaching in my car the corner of LaSalle, Clark and Eugenie Streets at the southwest end of Lincoln Park—I was lying in bed in a house on Eugenie, one block from this intersection, and I was suddenly, under the stimulation of reading some work of C. Wright Mills', seized with a vision of a developing totalitarianism in this country and, along with it, a developing revolution over the next nine years. I don't know why but my vision set 1969, or thereabouts, as a sort of dénouement for this development in which the revolution lost, but I sided with it: a revolution that I felt to be different in that it could be at once militant and tolerant of diversity and even find its pulse in all such paradox. But

perhaps it needn't lose. Naturally, I leaped out of bed
to start a magazine to evangelize this vision, thinking
myself the sole agent. What I had come up with, in fact,
was the basic feeling of the New Left, growing among
a few people about my age at that time who could not
tolerate the belabored robotics and the intellectual cowardice of the Communist Party, as we knew it. We needed
to give substance and spirit to the inevitable. New ideas,
it seems, occur at about the same time to different people, unknown to each other: human responses to the uni-
versal situation. On the other side of the Veil of Death,
in 1960, Students for a Democratic Society (SDS) was
not yet formed, not quite yet, and civil rights workers
in the South were just beginning to insist on their right
to eat hamburgers in any old restaurant. I was paying
little attention to John F. Kennedy. The Cuban Revolution had been won a little over a year ago, and all of
its paradoxes—its mythic departures from other revolutions, its existential making it up as it went along—gave
us exuberant attitudes about ourselves. I discovered
Studies on the Left (now defunct) in Madison, Wisconsin, and when I read it I saw that it was doing pretty
much what I'd wanted to do, though there was no literature or art in it. But there it was, the seminal magazine
of the New Left, and the issues were very good, and I
wrote the editors and told them so, and sent them the
one piece that I'd collected for my magazine—an interview with the now exiled black leader Robert F. Wil-
liams, which they published, and not without its effect
and its indication of the direction of the black movements. My own magazine was re-born years later as f^1.

I am here, one block away from the other side of the
Veil of Death because the vision never left me, though
its content grew and its territory widened. I am here

because I suspect a fruition, swan song, end in beginnings. I am here because I have a notion about story: that it is an event that happens and ends of itself, being the way a people keep themselves clear in the common soul and moving—where they come from, who they are, and where they are going. I am here because I have found and am following the movement of a story. I am here, Wednesday midnight, as I've been here every midnight for a week because I believe that I am in a story that no one else has seen. I am here because I asked Fred Jordan of Grove Press to get me credentials so I could do an article for *Evergreen Review* on a story I only sensed, as if it were already the memory of a dream that haunts and compels by its very incompleteness. I am here not only because I live in Chicago but I live in Lincoln Park, the scene of the crime itself. (Lincoln Park is an area of the City, as well as a park.) I am here because the Democratic Convention was not moved to Miami, thanks to Mayor Daley's throttlehold on the Party's decision-making areas. I am here, Wednesday midnight, because "the clearing of the Park"—namely, the cop attack on the kids in the Park—begins around midnight. I am angry, very angry, and I am stubborn about this story, as if I feel that history will be warped forever if I don't see all that I can see.

But the Park was empty. Lincoln Park had not been empty, except when the cops forced it to be empty, for three nights. Its emptiness on Wednesday midnight was a way of saying that the job was done—the job that began Sunday and carried with increasing violence through Monday and Tuesday. Vice President Hubert H. Humphrey had just been nominated for the Presidency at the Amphitheater, the peace plank had been defeated earlier, and Humphrey had just kissed jubi-

lantly the TV screen on which loomed the image of his
wife Muriel, while tear-gas sniffed around his walls. Kids
were massed on the corners of LaSalle, Clark, and Eugenie Streets, at the south end of the Park, where broken
glass riddled the large intersection as if someone had
dumped a truckload of cracked ice—the result of the
kids' stoning of a couple of cop cars. There were clusters
of kids on every corner near Lincoln Park.

I had to check to make sure the Park was empty so
I parked my car near Oxford's Pub and went into the
Park alone, and I felt more alone the deeper I went
under the trees in the dark. No bonfires tonight, no
drums, no caucuses, no masses of Yippies, students, and
other people milling back and forth in fear and fascination, readying for confrontation with the cops. I reached
the embankment of Stockton Drive inside the Park just
as banks of floodlights on Fire Department light trucks
sent their white blaze springing through the trees. A few
demonstrators hiding nearby quickly danced into cars
and onto cycles parked on Stockton Drive, and drove
away, as the skirmish line of Guardsmen and cops began
to sweep the Park. This was the first time the Guard was
used to help clear Lincoln Park, and whether that was
good or bad, no one could tell. A flare arched over the
trees, lighting a wide area, no people in it. I waited and
then walked slowly out of the Park about a hundred
yards ahead of the Guard skirmish line. I enjoyed, ab-
stractly, the image of all those armed men and equipment driving one man out of the Park. I walked slowly
because if I ran I knew I stood a chance of being beaten
or shot at. I glanced as coolly as possible over my shoulder at the skirmish line. I was dressed very straight, suit
and tie, though that did not generally make much difference to the cops. I walked slowly also because by

now it was important to let them know and to let myself
know that their invasion was not only being repulsed
in the mind but other powers were rising everywhere
against it, too. A second flare spit up into the sky,
bloomed, and fell dreamily, its light frosting grass and
trees. A helicopter beating around overhead fingered its
searchlight through the trees up and down the length of
the Park. The searchlight stopped on me, and I stared,
still walking, up into its eye, into a glaring shimmer that
became a whine in the eye. A third flare went up into
the night sky, and I watched it, and I watched it, and I
saw that it was falling directly toward me, that frosted
light blooming and quivering all around me. They
wanted to make sure if I was alone or part of a group,
or they were pissed-off at my slow pace. My throat
caught with the jump of a thrill, part fear, part expectancy. Then the flare, in a kind of slow motion, splashed
out in the grass a few yards behind me.

I reached the sidewalk at the edge of the Park along
Clark Street. Technically, I was now outside curfew
territory. But that never stopped the cops. They made
up law as they went along. I walked north on the sidewalk trying to keep the same speed, as the skirmish-line
of Guardsmen also turned north, pushing closer and
closer. I crossed Clark Street and stood on the small
grassy triangle, with flower beds, where Clark, Wells,
and Lincoln come together. I stood there with three
Chicago newsmen watching the lines of troops and cops
sweep the empty Park. The helicopter yammered overhead and jabbed its searchlight through the trees and
the streets and stopped the light briefly on us. One of
the Chicago newsmen said, "This whole thing has moved
me so far Left I can see the back of my head. Do you
realize I started out Sunday as an Adlai Stevenson Dem-

ocrat?" Everyone laughed. Then we felt quiet and quick
—meditative—before the sight of the lines and lines of
Guardsmen moving at a slow, mechanical pace, with no
distinction of individual movement or individual energy,
followed by lines of cops, then trucks with banks and
batteries of floodlights, and the helicopter overhead, all
massively sweeping an empty park. There could be gas,
there could be clubbing, there could be worse. There
were a few arrests in the parking lot in the Park down at
LaSalle Street, but otherwise the Park was empty for
the first time in several nights.

Just south of the grassy triangle, kids were clustered
around the front of the Lincoln Hotel under the marquée
and by the drugstore at the corner. A lone patrol car
came gliding down Clark Street, with one window
broken, and I saw the cop in the car look at the cluster
of kids and reach for his radio. By now, demonstrators
and other enforced participants such as Lincoln Park
citizens were hip to many of the ways that the cops
worked, and we knew that the cop was calling for more
cars to attack the kids. He cruised away innocently down
Clark Street. I said that somebody should tell those kids
to get out fast, and one reporter jogged across the intersection and told the kids, who slipped away, leaving
nothing but bare sidewalk and plateglass inside which
the night light burned among the drugstore racks. Then,
sure enough, around the corner from the rear came three
patrol cars, an attack unit, coasting silently. The cops,
with shotguns, stared at the empty corner and kept
staring until they knew the corner was empty both ways,
then looked up and down the street, looked at us, and
we looked quite blandly back at them. They cruised
away. The reporters in the grassy triangle chuckled again
that night. The Pig had been fooled; and the courts

had been robbed of an incident where there would have been four eyewitnesses.

But the cops were not going to stop their attack because the Park was empty. The kids in the streets would not go away and so the cops had been escalating their attack every night. What kind of escalation, what fear, what satisfaction, could we expect tonight? I crossed from the grassy triangle to the sidewalk in front of Oxford's Pub and The Theater—an aid station and Movement center for the kids—both now demolished to make way for a highrise. In front of Oxford's Pub my fellow Lincoln Park residents—among them the composer William Russo and theater director Paul Sills and several ministers—were furiously talking about whether they should go as observers in police cars. The local Police Commander of the 18th District had offered this as a means of deflecting the intense anger flying at him from the citizenry. He was a cool, impenetrable, professional man, lean and smart. When told by citizens of the incredible police violence, he wore a fine concern and asked for names and badge numbers. That, of course, is the first thing a person being clubbed looks for, the name and badge number of the cop clubbing him. If no one could give the Commander names and badge numbers or car numbers, he intimated that the protesting citizenry must have been dreaming. Neighborhood leaders—ministers, lawyers, artists, appointed largely by their intense concern about the police invasion—found themselves stammering in the face of his absolute pretense, as if meeting an impossibility only met before in dreams. Hadn't masses of people, kids and general citizens, the whole neighborhood, been clubbed, gassed, terrorized? The Commander asked for proof. Now he offered to let citizens ride in police cars and police buses

and see for themselves. "Our presence might at least restrain the police in a particular car," one fellow said. I
was asked by a friend, who was the main organizer of
this citizens' attempt to mitigate the police violence, to
go with him as an observer. I reacted with a fury, not
at him but at the idea of it, saying that if he went he
would certainly see nothing, the police would make sure
he saw nothing, and he would have to report that he saw
nothing, and thereby he would end up playing the Pig's
game. I said that even to go and talk to the Pig, to try
to prove to him what you know happened and what he
knows happened, is playing right into the Pig's game:
garbage-making. (Pig at this point meant all the representatives of a general oppression, from the cop on the
corner to Lyndon Johnson in the White House: and I
saw snouts and jowls all the way from Chicago, to
Prague, to Moscow, and around the world and back
again.) I told my friend that the media had capitulated
to the police yesterday and stayed behind the police lines
and saw nothing. Others also reacted furiously to the
suggestion of being an observer. One minister said he
was ready to pick up a rock and throw it at the cops. It
was as if our anger, so hard and true-feeling, was pre-
cious, a flagrant gift to be used where it could see its
right result, anger with the strength to bide its time, not
to be spilled on the ground. Two of the citizens went as
observers in police vehicles that night. They saw nothing.

But a few minutes after the talk, I was driving alone
down Clark Street back to the Hilton, following one of
those sinister CTA buses, with its lights out, huge and
packed with cops. A couple of newsmen were still standing on the grassy triangle. A rock, thrown from the corner
of Clark and Wisconsin, banged against the side of the
police bus. "Pig," someone yelled. There were no head-

lights on the bus, no interior lights, but all the cops looked toward the corner and the bus slowed to scare whoever threw the rock. I followed the bus two more blocks to the corner of LaSalle and Clark, where a mass of kids, residents and tourists were congregated, milling and looking around, taunting cop cars and taunting the Guardsmen who stood in lines on the edge of the Park with their rifles. They looked at the crowd. The kids had every right to be on that sidewalk, just like the kids a few minutes before in front of the Lincoln Hotel, but no one thought anymore in terms of civil rights and liberties. We thought in terms of citizens' protection and a citizens' underground, and the makings of it were showing fast in the Lincoln Park area.

The cops came out of that bus as if they were shot from a gun, howling and running as hard as they could after screaming kids who were running as hard as they could to get away. The Guardsmen simply stood on the edge of the Park across the street and watched. The cops were beating everyone in reach with their clubs, jamming them up against the wall of the building, against the iron fence of the Georgian Court, ramming them in the groin, and if a kid were caught in a no-exit situation between cars he was beaten senseless. Kids were running and screaming to get out, get away, and cops were swinging in haymakers with the clubs and catching people flat on the sides of their heads. One kid, caught scrambling between two cars on the east side of the street, screamed, as the cop beat him, "I'm *going*, sir, I'm *going!*" As he spun out of the trap and fled, the cop swung wide to catch him hard on the side of the head and hurry him. A group of medics—possibly from the Medical Committee for Human Rights—was hit, and hit, and hit, as they ran hard, blood all over their faces, their white coats billowing. They were screaming, "We're *leaving*, sir, we're *leaving!*" There were several hundred kids on this intersection. The cops were telling them to get out of town, though most of them came from Chicago.

Rights in Conflict, or as commonly known, The Walker Report, gives the impression that after the Guard sweep of the Park at 1 AM Thursday morning, everything was quiet in Lincoln Park. In fact, the attack was more intense and more concentrated than the action downtown, except for the 17 minute battle at Balbo Drive and Michigan Avenue in front of the Hilton. The Walker Report is intent on terming the events during Convention Week in the streets and in the parks a "police riot." The word "riot" connotes a lack of superior responsibility, while the violence in the midst of which this parenthesis occurs, was quite apparently concerted and ordered. To term the street and park events a "police riot" is to shirk what happened and the implications of it—a way in which one establishment area, which believes the general system to be potentially more "just" and workable, serves definitive warning on a political area, namely the City Administration and the likes of it across the country, without directly indicting it. The Chicago police were acting under orders, and they said it outright again and again. It is ridiculous to think of conspiracy in terms of superior authorization for every clubbing and every action. What was ordered by the City—and that means Mayor Daley, as the cops themselves would tell you if you asked them during Convention Week—was the posture, the latitude, the context, and the use of any violence short of shooting to kill, which gave wide room for the play and acting-out of very revealing impulses. The Walker Report is an extraordinary example of "Federal Committee" findings that duck many facts and distort others, in order to transform all perception and feeling about an event—to coopt the issues and re-direct the indignation aroused by the street and park events during Convention Week in Chicago. The Walker Report investigators knew about the cop violence in Lincoln Park after the Guard sweep early Thursday morning—I told them—but they, who meticulously exaggerated demonstrator provocations, chose to exclude it totally. I suggest that the reason is that the cops had not a smidgen of excuse on their side for this attack, and that the attack, as with other attacks during the week, was ordered by superiors. The cops were systematically trying to drive these kids on the corner of LaSalle, Eugenie and Clark out of town: these kids who had made such fools of them and the City and the Democratic Party by exciting them to the use of preposterous violence.

Up and down the streets traffic was stopped by all the chasing of kids by cops, and the cops were incensed at the stopped traffic—guilty rage at the sight of the appalled witnesses in the cars. They hit cars with their clubs and told them to *move* even when the cars couldn't move because the car in front of them couldn't move and the car behind couldn't either. A cop hit the window post on the right side of my car with a club and told me to *move*. I'd already been hit on the head once, and I'd come to regard getting clubbed as a practical problem, devoid of any social or political implications: a ghetto attitude. No media were nearby, no cameras. The wounded were making their way or being helped to the improvised aid stations—such as The Theater—in the neighborhood. The violence here happened after Humphrey's nomination and after the great event of the Battle of Michigan Avenue on national TV that evening. Up here in Lincoln Park, hardly anyone was talking

about the Convention itself. There was nothing compelling about the Convention. All reality was out in the
streets, anger on all sides, *exhilarating* anger.

I reached LaSalle Street where cop cars were making
mighty believable attempts to run down groups of kids.
One cop jumped out of his car before it even stopped
and he continued to chase a bunch of kids down the
sidewalk while his squad car wobbled and jounced in
gear to a stop on its own. There were cars stopped all
along LaSalle Street, with cops frisking and searching
youngsters who were stretched across the cars or up
against walls. There was the justice of no exemption in
the cops' attitude. Some of the cars were new converti-
bles, with Illinois license plates, and the kids were as
casually straight as the homes they came from. To be
young was to be suspect, to be a target. I drove now
subject to a gut-urge, a gut-dream, a gut-rage, my fingers
sensitive on the wheel as I looked into the side streets.
I wanted to find a lone cop on a back street and run him
down. Us and Them. To wear a uniform was to be suspect, to be a target. No wonder this night (as last night)
kids were ambushing patrol cars and smashing their windows with a storm of rocks. No wonder the cops were
trying to drive everyone somewhere else. There was a
rightness about it. Us and Them. In Lincoln Park, in
front of the Hilton, at the Amphitheatre, three widely-
spaced places in the city, there was the feeling that
planets were colliding noiselessly but with terrific final-
ity in the air above our heads.

Confrontation Attitudes

This was a white man's convention. It was a battle
inside and outside—in the Amphitheatre and around the
Hilton, in the streets and in the parks—between white

owners and managers of the country and their white minions and their sons and daughters. The owners and minions came from within Chicago and from outside the city, just as their white sons and daughters came from here and elsewhere. Proportionately, there were far more people from out of state within the Convention itself, delegates, aides and media persons, while in the streets more than half of the participants came from Chicago or nearby areas. The police invasion, almost entirely white in the Lincoln Park area, came from within the city; and some cops knew that their sons and daughters and kid brothers and sisters were on the other side. There is the report of one sad cop who haunted The Theater on Wells Street opposite the Park, asking Yippies and neighborhood people to watch out and take care for his daughter. The Chicago black community, where a variety of separatist movements and attitudes are strong, shunned the Convention, snubbed it. The pigs were cracking white skulls for once. This was white family war, family rage, family fight over family destiny, miraculously stopping short of killing, though concussions and broken bones and arrests and beatings on the streets and in police vans and stations went beyond numbering. Many demonstrators who sought aid at hospitals gave such reasons as having fallen downstairs for cause of wound, and the nurses and doctors accepted it and asked no questions because the police would take away those who were declared to be hurt by police violence. The Mayor of Chicago has talked about restraint on the part of the cops. It was the Yippies and demonstrators who always pulled back at the point where cops would escalate to killing and, necessarily, Yippies and demonstrators would, too. The blacks were wry and astonished.

There were very few blacks among the Yippies, even

fewer among the New Left and the Mobe, and blacks
were hardly present at all among the McCarthy workers.
Blacks were more in evidence in the Convention itself,
where every effort was made to immobilize them as a
major force in this country by grudgingly giving precedent for representation according to population per-
centages. The blacks within the Convention—such as
Willie Brown of California and Julian Bond of Georgia
—were generally brighter, quicker, more aggressive, and
more robust in feeling than their white counterparts. The
young whites, particularly among the McCarthy workers
and often in the New Left, were cool, manipulative,
naive, arrogant, and with small presence of feeling. They
didn't know yet that they had cops in their minds. It was
unsettling to see how much this cool, controlled, manipulative, naive, arrogant mind, with skinny presence of
personal feeling, a puritanical exclusion of spontaneity
and complex response, pervaded the McCarthy people
and the New Left. It was the seeming opposite and yet
the complement of the conventional politicians who were
made stupid by their bullish necessity for control. It was
the impression of the drugheads, too—skimpy personal
presence—as if most feeling in these young people were
channeled by some means into the volcanic beauty of the
music, leaving behind a wisp and whisper of a man or a
woman to lead the bodies into dance. It was an impression that I tried hard to shake. It suggested, in combination with the Piggish, a nightmare society self-satisfying
in its pluralistic conflicts and far subtler than any Orwell-
ian comprehension of a 1984 totalitarianism. The blacks
were personal, strong and quick in feeling, and the forms
of personal attack were as close as they came to the manipulative. Come Tuesday and Wednesday, the whites,
too, would be personal, at least temporarily.

But as moment was booted into moment, and day into day, and we who stayed in the events didn't know where the toe of history was going to kick us next, a number of black kids, made wonderfully curious by the sights on TV, began to show up both in Lincoln Park and in Grant Park by the Hilton. Most of them thought the Yippies in Lincoln Park were taking risks so dumb on the face of it that participation on their part was impossible. A few blacks were in the forefront of some marches. There were black guys who spoke through the demonstrators' speaker in Lincoln Park and in front of the Hilton. The Yippies and the demonstrators gave more than token appearance in support of a black CTA workers' strike. But the number of blacks involved in the events of Convention Week did not increase much. Black spectators and comments on the sidelines increased, though.

On Thursday afternoon and night, two marches went into the fringe of the black ghetto before they were stopped by a wall of soldiers—Illinois National Guardsmen—with bayonets and barbwire-enclosed jeeps and a .30 caliber machinegun on a personnel carrier. The first march was stopped under the viaduct at 16th Street; the second, at night, at 18th Street. Black people answered the white marchers everywhere with the V sign. The reason the march was allowed to go only as far as 18th Street was not because Mayor Daley feared what the demonstrators would do at the Amphitheatre, which was well-protected and exhausting miles away, but because beyond 18th Street is deep black ghetto and God and Mayor Daley knew what might happen.

But the riots and the insurrections of the black community in the past three years did influence events during Convention Week in that Pig responses—from professors-on-commissions-to-study-riots down to patrolmen

—determined the style and magnitude of police tactics.
The Chicago cops gave warning what they would do
during Convention Week in the way they had responded
during the April 1968 black insurrection that sprang up
in response to the killing of Reverend Martin Luther
King, Jr.—which elicited Mayor Daley's famous "shoot-
to-kill arsonists and shoot-to-maim looters" order—and
in the Peace March later in April that was arbitrarily
clubbed and driven out of the Civic Center Plaza in
downtown Chicago. The cops were more prepared during Convention Week for an uprising in the ghetto, or
for 200,000 Yippies freaking out on acid in the streets.
They were not prepared for what actually happened.
The Chicago police were at a peak of expectancy and
readiness, and their tactics were fermented from what
comes out of the heads of some of our most prominent
sociologists—such as Professor Morris Janowitz of the
Department of Sociology at the University of Chicago—
who are letting their brains be turned into pork lard by
believing that any problem will yield to a prescribed or
acceptable solution if we just apply sufficient brain-
power, man-power, machine-power, fire-power, money-
power, or just plain force. Read the chapter called "Control of Disorder" in the U.S. *Riot Commission Report,*
and see how the cops took its advice literally in some
places, and understood it by reading between its lines
in other places. Then, you students of sociology, go and
listen to those professors of sociology far down the garden
path, where well-dressed "social control" recommendations are dreamed up for our militarily repressive forces
everywhere. Professor Janowitz is capable of extraordi-
narily benign, almost undetectable, irony, when he uses
such sentences as: "In the management of violence, there
is a wide gulf between official doctrine and actual prac-

tice." (*Social Control of Escalated Riots* by Morris Janowitz. 1968. University of Chicago Center for Policy
Study.) He also uses such fingertip phrases as "selective
response," which, in the context, means sending a hundred accurate bullets ripping through the body of a man
conceived to be a sniper. After Convention Week, Dr.
Janowitz would say that the Chicago police should have
showed more humor, whereas, in fact, much of the time
they were in wonderful humor—just not at the point of
the confrontations. However, sociologist Janowitz, after
the April 1968 black insurrection in Chicago, also appeared on TV to speak against Mayor Daley's shoot-to-
kill order. It seems that Chicago's riot-control forces and
their superiors are always misinterpreting the helpful
servant from the University of Chicago. Yet Professor
Janowitz and many of his peers are in the very forefront
of those liberals who would invest a large portion of the
country's resources in huge programs for the ameliora-
tion of social and economic troubles. How is it that repressive governmental forces in our society, that couldn't
care less about such programs, find these professors so
useful in their more immediate recommendations for
"social control?" The professors are constantly misinter-
preted and then asked to correct the misinterpretation.
Ah, they would be Romans among Romans in a modern
Roman Empire. That a problem might be even helped
to generate its own solution is too paradoxical and too
threatening and much beyond these men. Nothing scares
the Monster-Who-Needs-to-Solve-All-That-Moves more
than letting people do what they want to do, what they
need to do. Such sociologists are going to say that the
cops did not use their advice correctly and that the Illinois National Guard did because the Guard didn't draw
blood with the general fervor of the police.

The fact is that by the time the Guard came into the action of Convention Week, the great and deadly energy had been turned, by force of fear and will on the part of many demonstrators, particularly the public leaders, back into dissent. The Guardsmen were very different from the cops. Most of them were about the same age as the demonstrators, and most of them belong to the Guard because they do not want to go to Vietnam, a form of passive protest in itself. Many were openly sympathetic with the demonstrators. On Thursday afternoon, truckloads of Guardsmen moved past the marchers on the sidewalks of Michigan Avenue, heading toward the 16th Street viaduct where they would become those anonymous figures behind fixed bayonets blocking the march. Many Guardsmen in the trucks were giving the V sign—the peace sign, the Yippie sign, the victory sign —in answer to the demonstrators shouting "Join us." Sometimes several Guardsmen in each truck would answer with the sign, or two or three, or just one. Just one is important. The fact that only one man in a truckload wanted to give the sign at that moment is something to consider, because it is not easy for men to make any declaration alone without at least implicit support from those in whose company they must survive. (Cops would give the V sign to mock or to indicate they wanted to talk peaceably—a sort of white flag. I saw only one cop during the whole week give the sign seriously, a skinny, short, remarkably slight cop, who seemed scared, in front of the Hilton.)

It has been reported to me that, in Guard training for "riot-control," Guardsmen are required to stand or move in formation, anonymous, unyielding, and just take it, while another company of their fellows, dressed as demonstrators, abuse them, throw rocks, bottles, worse things, spit on them, etcetera. The Guardsmen physically repel only direct attack. The Guardsmen agree that in this training it is more fun to be a "demonstrator." In the present "state of knowledge" of tactics for handling dissent, the Guardsmen block and attack in formation, impersonally. Their first and major form of attack is gas, poured out so heavily that only para-military demonstrators, with gas masks of their own, could force the Guardsmen to personal, physical attack on a large scale. Many people believe that if the Guard had handled the situation in Chicago during Convention Week from beginning to end, the results would have been very different, more pacific. I believe that something else would have happened. In Lincoln Park, what amounted to new law was being enforced, the 11 PM curfew—new law because it had been only lackadaisically enforced by the police up to now and citizens largely used the Park as they wished after 11 PM. I believe that the Yippies might well have forced a partial revolt in the Guard (if the young Guardsmen were required to act with the general vicious aggressiveness of the older cops) and the situation in Chicago would have been even more dramatic. Imagine the Yippies and Guardsmen side by side day and night in Lincoln Park: the temptations of music, pot and women, plus the angers of not-so-brotherly Guardsmen and Yippies. Yes, in Lincoln Park the Guard could not have hidden in the continual anonymity with which it approached the situation downtown.

But the social scientists, those who make their plain and desperate bread by performing study services for the military and the police, and who must defend these services, will say that the Guard did it right. The main contribution of such social science to the tactics of stilling dissent is that there should be a massive show of force, of manpower, and quick stamping out the instant "trouble" starts.

In *Social Control of Escalated Riots*, Professor Janowitz states that "the operational code of the police in New York City under Commissioner Howard Leary and in Chicago has been to intervene with that amount of force judged to be appropriate for early stage of the confrontation. The objective is to seek to prevent the spread of contagion. No special steps are taken to prevent routine police performance from developing into incidents which might provoke tension. But if an incident becomes the focal point for tension and the collection of a crowd, the police respond early and in depth in order to prevent the second stage from actually expanding . . . The police seek to operate by their sheer presence, not to provoke further counteraction." Author Janowitz does not seem to question the basic assumption here that the actions of everyone under the sun need to be controlled by sophisticated and firm police tactics. That it might be the "control" exerted by the first actions of "routine police performance" on up the scale of police intervention that itself causes the escalation is not to be considered by minds made smooth as wood by intensive academic training. It is one of the most intensely played games of our society that everyone must justify his job, and that includes sociologists and police undercover agents. Each one must make the subject of study—in this case, demonstrators, hippies, and ghetto dwellers—produce evidence that the job is necessary. Surveillance agents must find conspiracy in the tread of angels. Sociologists must see patterns in the actions of people that can be manipulated to the profit and advantage of all those concerned with "control."

The Chicago cops feel that they used massive manpower and minimum force, and when the moment came, they used non-lethal gas instead of guns. Police Superintendent James R. Conlisk Jr. is quoted as saying that the police made the great discovery of the effectiveness of gas, and that they should have used gas even more heavily during Convention Week.

The police took it all so seriously that they began stamping out trouble before trouble started. In the Army, it is often felt that the best way to disobey an order is to obey it to the letter. The spirit of application is all important. If there was one thing that characterized the Chicago cops, it was energy, tremendous energy, a high pitch of personal energy, and a nonchalance that could change on the instant into white-faced fury. It was amazing to see men with such bellies run so well, even if they couldn't run as fast as some of the speedier kids. The cops didn't like the 12-hour shifts, but most of them liked their work.

The moment the Yippies showed up in Lincoln Park in the week before the Convention, and the Mobe began training its parade marshalls on the baseball diamond there, they were watched over by platoons of police, with helicopters overhead, and with plainclothesmen mixing with Yippies and practically taking part in the marshalls' training program. Monday night, on the corner of Wells and North after the streets had been cleared by blocking off and gassing and clubbing, there were crowds on all four corners and a great many cops in blue shirts and blue helmets working their asses off blowing whistles and thumping cars with their clubs and waving on traffic and shoving back bystanders. An old police sergeant said to a group of media-men, "If my men would just quit blowing their whistles and take it easy, these people would go away." The reporters were naturally astonished and they asked why men under his command were acting against his wishes. He shrugged and said he had his orders. (He also said that the last three years —the riots and demonstrations and so forth—had been just too much for him and he wanted to retire and go to Canada. "I want to go fishing," he said, "for a long time.") Hundreds of times that week cops said, "I have my orders, *buddy!*" The Sergeant was right in one sense, and everytime I saw the police actually take it easy or go away, the demonstrators and Yippies also went away. How much employment is there for a sociologist in the Sergeant's observation? But the event went much beyond the Sergeant's wisdom, nevertheless. There was a magnetic attraction of provocation between cops and Yippies and demonstrators, within the established theater of the parks and streets. Poet Allen Ginsberg chided the Yippies, saying that if you call a man a pig you bring the Pig out in him. That was shrewd, too, but the event pounded way beyond Ginsberg as it went way beyond every leader. And it may be that you don't get rid of the Pig until you name it and call it and bring it out, and only after a purge that knows its own reason, are you able to meet man to man. That happened in some areas of Chicago. The Yippies, during the day, were the only group that some cops sought and talked with: big brother trying to straighten out kid brother and kid brother telling big brother why he was wrong. Many Yippies and cops were out of the lower middle class, impulsive.

The constant, massive presence of the cops to enforce the City's denial of permits to march and permits to use the parks after the curfew hour, exacerbated everybody with fear and hate. When I first came to Chicago in the late Fifties, its police force was then known as the worst in the world, too— but for a different reason. It had become so corrupt that the price of a bribe to go scot-free for any crime was sinking lower every day. There was a scandal about some cops who had discovered the profits and pleasures of playing both sides of crime, and a solution was found by hiring O. W. Wilson, the head of the Department of Criminology at the University of California, to be Superintendent of Police. The universities, again. The Pentagon can't get along without them to do research, and it seems the police can't, either. During Wilson's time as Superintendent, the Chicago Police Department was modernized and computerized and men with college degrees—the implication is that nothing is more to be trusted than a college degree—were sought to be policemen. There was a big recruitment drive in the early Sixties, and a large proportion of the men on the force seem to be in their late 20's and early 30's. It was said in an article in a Chicago newspaper—the name of which escapes me—that the police relaxed their psychological standards in order to fulfill that big recruitment drive. This is meant to imply that the violence of the Chicago cops had to be outside the range of "normal psychology." There was nothing abnormal about them. They were in fine fettle. They had their orders.

Modern police science and criminology, and the most sophisticated communications equipment, went into the making of this Department. Chicago cops are fast, they can answer almost any call in three minutes, often less; I have timed them. Many of them still take bribes, and still play both sides of crime, but they are different, and their communications technology is equivalent, in some respects, to the general technology that the United States has visited upon Vietnam. The use of such technology generates an attitude that people are merely components of a problem; hence, the hard rage on the part of the administrators when the "problem" refuses to let itself be "solved."

There was also an escalation principle at work between the cops and the Yippies. An insult from a Yippie demands one hard shove from a cop; a stronger insult means a club on the head; and a storm of abuse means wild beating. One Yippie kid hitting back with his bare fists means a whole neighborhood will be terrorized. Yippies finally arming themselves with rocks, ambushing cop cars and shattering every window and maybe hitting cops inside, means "search and destroy" missions will continue all night long.

So be it.

Let us now begin the story that ends of itself.

After midnight. Monday August 26. Lincoln Park. Photo by Fred Schnell.

the week before the convention: preparatory confrontations

Julian Bond Meets the Governor of New Jersey

It was hot the week before the Convention, hot as only Chicago can be hot, heat and humidity that holds you, irritates and makes you want to move violently or not move at all. It is the kind of heat that is traditionally thought to be a ready condition of riots and insurrections.

The talk among the citizens in Chicago was that if this heat held through Convention Week, the black ghetto would surely erupt in violent action. The heads of everyone reverberated with stereotyped expectations, as if in direct, though contradictory, response to the tremors from the unknown energies about to visit the City.

The air in the Hilton Hotel was muggy. The air-conditioning simply could not cope with all the bodies. The Credentials Committee hearings were jammed, and the McCarthy headquarters on the 15th floor was jammed with tense, energetic people. The coolest place in the Hotel was the Humphrey headquarters, where the long hallways were empty, no people to aggravate the air, except for a few Humphrey girls, who were sometimes pretty, but never with any style of living, as if they had flunked out of airline hostess training. The emptiness of the Humphrey headquarters indicated Humphrey's enormous confidence about winning the nomination: sewed up. A McCarthy aide, when he wished to cool off, would take the elevator to the Humphrey floor and stretch out in the empty lobby. Several miles north, in Lincoln Park, it was hot but more pleasant, near Lake Michigan, on the grass in the shade, under the sky. Cops, Yippies, self-defense training for demonstrators who would be parade marshalls, plainclothesmen, guitars, drums, caucuses, tree-climbing—everything in Lincoln Park happened under the wide, summer sky, on the grass. In the streets around the Hilton, the heat redoubled itself against concrete, asphalt, and glass. The City waited for what everyone had determined to be inevitable. Mayor Daley said that the City would not let disruption happen, and so made sure it would happen.

The Credentials Committee hearings, in the International Ballroom of the Hilton, were sweaty, swampy. Bodies and bright lights stuffed the place. It was air that leaned on you. In the center of this mugginess was a flushed face, the cause of friction right and left that generated more emotional heat, and this flushed face belonged to an irritable, domineering man, who was greedy about work and enjoyed it—Richard Hughes, Governor of New Jersey, Chairman of the Committee. The Committee's job was to hear the challenges of people who did not feel that their regular state delegation fairly represented the popular will and the legitimate interests of the Democratic Party in their state. There were two delegate representatives from each state and territory

seated on the Committee. They made decisions by majority vote, but a minority report on the decision could
be brought before the National Convention and there
the majority vote of the Committee could be overturned.

The Yippies were running a pig for President, and the
cops were pigs and politicians were pigs, and the Pig
was a proliferating force and growth in the mind and the
soul and in the society. Like cancer in the way it grows,
the Pig sickens and hardens all cells of common sense,
compassion, responsibility and sense of consequence, and
turns them to greedy, self-protective, oppressive ends.
Among those on the Left I would look for the skinny-
feeling, self-righteous man who was masking a bedrock
of frustrated, puritanical authoritarianism. I started looking also for the Pig, and it was a revealing game. How
much of the Pig in this man, that man? Not quite half
Pig, more than half Pig, almost all Pig, because no man
can be all Pig without being entirely of Satan, a human
impossibility; our limitations will not permit it.

I looked at Richard Hughes and found a man somewhat pinched and somewhat Piggish, who wrestled
with both the pinches and the satisfactions, a man
for whom compromise has a savor, a man who exercises his circulation by twisting and bending and ram-
rodding compromise solutions. He is also the man who
said during the Newark black insurrection in his state
in July, 1967 that there comes a time when we have to
draw the line between the law of the jungle and the law
of civilization and now is the time—or so a McCarthy
aide said to me with a knowing smile, as if it were a bed-
room secret about Hughes. The United States Riot Commission Report says that Hughes "decreed a 'hard line'
in putting down the riot." And we know the bloody re-

sults in Newark—23 persons killed, 21 of them blacks. Hughes was a man who was supposed to be manipulating the Committee hearings for the benefit of Hubert Humphrey and a possible vice-presidential nomination for himself. Yet Hughes acted as if he were the only Party regular who had a clue to the future, and he gave the impression of having his eye more on 1972. He was, in the week before the Convention, spot-welding connections between the old Party and some of the Young Turks. He did not pick just any Young Turk. He picked the best to come before the Committee. He picked Julian Bond—New Left hero, black member of the Georgia State Legislature, and head of the challengers from Georgia.

It was said before the Credentials Committee hearings began that the Mississippi challenge delegation— the Mississippi Freedom Democratic Party challenge headed by Fannie Lou Hamer—would be seated in place of the old-line Southern regulars, as a token to quiet black dissent, and the other challenges would be denied —such as Texas, Alabama, Georgia, North Carolina. I mention these four because, on the face of it, in any heavenly court of law, it seemed that their cases would have to win. The challengers were generally men of personal excellence and considerable professional skill. The basis of their challenges of the credentials of the regular (usually appointed rather than elected) delegations was that the regulars did not accurately represent the peoples of the state. The challengers understood the adversary system, and they gave well-prepared, closely reasoned arguments, with strong feeling, a good sense of timing, and a good sense for the listener. The regular delegates, the ones being challenged, were almost always slow,

florid, insistent men, Southern party hacks, accustomed
to delivering a mechanical rhetoric to courts that want
nothing else.

Hughes was playing a delicate, stubborn, frustrating
game with the challengers who could constitute a powerful cadre for the Democratic Party in the South. It
seemed that he wanted to lock them in a room with
their state regulars and throw the key away until they
bound themselves to one another with all the forms of
compromise. Hughes and the Credentials Committee in
general were passionately inquisitorial about the loyalty
of state delegations to the Party nominee—*whoever that
will be,* was their phrase. Most of the Southern delegations, especially the Maddox-Georgia delegation and the
Alabama delegation, were profoundly suspect to Hughes
and all national Democrats who feared the vote drain
that would occur with third and fourth parties. Despite
all the protestations on the floor and all the guarantees
given in the halls outside the hearings, the spirit of
George Wallace and his new party eavesdropped on
everyone. The McCarthy people dropped their challenges of the Pennsylvania and New York delegations,
where they had won popular preference in the primaries
but did not get that share of the delegations. They
dropped the challenges because they did not want to
alienate, apparently still hoped for, the support of the
big party bosses in the North. A mistake. There were a
series of confrontations inside the Convention and outside it. The challenger could either turn away from the
impending confrontation and hope the gesture would
bring about a desired response, depending on the good
will of cops and politicians, and it never did, or they
could go smack into the confrontation. *Every time a confrontation was avoided, in the Convention or on the*

streets, the challenger, on the terms of his own aspirations, made a mistake.

In another time, another situation, possibly even another convention, this might not be the case. But here in Chicago all the cells of good will and common sense were turned off in the Pig. The McCarthy people had been too much to school, and they made many such mistakes. Assuming, of course, that they really wanted to win, they should have challenged the composition of the Pennsylvania and New York delegations, and turned the hearings into a charged theater to scandalize and discredit in front of the entire nation any remaining pretensions of democracy in the processes of candidate selection. One reason the McCarthy people turned away could be that their case was that good, and they did not want to believe the implications of it, either.

It would seem that it was easy for Hughes to pick Bond because Georgia Governor Lester Maddox' disloyalty to the national Democratic Party was open and irredeemable. But that seemed to be true of Alabama, too. And yet, unless the Committee had not done its homework at all, anyone who cared to know could raise the question of Bond's loyalty to the national Party. He was the first black to win election to the Georgia State Assembly since Reconstruction, I believe. He had to fight the Assembly's attempts to deny him and his credentials then, too. He has been an organizer in peace and black movements in the South and elsewhere. He persists. Bond is slim, lithe, light-skinned, with an easy sophistication, a cool sharp anger, and he was surely the handsomest man to stand before the Committee. What could have closed the Committee's case against him was that he was a McCarthy supporter and that he made no bones about his complete opposition to

the Vietnam War. That he is a hero of the New Left
must have put a sick chill in the gut of many a Committee member, and leads to wonder about what was
going in the mind of Richard Hughes.

When Julian Bond first spoke to the Committee, something happened that had not happened with any other
person who came before it. It happened before Bond
even said his first words. It happened as soon as he got
up and started to the podium. The whole Committee—
conservatives and liberals alike—stirred and leaned forward in fascination tinged with fear, and gave to Bond
that warmth of attention that Americans, in most areas
of our life, give to a man whom they collectively recognize as a comer. The Committee had done its homework,
all right, or the few who had done their homework had
told the others. It was remarkable to see and feel. When
the members of Bond's delegation were asked what they
had done to help build the Democratic Party in the State
of Georgia, one member of the delegation, a fellow
named Brown, Humphrey supporter, told of their activities, and Richard Hughes said, with unusual unction
for him, "And that reflects credit upon you, sir."

When Bond was personally queried on the loyalty of
his delegation to the nominee of the national Party, whoever that might be, he, with that casual grace of his,
pointed at one member after another and showed the
variety of allegiances: a Humphrey supporter here, a
McCarthy supporter here, someone else over here, and
just at the point where it seemed that he would avoid
stating his own support and the Committee hardened
briefly, he casually pointed at his own head and said,
"A McCarthy supporter." If he had not done it casually,
and if he had stated his own allegiance first, he would
have incurred hard feelings. He made ground with short

runs and short passes, within an overall scheme, and you
were suddenly startled to see how near he was to the
goal line. He was seemingly casual, but in fact he paid
attention to every detail. He was seemingly unhurried,
but this simply gave him a moment to deflect his oppo-
nent and to make mental connections at great speed far
ahead in the game. When his delegation was finally
queried on its loyalty to the national Party, they made
their obeisance gracefully. At the very least, Julian Bond
would not support George Wallace. At the most, the
Democratic Party had let a Prince of the Left into its
fold and given him prominence above almost anyone
else, except the nominees, at the Convention. There must
have been a lot of people, on all sides, counting on their
luck. Hubert Humphrey is finished—even if he becomes
a senator from Minnesota—but Julian Bond is alive and
working inside the Democratic Party.

Bond has the air of a man who feels assured of his
luck and of a destiny, a personal destiny inextricable
from the movement of a social destiny. He is one of the
few New Left leaders who does not act as if he is waiting for someone else. He is nobody's right hand man. He
does not cater emotionally to anyone, but he affects other
people strongly. Bond supported McCarthy, with no
qualms about what his New Left brothers might feel,
but when Bond was on the stand with McCarthy, he was
Julian Bond and that slightest touch of the usual subordi-
nateness was absent. This was also true when he spoke
to the demonstrators: he did not cater to them either,
though all other speakers did. He received admiration
cleanly, and exacted no price for it. He could walk
among the demonstrators wearing an absolutely straight
suit and wearing it well, and have their unreserved
affection and admiration. He could walk in the Hilton

and the same admiration was given, excepting the obvious racists. A retired Army major in Bond's delegation spoke of "Julian" with the simplicity of feeling that men give to a rare sort of man: a man who seems to ask simply that you give because the movement of history is beyond price or agreement. In some ways lines are drawn more cleanly in the South, but it is important that the Major did not feel that he had to hock his soul to ideology or style of life. Bond never showed any qualms about working both inside and outside the established system. He trusts himself. Bond never catered to Hughes, but he met Hughes right where Hughes lived.

The Credentials Committee was, in its chary way, working. There was a group of liberals—particularly Mrs. David Hoeh of New Hampshire, William Hochman and Mrs. Arlie Taylor of Colorado, Willie Brown of California, Philip Stern of the District of Columbia—who kept putting ginger up a few asses. They were insistent; and they wouldn't go away. Mrs. Hoeh's husband would be the man who, later in the Convention itself, tested the computer security apparatus and found it would pass any old card, raised hell about it, and was dragged away thrashing and accused of biting those who arrested him. Yes, despite the rhetoric of the general discreditation of liberals in the past few years—and perhaps because of it—there was spunk in some of these people. They were angry and they stayed angry, and their anger was neutralizing the Pig's hold on some common sense.

It could be that Hughes was the best theatrical manager within the Convention itself and that he labored to keep alive the air that the Committee was not one of wholly foregone conclusions. It was certainly adept at hearing cases and postponing decisions that would set precedent for other cases. They were, nevertheless, forced to meet the possibilities that came before them, even if to stun and drag them away, and all of this made new forms of accreditation almost a certainty for the future. Hughes seemed especially interested in this. He seemed to know that McCarthy would lose the nomination, and rather suspected that Humphrey would lose the election. It must have been an interesting game, seeing a winner who would be a loser, and a losing side that might win in time to come. He was jumping back and forth across the widening split, and writing his claims on all kinds of territory in the future.

The Platform Committee, on the other hand, where the national issues were verbally belabored and the decisions were to be made on how the Party would stand rhetorically for this campaign, plodded through a ritualistic hearing of grievances and recommendations at the Amphitheatre, coming up for air now and then to wave the flag and lust for the blood of other nations. The way in which the two Committees sat accentuated the differences. The Platform Committee sat in a solid bank, as if blocking all approach. The Credentials Committee sat in a broad U-shape, where each person had to face everyone else. No doubt this was dictated by the rooms in which the Committees met. But in the Credentials Committee, there was a suggestion of what a democracy's court of last resort could be, if properly constituted, and how it could work. That was a small favor, too.

The Georgia challengers were impressive. Horne, their counsel—an American Civil Liberties Union lawyer from Atlanta, a white man—was the most skillful, the most articulate, of all the counsels for challenge delegations. But other challenges were also sound and impressive. Ferguson, the counsel for the North Carolina challengers—a tall black man, with a hint of the physical

disposition of Malcolm X about him—presented a fine
case for that group, with methodical, convincing, low-
key warmth. A McCarthy aide told me that all of the
other challenges received considerable help from the
McCarthy staff, but that the North Carolina challengers
had put their case together alone. Plainly, Hughes
wished to rid the Convention of Lester Maddox—Georgia Governor and definite renegade from the national
Party—and wished to accept Julian Bond. The reasons
for the former were patent; but the reasons for the latter
were more speculative.

The Credentials Committee went into executive session on the Georgia case in the Waldorf Room of the
Hilton. They were in session many hours, up to midnight, and then into the early morning. Crowded outside
the doors of the Waldorf Room were reporters and political aides of all kinds, waiting, waiting, waiting, sitting on the floor, sitting on the edge of cylindrical hall
ashtrays, smoking, smoking, chatting out of boredom,
smoking, waiting, waiting. I got the image of professional journalists being men who spend long hours waiting for their life to begin when a door opens. It was crucial that they get the news the second it came out of that
door. There was the same sort of tension and boredom
that afflicts an outlying Army post. Men were smoking
one cigarette after another to stave off their sense of
time. Now and then the door did open, and out came a
desperate man, a man who could hold it no longer: he
would lunge down the hall toward the Men's Room more
desperate the closer he got to release, with a pack of
galvanized reporters after him asking questions, and the
man saying he could not answer any questions. He was
hounded by reporters up to the stall where he found
relief. Hughes did not like to sleep. Hughes liked to

work. Hughes was twisting and bending a compromise together. Hughes was enjoying himself. Hughes, so far as I know, never emerged.

Then the former Governor of Florida, Farris Bryant, one of the conservatives, came out, doing a slow Southern burn over what had happened in the session, and rather tightly indignant about answering the reporters who tied themselves in knots around him. But the talk in the hall was that apparently Hughes had called upon a debt or two and Bryant had aided him. Then the liberals came out, in an open huff, people such as Mrs. David Hoeh of New Hampshire and Mrs. Arlie Taylor of Colorado. It was explained that Hughes had got on his steam-roller and flattened both the conservatives and the liberals. "That man," they were saying, "that *man*." Now he was going to hold a press conference down on the first floor of the Hilton. "I'd just like to see how he's going to explain this to the press," said Mrs. Taylor. Hughes was not at all perturbed about his ability to explain the compromise to the press.

In a quickly arranged press conference, Hughes came, bullish, to the microphone. He always came to the microphone as if he were going to butt it. He announced a compromise solution, a new delegation to be formed half with challengers and half with the old regular Democrats of Georgia. When asked why Lester Maddox couldn't be one of the delegates, Hughes said, "He would have to pass me, and I don't think I would let it happen." Hughes would head the small committee that would approve the members of the new delegation. He enjoyed his bullishness and he was blunt about it. When asked by another reporter if the compromise was his idea, he allowed that, yes, he had had quite a bit to do with it, and then, again, he decided to be frank. You might even say,

he said, that I initiated and carried it. He was anxious
to let his actions and his quality be known to someone.
I watched him and thought of those people killed in the
Newark insurrection in his state, and wondered in what
ironical way was history finding him useful.

Now it was up to the two parties—the Bond group
and the Maddox group—to see if they would accept the
compromise. Bond made the statement for his group,
keeping his cool but he was excited, so was Horne,
though they were all trying to hide it. Bond said that
they were happy that the Committee had, in principle,
recognized and accepted their challenge, but a decision
on acceptance would have to wait until the next morning. That was all. It seemed to suit everybody, including Hughes.

I walked out the door of the room into the hall, in the
dry fever of long waiting and two o'clock in the morning, and found myself walking beside Hughes. He
walked with a pinched shufflle, small quick steps, as if
he were in a hurry and yet it would be painful for him
to stretch his legs. I thought, given my nearness to him,
that it was a wonder that public figures were not assassinated every day. He was pleased with himself and smiled
at me, as if wanting me to ask him a question, as if, in
the flush of a victory all his own, he wanted to go on
talking about it. Just then, at the turn of the hall, Julian
Bond, with a few members of his delegation, came
quickly up to Hughes. Bond asked a favor that had to
do with money. When the reporters saw the heads of
Richard Hughes and Julian Bond together, they rushed
from all sides and jammed around the two, practically
climbing each other's backs to grab a juicy bit of news.
Richard Hughes' face lit up with purest pleasure when
he heard Bond's request. "Well!" he said exuberantly,

pleased that he was able to do Bond a favor, "I'm a poor man myself! Let's go talk to Reverend Martin!" (Louis Martin held an office in the Democratic Party out of whose funds he could give some money to indigent delegates and delegations.) Hughes was seized with such energy and pleasure that the pinched shuffle dropped away. Blinking rapidly, as if he were in a B movie of the Old Politician accepting the Young Turk, he strode beside Bond. But Bond was aware that the theater was of the absurd—perhaps of cruelty, verging toward the heroic—and that there is nothing more absurd than heroism, being acts done by men. Bond kept his cool, and pulled ahead of Hughes along with his Georgia delegates, who were all trying to keep their cool, but they skipped in spite of themselves. It is the most natural thing to do, to skip, when you have won something. Bond himself did not skip, but he could not wholly restrain the gleeful energy in his body and he turned this way and that.

The next day they accepted the compromise solution; and Lester Maddox, in a press conference in the Hilton the next day, intimated that if he had been fucked, there were bigger fucks to come in the South. Richard Hughes would take the report before the Convention, and the report would win, despite efforts of liberals to unseat the entire regular delegation. Also, the regular Georgia Democrats would be foolish enough to try and deny Bond and his delegation their seats simply by sitting in them. Altogether, following absurdity seriously, through one presentation and confrontation after another, Bond would emerge with near heroic credit everywhere.

I told this story to an SDS friend of mine who came into town from New York the next night. He said, "So now we can't trust Julian Bond any more." I had not thought that he was among those who felt that there was inherent corruption in shaking the hands of some people, or that success, in Ambrose Bierce's definition, was the one unpardonable sin that one could commit against one's fellows. Why not at least wait until Bond gave reason for judgment? Certainly, for the rest of the week, Bond acted the part of the legislator who knows where he comes from, who he is, and where he's going. It took me aback. Maybe my friend was right.

But as Convention Week developed—with its extraordinary up-for-grabs power, a movement that was as inexorable as a Biblical epic and yet could not be anticipated—it became apparent that the Left, in gaining some of the power that it sought, was coming into sharp friction with some of its most cherished, most useful attitudes and ideas. Do you work inside the system or outside it? Why not both? Do you try to change existing institutions or create alternative institutions? Why not both? Can drugheads be clear-headed radicals? Apparently. Are there important numbers of liberals who are not just the most well-packaged of sell-outs, the subtlest instruments of the Devil? Apparently. It is interesting that many liberals went away from Chicago thinking that the system could not work, and many New Leftists went away thinking maybe it could work. Perhaps there was as much fantasy as gas in the eyes of many people? The "system" is never well described; its dynamic element, that can make connections below the surface, is always left out. Is middle-class spiritual deprivation, the middle-class drop-out, the most important force in the possible revolution? Is the working class, among whom were those who gave the finger to the marchers on Michigan Avenue Thursday, largely lumpen? Or are middle-class radicals deliberately patronizing? What do you decide about making a revolution in a country that is so hugely "middle class"? Before Chicago, it was possible for whoever to stand on whatever side of a debate that he wished, and call himself correct, without ever being seriously challenged. The New Left, while it has never had a wholly agreed on ideology, has, necessarily assumed certain self-protective attitudes and ideas, behind which it has nurtured its growth. But the cops were quite accurate about whom they knew to be the enemy. In the focus of common danger during Convention Week, unexpected neighbors, bedfellows and comrades showed up on the side of Us. A new concept of an American revolution began to come out of the woodwork. It remains to be seen if those pointed out are clear enough and brave enough to follow it and let it happen.

Cops and Media Watch Over the Festival of Life

In Lincoln Park, Yippies were gathering, a few more every day, but not nearly the numbers expected or hoped for. Between Lincoln Park and the beaches of Lake Michigan runs the Outer Drive—Chicago's lakeside north-south expressway—generating a constant roar of tires and motors that numbs the air even under the leaves of the trees in the Park. Lincoln Park lies a couple of miles north of the Loop, but other than during rush hours, transportation is quick on north-south thoroughfares between Lincoln Park and the area of Grant Park that faces the Hilton Hotel at the south end of the Loop. This would be important later in the week. A lot of the kids in Lincoln Park wore McCarthy buttons and had big blue-and-white McCarthy flowers printed on the backs of their leather jackets. The cops noticed this and would act upon it later.

The Yippies had plans to turn Lincoln Park into a carnival of music, dance, poetry, political and drug workshops—a Festival of Life, they called it—to raise a show of hope and celebration against the Festival of Death, as they called it, in the Convention in the Amphitheater. *

The Yippies were still working and hoping to get a permit to sleep in the Park after 11 PM—the curfew hour that up to now had never been really enforced.

* A description of the activities planned during the Festival of Life—only a few of which actually materialized—is contained in this leaflet handed out by Yippies in Lincoln Park during the week before the Convention:

August 20-24 (AM): Training in snake dancing, karate, nonviolent self-defense. Information booth in Park.
August 24 (PM): Yippie Mayor R. Daley presents fireworks on Lake Michigan.
August 25 (AM): Welcoming of the Democratic delegates— downtown hotels (to be announced).
August 25 (PM): MUSIC FESTIVAL—Lincoln Park.
August 26 (AM): Workshop in drug problems, underground communications, how to live free, guerrilla theatre, self-defense, draft resistance, communes, etc. (Potential workshop leaders should call The Seed, 837 No. LaSalle Street, 943-5282.) Scenario sessions to plan small group activities.
August 26 (PM): Beach Party on The Lake across from Lincoln Park: Folksinging, barbecues, swimming, lovemaking.
August 27 (Dawn): Poetry, mantras, religious ceremony.
August 27 (AM): Workshops and scenario sessions. Film showing and mixed media—Coliseum, 1513 S. Wabash.
August 27 (PM): Benefit concert—Coliseum. Rally and nomination of Pigasus and LBJ birthday—Lincoln Park.
August 28 (Dawn): Poetry and folk singing.
August 28 (AM): Yippie Olympics, Miss Yippie Contest, Catch the Candidate, Pin the Tail on the Donkey, Pin the Rubber on the Pope, and other normal, healthy games.
August 28 (PM): Plans to be announced at a later date. 4 PM —Mobilization Rally scheduled for Grant Park. March to the Convention.
August 29-30: Events scheduled depend on Wednesday night. Return to Park for sleeping.

All of a sudden, in the week before Convention, signs appeared everywhere around the Park: PARK CLOSES AT 11 PM. The citizens of Lincoln Park regarded the appearance of these signs with some amazement. The City had the one excuse of not having appropriate sanitation facilities for so many people, and yet the thousands who were in the Park during the day—from morning until late at night—managed to find some place in the neighborhood, and if a few went to the bushes, it did not worry the Department of Sanitation during the day. The denial of the permit to sleep in the Park would heat up the conditions that would furnish the fever for the confrontation Sunday night that would trigger everything that happened in the streets during Convention Week. Both sides needed a pretext, real enough and absurd enough to touch the centers of rage.

The Yippies' Festival of Life was planned to end in the nomination of Mr. Pigasus, a hog, their mock candidate. Friday, in the week before Convention, Jerry Rubin—one of the three Yippie founders—singer Phil Ochs and other accomplices were arrested in the Civic Center Plaza in the Loop, on charges of disorderly conduct, as they steered Mr. Pigasus, the candidate, out of a station wagon. Late Friday afternoon, in Lincoln Park, the training of the parade marshalls continued on the baseball diamond, largely, it seemed, for the benefit of the incredible massing of media cameras, media mikes, media reporters, who gleaned all of the sensational visual images they could contrive from the Yippies and the training of the parade marshalls. Then they televised it to put a little carbonated zing into the fears of the viewing public. "I am an actor for TV," said Abbie Hoffman, another Yippie founder, whose friendly, hectic energy gave a good tone to Lincoln Park in the week before the

Convention. It was reported that when he went to stay in a house he always asked first if it had a TV, keeping in touch with his craft. Hoffman even began to feel that the Yippies should get some payment for their services to the media, and he bargained some of the larger networks into agreeing to bring loads of soft drinks, balloons, etcetera, to a Yippie party that never happened because, by that time, something else was happening in the streets. TV seeks such actors, news actors, and the self-conscious Yippies played it for all it was worth. If the McCarthy people shied from creating a national theater of scandal for the TV cameras in the Credentials Committee hearings, there were people in Lincoln Park who knew how to feed exalted garbage to the Pig. Education begins wherever the Pig is at, and the student is on all fours eating garbage.

You could not count the times that the parade marshalls were asked to perform for the cameras the exotic import: the snake dance used by Japanese students to break through police lines in their demonstrations. The American marshalls, training for a march that never happened, could not break through a line of ten of their own men, so an important element of the snake dance must have been left behind in Japan. "Wa'*shoi!* Wa'*shoi!*" —left, right, left, right. The first time I saw the snake dance I said that a drill sergeant would envy their cadence. The compliment seemed wry to the Yippies. But a para-military attitude was showing everywhere, expectancy of police violence, though all the training was strictly self-defense. Imagine *that,* daring to try to train yourself in self-defensive tactics, how to kick in the groin, how to deflect a club, how to use first aid. The City dared to use *this* as a justification for the police attack. The City dared to revere suddenly non-violence and the memory of Martin Luther King, Jr. The student, the viewer, is indeed on all fours eating garbage. The Yippies knew how to despise the media openly, and thereby draw them deeper into the game.

Late Friday afternoon, the parade marshalls were scattered in workshop groups over the baseball diamond. There were almost as many plainclothesmen and mediamen as there were marshalls. There had been talk of the arrest of Pigasus in the morning and of Rubin now being out on bail. A sudden melée occurred just north of the Park building. Yippies and marshalls streamed, at first uncertainly and then faster, straight toward it. Blue shirts and blue helmets were moving in it. The first astonished cries from Yippies caught off guard were, "Police! Police!" (They didn't even use the word cops, much less pigs!) The cries were frightened; and it was a moment before the Yippies realized, having been taken by surprise, that they were not acting their parts. Then they assumed their roles, and changed the cry to: "Pigs! Pigs! Pigs!" Assuming the roles changed the tone, too. Now the Yippies were not so frightened, now they were assertive, now they walked with more assurance. *"Pigs! Pigs!"* Cops and Yippies rushed upon the center of the melée. (The day before, an Indian boy, Dean Johnson, a hippie, had been shot to death by the cops in Old Town across from the Park, apparently because in his fear when he was stopped by cops, he had pulled a gun out of his flight bag on the sidewalk. This one killing at the time seemed to presage more, and it weighted the fear in the Park.)

The melée was all because Mrs. Pigasus—somebody said she was actually a small boar—had been brought into the Park and released near the building by the baseball diamond. A Yippie monitor with a speaker strapped on his back, was giving directions and talking to the crowd. If he was inciting to riot, his language was too subtle for me. I was about ten feet behind him. He was tapped slightly on the arm from behind by a cop; the tap was slight indeed but the boy did not even look around, he knew immediately that it was a cop, and he let his arms go limp and gave no resistance as he was arrested. Another cop was carrying Mrs. Pigasus, like any farm boy would carry a pig, against his body with his hands under its frong legs, the pig bumping against his thighs. Mrs. Pigasus was snorting delicately. "Be gentle with the Presidential Candidate's wife," Yippies were saying. Or, "Look at the way you're treating the next First Lady." The cop stared sometimes stolidly ahead, sometimes laughing, followed by a crowd of Yippies. "Pig! Pig! Pig!" Sometimes the Yippies pointed at the hog and sometimes at the cop. It was too much for the cops. From all directions, the put-on came at them. They made savage motions, short charges, and head-cracking was felt to be imminent—or worse. Mrs. Pigasus was heaved into a paddy wagon parked on the green grass of the Park. A couple of Yippies were already arrested for disorderly conduct and pushed into the wagon. Now, with the back doors of the wagon still open and a crowd gathered, one or two of the cops—one a sergeant—actually asked *who wanted to be arrested and go with the pig*. A few Yippies volunteered—to take care of their candidate's wife, they said—and climbed into the back of the wagon. It drove away. The remaining cops waved and shouted for everyone to disperse.

A feeling was there as if something terrific and terrible in the air had just leaned toward us at great speed and then skirted by. A few Yippies were worried whether the cops had got all their pigs. "Oh, man," one fellow whispered, "we've got a whole farm-full of pigs outside of town." That was most likely a put-on, too. A radio interviewer was holding his mike out to the mouths of any Yippies willing to talk. He looked puzzled, and a little worried. He asked, parentally gentle, as if talking to small children who had just lost their pet, "How do you feel about losing your pig?" The kids' faces squirmed with suppressed delight at the great success of the put-on. "We want Secret Service protection for our Candidate." But otherwise they had difficulty answering the question; so the radio-interviewer tried another approach, tenderly, parentally, cautiously: "What does the pig mean to you?" Right out of Literature 101, symbolism.

"Food," one Yippie said.

"Ham," another said.

"A pig is a pig," another said.

"Pigs are cleaner than people."

"Our Candidate should be allowed to walk the streets."

"Streets belong to people."

"Parks belong to people."

"Pigs belong to people."

The radio interviewer had just seen the cops taking the matter with terrifying seriousness. But he could not cope intellectually or emotionally with kids who were willing to take physical risks for a put-on. He was in a bind and he could not see the bind; he could only feel it, dimly. He thanked the Yippies cautiously and turned his back on his interviewees and began talking into the mike himself, as if speaking privately behind his hand into the ear of all that part of America that could not understand the bind, either. "I am in Lincoln Park, where the police have just arrested the Yippies' pig. . . ." It was the same for the City when the Yippies threatened to put LSD in the city's water and turn on everyone, or threatened other acts that would shake people loose from their careful control of their lives. That was the fear. There was the put-on. If revolutions occur when ruling groups lose touch with people, then the chasms are ripening in many areas.

It seemed that the Mrs. Pigasus incident, with its absurd terror, was gone, and then, in only a few minutes, a stronger aggravation surged between cops and Yippies at the corner of the building containing rest rooms near the baseball diamond. The cops shoved with their clubs. A Yippie, who would not swallow an insult, came toward one cop yelling, "Pig! Pig!" He moved back again and the cop told him to *move*, meaning not just walk. The Yippie said, "I am moving." The cop yelled, "I said *move!*" and hit the kid hard on the back of the neck with his club. I was only a few feet away, expecting a club on my head any second, and I was amazed that the kid stayed upright. He did not run, he walked away, and I walked carefully away with him. Often the cops were most provoked by presence of mind, and other times they were most provoked by helplessness and presence of mind would dissuade them. The cops charged again, snarling, and then lined up with their backs to the building, stirring among themselves. "Up against the wall, motherfucker," a Yippie shouted, almost sobbed, and it sounded more like helpless frustration than a promise of things to come.

Platform Committee, Hale Boggs Presiding, Faces the Nation

"Out at the Amphitheatre . . ."
"Out at the Amphitheatre . . ."
"What's happening at the Amphitheatre?"

"Man, the Amphitheatre is *not* where it's *at!*"

There were three main locations for possible activity during Convention Week—Lincoln Park, the Hilton Hotel facing Grant Park, and the International Amphitheatre, each a few miles distant from the other. Most of what occurred in the Convention itself in the Amphitheatre seemed about as relevant to the situation in Chicago as what went on in the Tsar's household must have seemed relevant to Russians in the February Revolution. The Convention was a main focus, a symbol of the power that could be brought to bear against people, and yet it seemed unimportant. Yet because of the separation of the three main areas of activity, energy could take electrical leaps, storm leaps, fire leaps, gaining power in the leap over space. The distance between the areas permitted a dynamic interplay, a variety of confrontations, and the growth of legends. If everything about the Convention had been concentrated in one spot, the event of Chicago might still have been interesting, but it would have been more stolid, more manageable. The Yippies initially wanted to do their Festival of Life in Grant Park, and there must have been a greater wisdom that made them shift to Lincoln Park. The demonstrators and Yippies were on horseback, plying between the Hilton and Lincoln Park. It is natural for Americans to be on the move. We gain energy on the move.

The Amphitheatre is a huge block of a building stuck right at the source of the smell that plagues Chicago when the wind is right: the smell of the Stockyards. The Amphitheatre was guarded stupendously, and yet stupidly, with no real awareness of how to fashion security. A blind man—wearing huge black glasses, with an enormous black cape, a shotgun under his arm, and a tall

Afghan hound as a seeing-eye dog—could have negotiated the security and assassinated whomever he chose,
if he also wore on his back and front a WE LOVE
MAYOR DALEY sign. There were men who have no
love for Daley, who accepted ten dollars in a bar to
carry a WE LOVE MAYOR DALEY sign into the Convention, which they wanted to see, and they even
walked the floor. Security breaks down before the great
need of politicians for the evidence of public support.
Americans are not good at security. We have our Min-
utemen, KKK, CIA, FBI, etcetera, but secret organizations and real security violate the needs of the democratic charade, and the charade is important within its
own theater. Security is usually a play-act full of holes,
a part of the charade. The stupendous play-act had to
be put to some use, and so it became *a harassment of
people other than Administration regulars,* McCarthy
people, peace plank people, outspoken liberals.

I stopped at a gas-station on South Wabash on my first
trip to the Amphitheatre, which is located about five
miles southwest of the Hilton. You drive through black
ghetto to get there, where, around the Amphitheatre
itself, the residents are Irish and Polish, "etcetera whites."
All of the attendants were Negro, and one filled the tank
of my Volkswagen. I gave him a $5 bill, in something of a
hurry, but he carried no money to make change. He
had to go find the owner-manager who kept all the station money in his pocket and made all the change. This
occurred for every transaction with every black attendant. This is common in black areas where the white man
owns the business. In Lincoln Park, where I live, the
attendants at a nearby gas-station are white, mostly hill-
billies, and they usually have as much as $100 or more
in their pockets for change. The implication is that if

there is any stealing to be done it will be done by white hands. You cannot hold the money, it says to the Negro, even if it means the white man must waste a lot of black and white time and energy shuffling back and forth, making change. One of the main demands of black power groups is that they hold the money, incoming and outgoing, allocate it, make the change, and if there is any stealing to be done they can do it as well as any white man. Equals.

The owner of this gas station on South Wabash— greasy from working on a car that he had crawled out from under to make the change—thumped the back of my car, where the bumper sticker was, and said, "*Hey, McCarthy!*" It was hard to tell whether he approved or disapproved. He was obviously used to speaking loudly in an ambiguous tone to keep others on the defensive. I was not going to tell him that the sticker was there because my wife was working for McCarthy, while my own feelings were quite ambivalent.

On the route to the Amphitheatre where the redwood fences and pastel-colored plastic cloth fence coverings put up by the City to shield unsightly spots. There were reports of these fence coverings being used to hide slums. I wish our Mayor were enough aware of slums that he would want to hide them. In most cases that I saw, the fence coverings were used to hide things as unsightly as a lot full of machinery, or a coal pile. Our Mayor's motive was not so elevated as that of hiding slums. His attitude was more that of a mortician. He wants his visitors to see nice colors in Chicago, smell nice things. He would, if he could, plant tuberoses around the Stockyards.

An explosion of red-white-and-blue pennants and banners roared and rattled in any breeze around the Amphitheatre and the Stockyard Inn next door. It could have been the biggest gas station, the biggest discount sale, the biggest used car sale in the world. It was reported that every rock above the size of a pebble had been removed from a several block radius of the Amphitheatre. Imagine all those city employees scouting and sifting the area for rocks. In the wisdom of the great unconscious that ruled all events during the Convention and made conscious decisions, they did not waste their time picking up rocks around the Lincoln Park and Grant Park areas. I parked in a lot where there were plenty of cinders if anyone wanted to throw anything. In back of the Amphitheatre, trucks were unloading fine potted trees and endless pots of great yellow mums, stacking them in ranks and files. The Mayor was going to make sure that it would be the best funeral that money could buy. Cops were everywhere, light blue, as if the sky had fallen in. In the Amphitheatre, I saw a cop who is known in my neighborhood to be a killer, who will take the first excuse offered to shoot someone, usually a Puerto Rican or Negro kid whom he is chasing. There was a shifting glance of eyes between me and him. I didn't like it.

In the Amphitheatre were the Platform Committee hearings, Hale Boggs of Louisiana, Chairman. He was a man who was always trying to look quizzically or sternly out of the top of his head, above his glasses, a sort of beseeching threat, possibly hoping to conceal his face and its constant flush. Blue, blue everywhere, it seemed that most of the available surfaces in the Convention hall were painted blue. Recessive. A color that helped to keep you from smelling that the body had been above ground much too long.

The Platform Committee sat dully in the rows of its solid bank against the waves of protest. It had none of the energy of the Credentials Committee. Yes, there would be verbal heat and worse over the peace plank, but there was an underlying dead silence, in which any speaker could say anything, but with the profound sense that nothing said would influence what the platform would be. It was known that the position on the Vietnam War was being written by the Johnson Administration in Washington. In the Credentials Committee whether people were accredited or not became very important—something to be fought for or fought against—because to accredit a man is to give admission to his ideas, and he may be around for a long time and you can never tell what he will do. The effects of accreditation may be geometric in progression over time. In the Platform Committee, grievances and recommendations were recorded in heated boredom.

Chairman Hale Boggs, a man mostly Pig, lying in the shade, cared only for his lunch and the complacent good will or acquiescence of his compatriots on the Committee. Lyndon's man. Lyndon's vendetta. Lyndon Johnson would not be discredited by the Party that disowned him. Lyndon would dance on the grave, a good old Texas stomp. It was the best thing Lyndon ever did for us. Good for Lyndon. Hale Boggs was a tired actor who was required above all to do nothing. It was most important, using the forms of parliamentary order, that he do nothing. With the humor of the county courthouse, he did it up right: he did absolutely nothing. And the South, tongue in cheek, lying in the shade or riding the range, won again, blocked again. Hale Boggs. Repeat the name. Hale Boggs. Repeat it again. Hale Boggs. Vary the tone. Hale Boggs. Henry James could not have named him better.

I was stopped on entering the Platform Committee

by the underlying cacophony of four different styles of life in the room. Lots of broad blue here, too. The enthusiastic black ladies—who were either large or emaciated, sitting in the spectators' seats, stamping the floor and singing out—were the church-meeting style, with their floppy black and white hats saying BLACK IS BEAUTIFUL. Another style was at the podium, where two Negro women, with one Negro man between them, were speaking to the Committee, angry, accusatory, deliberately exacerbating white guilt, yet with the feeling of being constrained and angered by "self-education," with all of its envy and hatred of those at ease with the forms. They were all of the NATIONAL WELFARE RIGHTS ORGANIZATION, and they wore buttons to prove it. They were all women, except for the Negro man, who had quit his job as a chemistry professor at Syracuse University, I believe, to lead them, and this was mentioned more than once. "Dr. Wiley," the ladies said, "Dr. Wiley," as if emphasizing their total reverence for standard credentials. The Committee *had* to listen to such a good lad, who had made good, and then given it up to help them, the ladies. They are clapping their hands in support of the two women and the man at the podium, "Yes, sister, that's the way it is. Tell it like it is, sister. You listen up there. She's telling it like is, yes, sister." Up there, above the broad blue, sat the white folk of the Platform Committee, with so few blacks among them that you had to search for them, except for one wonderfully handsome brown woman in a yellow dress, stonily graceful and aloof, in the top row. She asked few questions, only sat there, as if accustomed to being worshipped, but damned if she would ask for it. The Welfare Rights people were following the now familiar gambit of verbal abuse and accusation that

makes a liberal squirm in his guilt and come through
with the goods faster. It also brings out Piggish anger
faster, and that can be considered a boon, too. It would
seem that the Welfare Rights leaders thought they were
talking to liberals. They weren't. Hale Boggs, and almost
all of the Platform Committee members, stared stiffly
at nothing, at space, at their hands or at something on
the table before them, and if they glanced at each other,
it was in the way of parlor-room killers making a silent,
deadly agreement. A few, the liberals, leaned forward
as if with terrific attention, trying to make up for the
others. The only guilt felt here, constrained by the forms
of this particular sort of theater, was that which might
have been felt by the cops in the streets, the kind that
made the cops go crazier and bring the club down
harder. The media men—TV and newspaper reporters,
the fourth style of life—were coolly taking notes and
shooting film, with an occasional smile or a glance exchanged among them, particularly among the Negro reporters, as if with the feeling of there but for the grace
of God go I. The Committee stared that way until the
roisterous Welfare Rights ladies, thanked stiffly but with
a certain smile by Boggs, after a few questions, went
away.

They didn't have to go away. They had every right
to their spectator seats. It happened about one foot away
from me. He, their leader, the former chemistry professor, said to his cadre, mostly young white girls, "Let's
get our people out of here." The white girls said, "No,
let's stay: Connally is going to speak on Vietnam." And
he, tired and insistent, said, rather urgently, "No, let's
get our people out of here." The white girls said: "Let's
stay, Connally is going to speak in support of the Vietnam War. Let's not let him get away with it." But he,

the former chemistry professor, got them to leave, all of them. And that was a shame.

They should have stayed. They would have seen the Platform Committee smile and relax breezily among themselves as soon as the Negro Welfare Rights women were gone, except for the handsome brown woman in the yellow dress in the top row, aloof, so aware of something, god knows what: she was like a silent thunderclap in the room. They would have seen the lady white delegate from a Southern state, all fluff of Southern sexual tease, smiling discreetly to acknowledge what everyone on the Committee knew: we're home free again. They would have seen almost every member of the Platform Committee smile and lean forward in eager welcome of Governor John Connally of Texas, presumed by all parties to be Lyndon's hatchet-man—who entered briskly— a blue-ribbon razorback right off the range, cleaned up for the folks out east to see, with the scars of a bullet in Dallas under his clothing. They would have seen every member of the Committee look Connally in the face the way they did not look the black people in the face. It is nice to be welcomed by people, and Connally felt it. They would have heard Governor Connally ride the range on why the Johnson Administration's policy was correct and must be supported in Vietnam. Those loud, uninhibited, nothing-to-lose black ladies would have minced Connally: "That's right, Governor. Sing it like it is." They would at the very least have required Hale Boggs to call the cops to clear the "demonstration" from the hearing room, for any outburst of feeling or applause that did not support an Administration position was called a "demonstration." And out in the halls was the killer cop, with fellows, waiting for another excuse. Another confrontation was avoided, and Connally bathed himself freely and easily in the adulation of Committee members.

When Connally first stepped to the podium, the male delegate from South Carolina rose and asked, absolutely deadpan, "Have you ever written a book, Governor?" There was laughter from the Committee. Connally, taken only slightly aback, registered the game, registered the immediate gains to be made, and said, with a smile meant to be seen across a mile of heads: "*No.*" General laughter and applause came again from the Committee. Only a few were silent. All of this was because a number of witnesses, including perhaps the chemistry professor, had offered as a part of their credentials, a list of their publications. The male delegate from South Carolina reminded me of my border-state boyhood and of men who play a large part in the Green Berets and other counter-insurgency operations, many of whom despise educated, writing white men as much as they despise educated or self-educated, writing or not-writing black men, but in a different way. Connally mentioned that he had met the male delegate from South Carolina and he remembered the place of meeting, and they exchanged a pleasantry. Hale Boggs also remembered the Governor warmly to everybody. The South Carolina delegate was obsequious toward Connally in that way of male Southerners—though down home they call it respect—and Connally accepted the homage, cautious not to show how he actually felt about it—because the South Carolina delegate is the dupe of men like Connally, and it was obvious that Connally regarded him as material of limited use, but useful, nevertheless. The South Carolina man, and most of the Committee, listened proudly while Governor Connally, Lyndon's man, soaked the flag in blood and glory in Vietnam, freedom, anti-communism, and lasting peace with honor. He preached "total antagonism to communist untruth."

Such Southerners are serious only about food, women, color, war, and the sense of honor that tars all of those allegiances with a maudlin brush. They are also tongue-in-cheek about everything, or stuffed with a suffocating righteousness. It is a mistake to see them as men who shoot from the hip. No, sir. They do things in the dark at the dead-end of a country road. Mark Twain said much the same thing a long time ago. And the tongue-in-cheek feeling is always somewhere in it, as it was in Connally as he gave his speech in support of the policy in Vietnam. There were kids in Lincoln Park ready to play Tom Sawyer with Connally's tongue-in-cheek indifference.

Michael Harrington—author of *The Other America*, the book that helped publicize the issues of poverty in 1961–62 and now a columnist published by several large newspapers, apparently in their attempts to broaden their spectrum of opinion a little to the Left in the hope of helping to create a more stable, useful center—came brusquely to the podium next, as if he were late running onto the football field to take someone's place, struggling to get his helmet on. Harrington did not win any points when he said at the beginning, "I'm afraid I have published a few books." A short man, always up on his toes to say his say, he was not welcomed, and he himself did not respect the Committee. If a man is not welcomed, we don't see who he is, or how much he is, since generally what we welcome is a feeling or an idea that agrees with us in some way and leads us. Almost all wit and effect of feeling is in the interplay of welcome. Harrington was recommending a program of considerable social

reform, fairly specific, born of socialist insights, although
not necessarily socialist in application. Boggs, the Chairman, could not let it seem to his compatriots that he
welcomed, or even indulged, such ideas. In the middle
of Harrington's speech, he got up—a blatant discourtesy
—and walked out almost lethargically along the bottom
row, stopping here and there to chat with members of
the Committee, who enjoyed diverting attention from
Harrington, too. Harrington, unsettled a bit, proceeded
stubbornly. A number of people, among the spectators
and even among the press, clapped loudly for points in
Harrington's speech, a spontaneous but deliberate conspiracy to let the Committee know that there were supporters. Harrington responded to the support and was
better, at the end, than when he began. As soon as he
was gone, Boggs came back to resume his Chairmanship.

Then came Roy Wilkins, Executive Director of the
National Association for the Advancement of Colored
People, to testify, and Boggs let Wilkins and everybody
else know how much he respected Roy Wilkins, warmly
commenting on Wilkins' many appearances on Capitol
Hill. Wilkins, in his slight, tenacious way, appeared to
regard the welcome as somewhat onerous, and did not
let it bring out the best in him. He was greying in the
hair, and there seemed to be a grey cast to his light skin:
Ah, me, grey. He was slow, faintly legalistic, hard to
hear, and did not respond to such support as came from
the spectators and the press. He seemed tired of recommending his massive social and economic program to
secure justice for black people—perhaps he had been
here too many times for too many long, long years. Then
Hale Boggs needed his lunch.

When I left the Platform Committee hearings, the
violence that impended everywhere felt inevitable. The

rage of the righteous draws itself into a battering ram in the face of such blocking off. I walked around the Amphitheatre to get all of its blue into my mind, feeling that I would not be back, that what was going to happen would happen elsewhere in Chicago. I was glad that I didn't see the killer cop on my way out.

Sunday August 25. Lincoln Park. Photo by Joshua Moorehead.

sunday: overthrow

Chicago: The Prague of the West

Saturday and Sunday, Czechs were gathering around the invading Russian tanks and soldiers, asking: "Why are you here?" The Russian invasion of Czechoslovakia to suppress the liberalization of Czech life was seized as an example by every faction in Chicago. Connally used it in his speech to the Platform Committee to show why we must give vigorous support to such efforts as the Vietnam War. Senator Ralph Yarborough of Texas, speaking for the Texas challengers before the Credentials Committee, asked the Committee not to crush the "idealism of the young" with "political power" the way the Russians crushed the Czechs with "military power." Yippies and demonstrators felt the example of Czech bravery and began using such words as Czechoslocago and Prague East and Prague West. They were also alert for strong visual images of potential theatrical effect and they too gathered around the cops, saying "Why are you here?" The cops, without a trace of Russian queasiness, said, "This is my job."

It was assumed that the Czech question was levelled in accusation at the Russians. In fact, the question defined for the Czechs the area of their own consciousness; it defined for the Czechs who they are and where they are going, even if they lose, and nothing makes the Monster more uncomfortable than to be met at the border of real awareness. We Americans don't know our question yet. We can't duplicate the Czech question, but the question could not be asked unless there was first the answer.

Senator McCarthy, irritated no doubt at the fresh strength that the Russian invasion would give to the supporters of the War against Communism in Vietnam, said that the Czech affair was no great crisis, thus making what some considered the worst public relations error of his campaign. And it was possible to wonder if the Russians had not timed their invasion to affect the Democratic Convention, ensure the nomination of Humphrey and thereby have either Humphrey or Nixon as President of the United States, because there is possibly nothing the Russian leaders fear more than a progressive United States. Such a United States, not hellbent on turning half the world into an electronic shooting-gallery-disposal-area-discount-store, would invalidate the positions of the Russian leaders, and the unwelcome release from external pressure would cause unwelcome changes within the Soviet Union. And the cops felt that if the Russians were doing what they were doing in Prague, it was doubly OK to do it in a free country. They said so, to anyone who asked them in Lincoln Park.

Saturday and Sunday, the Mobe people—who had planned huge marches and demonstrations all over the city at places symbolic for protest against the War and against the Convention—found their plans largely empty. There were no people to fill them. Saturday, Abbie Hoffman and Tom Hayden were both quoted as saying: "My God, there's no one here!" Tens of thousands were expected, wanted, needed. But not so. The thing would be done by a few thousand at the most—3,000 or 4,000 up to perhaps 8,000 or 10,000 at the height on Wednesday—and more than half would come from Chicago and nearby areas. In a situation made responsive by months of needling play and counter-play in publicity, it was energy and unpremeditated daring that counted, not the weight of peace-marching numbers. Both the Mobe people and the McCarthy people had warned their supporters over the nation that coming to Chicago could be very dangerous. In retrospect, Mobe leaders would say that many more people should have come to Chicago and that the McCarthy people were to be blamed for cowardice or worse: complicity with the City and the Democrats in telling people to stay away. But at the time, Mobe and SDS spokesmen and some underground papers were all saying: you come to Chicago at your own risk. It seems that most people heeded the warning.

At the time, there was only one goal that SDS admitted of concern to itself, though originally SDS planned to shun the Convention in Chicago: that goal was winning over the McCarthy kids. They shared middle-class origins and since there were such a lot of the McCarthy kids and they worked hard, anybody would want their allegiance.

Carl Oglesby—former National Secretary of SDS and its only true speechmaker among a host of monotones—wrote a letter to the McCarthy kids and published it in *New Left Notes*, an SDS publication, which was handed out free in the Hilton. The letter was republished in *The Ramparts Wallposter*, the Convention

Week daily broadside, so the letter had extensive circulation in the Convention areas. But the letter was felt to be
patronizing, and the McCarthy people had no patience
with it. The potent New Left analysis of the liberal, built
up carefully over several years, began to sound uneasily
as if it had become as much rhetoric as analysis, static,
with perhaps a false bottom in it. A different sort of
teaching was coming fast, and it would hit the New Left
as hard as anyone else. On Saturday the McCarthy kids,
cool and well-protected with innocence and cynicism,
sneered at both the Yippies and the New Left, though
Yippies and New Left were considerably divided on the
puzzle of what they called the McCarthy phenomenon.
A great many kids in Lincoln Park were McCarthy supporters. The young McCarthy aides in the Hilton felt
themselves to be the advance guard of the new owners,
and they felt they could make the system work for them.
Wednesday their political orientation was broken, and
they were on the streets getting gassed and clubbed too
in their straight suits, and their arrogant naiveté was
gone, for the time anyway, with the answer blowing in
the wind.

McCarthy Arrives and Innocence Waits
on the Hilton Stairs

Sunday, Senator McCarthy arrived at Midway Airport, located almost in the fields on the southwest of
Chicago. I went out there to see McCarthy arrive on
the scene because I was convinced that he was the only
major political figure who might get killed in Chicago.
He was a puzzle, the meeting point of opposing possibilities; either he was finessing dissent on the War or
entering into a dynamic that could lead him past the
point of safety. On the other hand, Humphrey was a

foregone conclusion, a man with doldrums between his
eyes. And Senator McGovern of South Dakota had surely
been wound up and set going by parties, along with the
"Draft Ted Kennedy" rumors and efforts, who wished
to keep the liberals split up and disorganized. McGovern's sudden candidacy was the one thing that seemed
to indicate that there were people scared enough of
McCarthy to take him seriously, albeit that the two senators were supposed to be friends.

A media truck, in front of McCarthy's car at Midway,
tore down the wires that led to the stage where he was to
speak, creating difficulties with the microphones. Secret
servicemen rushed into the confusion to lead him to the
stage. Assassination would have been so easy at Midway;
the fact that McCarthy was still alive must have meant
that he didn't have a chance in the Convention, that
someone somewhere tolerated the annoyance of his presumption as the annoyance of Martin Luther King, Jr.,
Malcolm X, John Kennedy, Bobby Kennedy—one is
tempted to make the assertion either comprehensive or
insupportable—was not tolerated. If your presumption
gains the moment of definitive effect, there appears to
be no place to hide. From the time Bobby Kennedy was
killed, at the very moment it seemed the nomination
would certainly be his, McCarthy must have walked an
artful line. If he came too close to winning, he too would
surely be killed. If he did not come close to winning,
there would not be the base for the electoral renewal
that he sought, inside or outside the Democratic Party;
probably he still does not know which way he is going.
Oglesby, in his letter to the McCarthy kids, said that they
admired McCarthy's courage, but that his courage was
timid within "the system." Oglesby was not wrong in
suggesting that there was great courage on the New Left

—that would be amply demonstrated before the week was over—but the point was petulant within the dynamic of history and the reality of bullets.

McCarthy did not lose that touch of physical caution, particularly on entering any public place, until after Wednesday night, when Humphrey was nominated. Thursday afternoon, when McCarthy spoke to his supporters, he seemed positively liberated, perhaps in complicated ways. I came to look for robustness of feeling, it was so rare inside the Convention and outside it. I am not talking about demagogic passion. Personal presence. Cynical McCarthy might be, or might have been, but he had it: the feeling of more awareness than any candidate that I remember in American politics. Lean pickings, to be sure. It is almost impossible for a man of such personal awareness to survive in our politics. The Wilsons, Hardings, Coolidges, Hoovers, Roosevelts, Trumans, Eisenhowers, Kennedys, Johnsons, and now Nixon, all men with only one major gift, that they can, in their hunger, sustain prolonged public exposure, prolonged lack of privacy, prolonged manipulation of anyone and everyone, from the time they run for the state legislature to the time they run for Congress, up, up, step by step, using a personal fortune or developing a fortune in influence and debts—it leaves so little time for the meditative—until they survive, some one or two, and run for the Presidency. These are not men born of woman; they were shaken out of sleeves in cloakrooms. McCarthy may have been returned to humanity by the continual prospect of a bullet.

In the Hilton, the McCarthy girls' choir had been practicing for a couple of days, to welcome him. There has never been such fresh innocence ranged up staircases anywhere. No lipstick, no make-up, no hair work:

an enthusiasm so intense and so thin in its naiveté that you hesitated to touch it or breathe too hard: as delicate and whole as the puff of a dandelion.

Music in Lincoln Park/Invocation

McCarthy struggled wittily with the PA system at Midway Airport, while appointed and self-appointed regulars expanded their chests in the Hilton. Nevertheless, it was what happened with the Yippies Sunday afternoon and Sunday night in Lincoln Park and escalated Monday and Tuesday nights, that filled everybody's expectations with a stinging surprise and sent out an impulse that zig-zagged along the conduits of the real underground in our society: an impulse that jumped from the Yippies in Lincoln Park to the citizens of Lincoln Park, to the demonstrators in Grant Park and around the Hilton, to the McCarthy kids in the Hilton itself, and then into the Amphitheatre where, zeroing into the burn of liberal humiliation, it helped to sunder the Democratic Convention. It was an impulse that destroyed old defenses and old connections and left behind a strong trail of new connections of consciousness.

The alliance between the Yippies and the New Left was loose and uneasy, but also enthusiastic in places. Yippies, except for self-conscious leaders such as Rubin and Hoffman, hardly existed as an organization. Yippies were the suddenly political wing of a culture called hippie—or whatever else it may be called next year— but it is a movement that has grown from name to name since the early Fifties. Yippies were organized largely through the underground papers. In Chicago, separate streams of rebellion in the general society—the Yippie-hippie, the poets such as Ginsberg, the New Left, and certain left-liberals who need strong identification fig-

ures (such as McCarthy)—came together at last—a
volatile combination. These streams of rebellion originated in the cultural revolt in the Fifties—the drugs, the
poetry, Burroughs, Ginsberg, etcetera: the new literature published in *Big Table, Evergreen Review*—and in
the civil rights movement in the South, and in the birth
of the intellectual New Left in such places as Madison,
Wisconsin with *Studies on the Left.* It was in the late
Fifties that the gauntlet was thrown down by a few
artists and intellectuals to the Country of Death, and the
duel has continued to grow until now. These movements
shunned each other in their beginnings, even disdained
each other, generally siding with either "rationality" or
"irrationality." During Convention Week in Chicago,
their distinctions did not dissolve, but they began to
overlap, merge, blur, feed each other, and most important, *respect* each other out of the common purpose in
the action in the streets. The ramifications of being
steeped in the same stew will cause changes in all phases
of the general revolt for a long time. As Huck Finn observed, everything is much better when thrown into
the same pot and the juices swap around a bit. By general revolt I mean anyone anywhere who has perceived
and responded to the movement of something other than
the pre-determined, even if—and especially if—it happens in his own head: *that,* as an abstract generaliza-
tion, may be the shared perception of the artists and
intellectuals who began to liberate their own minds in
the Fifties. They may have then gained an inkling of
what the new American revolution will be about: consciousness over, above and beyond and yet firmly concerning ideology and material necessity and allegiance.

New Left people, with exceptions, don't dig the drug
scene—oh, pot, that's all right now and then, but none

of that zoom stuff. The Yippies felt in the beginning of
Convention Week that many people in the New Left
were the pigs of the revolution. New Left people are not
noted for agreeing among themselves, but they are generally of middle-class origin, and there were a lot of working-class kids who called themselves Yippies in Lincoln
Park. Yippies are impulsive, and New Left people try to
plan everything, even though they have had the tenor of
an existential ideology, making it up as you go along,
with a cautious basis in class concepts. Yippies and hippies feel that New Left people are often stolid and a
bit out of it. As with most groups who have fundamental
disagreements and agreements, they tend to talk about
the disagreements behind each other's backs and welcome each other with the agreements. On Monday afternoon, after the absurd breakthrough of the night before
and just before the dramatic seizure of the equestrian
statue of Union General John A. Logan in Grant Park,
there was a Mobe organized demonstration in Grant
Park in front of the Hilton which had proceeded from
Lincoln Park in protest over the arrest of Tom Hayden.
The demonstrators were donkeying around and around
an asphalt path in the familiar pattern, but a lot of Yippies were sitting on the grass inside the circle and outside of it, staring sullenly at the Hilton. An SDS leader
bellowed over the portable speaker, "If you are sitting
on the grass, you are liable to a bust. Join the march!"
The Yippies stayed right where they were sitting on the
grass and stared at the Hilton, unmoved by any New
Left exhortations, ready for something else, ready to
seize and ride the Logan statue.

There were other student war-resisters outside the
donkeying march talking with a small group of sailors
and Air Force men, all in uniform, about the War in

Vietnam and about war-resistance. One sailor, with rangy, ruddy face and blond hair, frankly admitted that he had joined the Navy to avoid getting killed in the ground-fighting in Vietnam. He was not affected by the brotherly, almost slavish intensity of the young, bushy-haired student's gentle, excited arguments. There were no conversions, but the feeling was easy between the students and the servicemen. The students were borrowing from Trotsky's description in his history of the Russian revolution of how the Russian workers successfully cultivated the Cossacks in the years prior to the February revolution, so that the Cossacks instead of murderously dispersing the rebels as they did in 1905, stayed on their horses in February 1917 and stood aside.

It was the Yippies, in their mercurial fear and daring, who finally in Lincoln Park confronted the power of the state at its raw base: the police. New Left people were here, too, and they were important when things finally got started, but the catalytic people had almost no previous experience in demonstrations. Their way of response was not yet formed. It was an exercise in the absurd. The Yippies were the first to name, absurdly, the enemy the Pig—the Monster in the mind and in the society. They were the first in Chicago to begin, absurdly, at the beginning. They wanted to sleep in Lincoln Park, where Chicagoans go to sleep on hot nights and are not bothered by the police. Even some policemen, in talks with Lincoln Park residents, admit that they were, during Convention Week, enforcing new law, arbitrarily, because the 11 PM curfew in the Park has never been enforced, except for neckers. Every now and then, the cops will ask neckers to leave, their pleasure being in the category of demonstrations. Yippies were denied permission to sleep in the Park but they kept

asking the City for a permit; while they were obediently
leaving the Park at 11 PM every night. Several times in
the week before the Convention, Yippies would organize
groups to pick up paper and trash on the grass to show
their good will to the City and in hope of the permit.

The training of parade marshalls continued every day
on the baseball diamond: defensive tactics, how to deflect a club, how to kick a man in the groin if he will
stand still long enough for you to do it. It was a charade
for TV, and a charade for the mentality of the marchers,
to put-on the City and maybe give confidence to the
marchers. The marshalls were supposed to be trained
within a few days to use these tactics for self-defense
and then to turn around and magically train all marchers
in parades to use them, too. Absurd. Hardly any of that
training was ever used. It went up for grabs, except for
the first-aid training, as did all the plans.

The fight was over space; the fight is always over
space; and the Pig eats space and will never be satisfied
until the last bit of space is gone. The anthropologists,
the bone boys, could have told the cops that they would
be beaten. The invader of space is progressively weak-
ened the deeper he carries the invasion, and the invaded
becomes stronger in direct correlation. Deep in the Park,
in cop territory at night, the Yippies were weak, but had
to go that far to touch things off. Driven back into the
streets, the Yippies became stronger, cooler, and the cops
went into confused fury, within the theater of a situation
in which they were not permitted to shoot—to kill *or*
maim. The Monster has carried the invasion very deep
into the American mind, and in Lincoln Park he tried
to carry it all the way. Yippies could not stay and sleep
in Lincoln Park, but demonstrators were permitted to
stay in Grant Park in front of the Hilton all night long.

In back of the demonstrators and among them a sizable number of Yippies and other tired folk were wrapped up in blankets, sleeping. Somehow they all managed to find sanitation facilities, somewhere, and the City did not raise that argument about Grant Park as they did with the request to sleep in Lincoln Park. It does not take long to draw the lesson about the Pig and space.

Norman Mailer, in *The Armies of the Night,* made famous as a harbinger of things to come, the phrase *revolution by theater and without a script.* Such an event needs a special dynamic of its own, that can hardly be predicted; it needs spiritual preparation, and it needs many months of cultivation by publicity: the needling of the groups necessary for the arena. The Yippies and the New Left could not have foreseen *that they too would have to be needled by outsiders, newcomers, some of them quite, quite young.*

The Yippies were increasingly pissed-off about leaving the Park every night at 11 PM and increasingly scared of what would happen if they didn't. Saturday night, when many Yippies were insisting on staying in the Park, Allen Ginsberg led a large crowd out of the Park, avoiding the police sweep, chanting Om, in a demonstration in the streets of Old Town—one of his many attempts to bring about peace. Some of the Yippies marched through Old Town, and were hit finally by brief police action, with some kids arrested.

On Sunday afternoon there would be a music festival, the first event in the Festival of Life in Lincoln Park. Plenty of the neighborhood citizens were out in the Park, with their children, their strollers, their friends. They like music, and it promised to be good music. The Yippies were there, and other people seeking to see or hear something happen. The trouble began when the Yippies

drove a flat-bed, cattle-style trailer truck, for use in the
Festival, into the north end of the area of the Park that
would become the contested area, between the Lagoon
and the Outer Drive. The cops were upset. They arrested
a man and dragged him through a mass of people who
had come to hear the music and who didn't like what
the cops were doing and told them so, from all sides.
The citizens are not always docile. The cops felt it was
now or never to stamp out trouble before trouble began
—they had been trying it for days—and they charged
here and there, they clubbed, they rode back and forth
on three-wheeler motorcycles to terrorize people, and
many were the neighborhood mothers with children who
fled the Park where they had come in hope of music.
One mother, with a group of very small children, was
letting them entertain themselves with pouring pebbles
into bottles, back and forth, while she looked out upon
the mess that was happening. Arrests and bloody heads.
Terrorized people. But the cops had made a mistake.
They had raised the most important issue: the issue of
bravery. It would be raised again and again that evening
up to the 11 PM curfew.

What were the kids going to do? There was a meeting
on the baseball diamond, and many recommendations,
but no agreement. Abbie Hoffman, with springy head
of hair, big smile and easy-jerky friendliness, conducted
one group sitting on the grass around him in a "workshop" in "dispersal-group tactics," a name borrowed
from the way the North Vietnamese handle U.S. air
attacks. One girl objected to the presence of "newsmen";
she was pale and bitter with anger at the recent cop
attack, and Abbie Hoffman said, "There are no secrets.
The pigs got paranoia; they're going to lose. Right? We
don't got paranoia; we win. Right?" The Credentials

Committee met in executive session behind closed, guarded doors; the New Left excluded newsmen but debated whether sympathetic reporters should be admitted and then excluded them too, except for *Ramparts* reporters; while the Yippies met on the grass where there are no secrets under the sun. It was heart-warming, but reporters *were* inhibiting the angry talk.

Sunday Night/Overthrow

The weather changed Sunday and became clear and perfect, in the 70's, as if it knew people would need to call upon their highest potential of energy. Throughout the week, the weather would hold this way—truly beautiful, unusual in Chicago—weather where you can feel yourself spun with the sight of your eyes up, up, up into the sky.

On Sunday night, trash fires here and there, in the Park reflected their light off the leaves of trees. The kids no longer made any effort to keep the Park clean. Drums were going day and night without ceasing. You could walk on the beat of those drums the way Jesus walked on water. Kids were climbing in trees—"Did you ever make love in a tree?" Allen Ginsberg, with the most intense, the most receptive, the most relaxed feeling in the city, was Omming with a small group sitting around him. People were dispersed all over the Park between the Lagoon and LaSalle Street. No one was speaking of what had happened in the late afternoon. Guitars. One large group was on the central sidewalk, drumming. Another group was down by the Lagoon with drums around a Chicago actor who was dancing, high as the clear night sky above him. Tall and thin, with a bizarre innuendo that shakes up anybody who does not know him, the actor had been taunting the Yippies for two days for cowardice—for obediently leaving the Park at 11 PM every night just as the police demanded, even though the kids presumably insisted on their right to sleep in the Park. He had really been working the Park, and now his taunts were digging home. Bravery. He was the sort of man who would destroy himself before your eyes, in order to make some bizarre point known only to the littlest angel in Heaven.

He lost his balance, dancing to the drums, and fell into the Lagoon, and then swam out to the island, where he taunted the Yippies about starting the revolution on the island and staying in the Park by holding the island against the cops. None of these groups in the Park at this point were much aware of each other. The caucusing group with a portable speaker was on the eastern slope of the Park under trees. They discussed different alternatives all night long, and could agree on nothing except that of doing your own thing. There were those who advocated simple avoidance of suicidal conflict; those who advocated resistance and staying in the Park; those who advocated hitting the streets in demonstrations; and those who advocated dispersal in small groups, a fancy concept of retreat, that we discussed earlier, sanctified because it was borrowed from North Vietnam. None of these tactics and yet all of them, in fresh and spontaneous combination, finally happened. One boy in the middle of the caucusing group was yelling, "Fuck the marshalls! Up the marshalls! Bullshit!" He meant the "leaders" were too cautious! A few agreed with him. Soon he and the Chicago actor were going to meet. No decision was made and at a quarter to eleven the caucusing group and everyone else began drifting out of the Park the way they had drifted out every night.

Then in the group on the central sidewalk, the drums stopped, then began again. There were cries of "Stay in the Park!" I was about 50 yards away. Suddenly a flood-light was turned on, a lane of light springing through the trees and then swinging as the man holding the light walked backwards back into the Park. At first, people thought it was a police light, and there was a static moment of being drawn toward it and away from it. Without that media light, nobody would have known what was happening. The cameras were hungry for news, and they could even help the news to happen. In the lane of light, a tall boy was astride the shoulders of a friend, with the Viet Cong flag raised high, and striding beside him on the ground was the Chicago actor, and they were chanting, "Stay in the Park! Parks belong to people!" The actor was crying, "Revolution, now!" They turned the drifting retreat back into the Park and the people massed by the park building near the baseball diamond. At this point, the leaders and the Mobe mar-shalls, whom the Chicago cops in their wisdom arrested and beat in vans and stations, began yelling, "This is suicide! Suicide!" They were trying to pull the boy, who later told me he was only fourteen, down off the shoul-ders of his friend, and they were trying to pull down the Viet Cong flag, and they were yelling to get back to Clark Street, while people keeping track- of the time, watching their wrist watches in the media light, were saying it was five minutes to eleven; and the crowd, in its fear of the cops at curfew, responded to the leaders and began heading back to Clark Street. Now the boy with the Viet Cong flag, seeing what was happening, turned the cry of back to the streets into the cry of "Onto the streets! Onto the streets!" And he hit the ground run-ning with the flag. This the crowd found itself willing

to do. It was much less fearful to hit the lighted streets
in a demonstration. The boy with the flag and the
drenched Chicago actor, who now walked with an air
of regal satisfaction, led the charge and the massing of
thousands on the intersection of LaSalle, Clark and
Eugenie Streets. The catalysis of the event, that would
burn its way finally through the Democratic Convention
itself, was almost accomplished. Not quite. A daring kid,
a bizarre and gifted actor with a sense of story, and a
media light. Hello, mom. Hello, dad.

It was not yet fully accomplished because the Yippies
had to re-enter the Park and, in violation of the curfew,
confront the sweeping line of cops. The march pushed
down LaSalle onto North Avenue, exultantly stopping
traffic, with some Yippies wrapping up in blankets and
lying down in front of the cars. Yippies were urging cars
to honk in sympathy. One laughing woman stuck her
head out the window and said to the Yippies standing
in front of her car, "I think you ought to be able to sleep
in the Park, too! But you can't fight City Hall!" The cops
were taken by surprise, they had to re-group, but soon
they appeared and drove the march off North Avenue
and onto the sidewalks where the Yippies melted into the
usual hippie crowd in Old Town. I followed with a few
Yippies several yards behind an attack line of cops moving west on North Avenue. The Yippies and students
were taunting the cops, "Look at the pigs in the street!
Streets belong to the people!" The cops turned suddenly
and charged and we ran in every direction and the cops
laughed, slapped their thighs with their clubs, and continued their push west on North Avenue.

Now began that surge and milling of attraction to
wherever something was happening. Arms were raised
on LaSalle Street and the crowd on North Avenue

headed back there, in intermittent movements. Raised
arms became the common signal during the week to
gather, to come back, to re-group. A signal that warms
the soul. A human signal. Any two or three people who
raised their arms and shouted, "Come back!" could turn
almost any panic or retreat into a new confrontation.
One group of marchers went south toward the Loop,
headed for the Hilton, and was clubbed badly at the
Michigan Avenue Bridge. The main group now gathered
again at LaSalle and Clark, now in fear again of going
into the Park: now again the tall boy, with the tall, thin
actor close by, raised the Viet Cong flag and carried it
into the edge of the Park. Traffic was stopped for blocks
on Clark and LaSalle, south and north, and their voices
were raised above the ecstatic, impatient din of car horns.
The crowd was uncertain, it needed urging, but its courage was up now, its feeling and energy high. The dark
under the trees in the Park was not so forbidding. On
one corner, there was a burst of smoke—some people
say it was a smoke bomb or tear gas—and cries went
up: "Roast pig! Roast pig!" and other cries of "Gas!"—
but it wasn't gas, or at least not much of it, not tonight.
The actor was taunting the crowd more exultantly than
ever: "Revolution!" Several kids moving along with the
actor and the boy were urging the crowd and yelling,
too. Then, with a cry, the crowd broke and streamed
across the intersection into the Park, re-christening it:
"Welcome to Ché Guevera National Park!" Those in
back in the crowd hardly knew what was happening in
front and simply let themselves be carried. They all
spread over the parking lot and down the embankment
on the east side of Stockton Drive, deep in the Park,
and waited for what the cops would do. Some brave
Yippies futilely wrapped themselves in blankets and pre-

tended to go to sleep. I saw the tall boy leaning against
the fender of a car on Stockton Drive. I went up to him
and told him that was quite something he had done
carrying the flag, turning the crowd on and around. "I
know I look older," he said, "but I'm only fourteen."
He was wearing his black hair cut like an Indian brave.
He came from an Italian-American "greaser" neighborhood, as he put it, located on Chicago's northwest side
around Belmont and Cicero Avenues. He said he had
been in only one previous demonstration, the Peace
March in Chicago in April, where he was thrown into
an elevator by the cops. "My parents can't do anything
with me. I run amuck." I told him to take care, and he
said, "I'll probably never get to be twenty-one." He said
it with a swagger.

Then the police skirmish line, three deep, came
through the Park. The cop bullhorn bellowed that anyone in the Park, including newsmen, were in violation
of the law. Nobody moved. The newsmen did not believe that they were marked men; they thought it was
just a way for the cops to emphasize their point. The
media lights were turned on for the confrontation. Near
the Stockton Drive embankment, the line of police came
up to the Yippies and the two lines stood there, a few
steps apart, in a moment of meeting that was almost
formal, as if everybody recognized the stupendous seriousness of the game that was about to begin. The kids
were yelling: "Parks belong to the people! Pig! Pig!
Oink, oink!" In The Walker Report, the police say that
they were pelted with rocks the moment the media lights
"blinded" them. I was at the point where the final, triggering violence began, and friends of mine were nearby
up and down the line, and at this point none of us saw
anything thrown. Cops in white shirts, meaning lieuten-

ants or captains, were present. It was the formality of
the moment between the two groups, the theatrical and
game nature showing itself on a definitive level, that was
awesome and terrifying in its implications.

It is legend by now that the final insult that caused
the first wedge of cops to break loose upon the Yippies,
was "Your mother sucks dirty cock!" Now that's desperate provocation. The authors of The Walker Report purport to believe that the massive use of obscenities during
Convention Week was a major form of provocation, as
if it helped to explain "irrational" acts. In the very first
sentence of the summary at the beginning of the Report,
they say ". . . the Chicago Police were the targets of
mounting provocation by both word and act. Obscene
epithets . . ." etcetera. One wonders where the writers of
The Walker Report went to school, were they ever in the
Army, what streets do they live on, where do they work?
They would also benefit by a trip to a police station at
night, even up to the bull-pen, where the naked toilet
bowl sits in the center of the room, and they could listen
and find out whether the cops heard anything during
Convention Week that was unfamiliar to their ears or
tongue. It matters more *who* cusses you, and does he
know you well enough to hit home to galvanize you into
destructive action. It also matters whether you regard a
club on the head as an equivalent response to being
called a "mother fucking Fascist pig."

The kids wouldn't go away and then the cops began
shoving them hard up the Stockton Drive embankment
and then hitting with their clubs. "Pigs! Pigs! Pigs!
Fascist pig bastards!" A cop behind me—I was immediately behind the cop line facing the Yippies—said to
me and a few others, in a sick voice, "Move along, sir,"
as if he foresaw everything that would happen in the

week to come. I have thought again and again about him and the tone of his voice. "Oink, oink," came the taunts from the kids. The cops charged. A boy trapped against the trunk of a car by a cop on Stockton Drive had the temerity to hit back with his bare fists and the cop tried to break every bone in his body. "If you're newsmen," one kid screamed, "get that man's number!" I tried but all I saw was his blue shirt—no badge or name tag—and he, hearing the cries, stepped backward up onto the curb as a half-dozen cops crammed around him and carried him off into the melée, and I was carried in another direction. A cop swung and smashed the lens of a media camera. "He got my lens!" The cameraman was amazed and offended. The rest of the week the cops would cram around a fellow cop who was in danger of being identified and carry him away, and they would smash any camera that they saw get an incriminating picture. The cops slowed, crossing the grass toward Clark Street, and the more daring kids sensed the loss of contact, loss of energy, and went back to meet the skirmish line of cops. The cops charged again up to the sidewalk on the edge of the Park.

It was thought that the cops would stop along Clark Street on the edge of the Park. For several minutes, there was a huge, loud jam of traffic and people in Clark Street, horns and voices. "Red Rover, Red Rover, send Daley right over!" Then the cops crossed the street and lined up on the curb on the west side, outside curfew territory. Now they started to make utterly new law as they went along—at the behest of those orders they kept talking about. The crowd on the sidewalk, excited but generally peaceable, included a great many bystanders and Lincoln Park citizens. Now came mass cop violence of unmitigated fury, descriptions of which become redundant.

No status or manner of appearance or attitude made one less likely to be clubbed. The cops did us a great favor by putting us all in the same boat. A few upper middle-class white men said they now had some idea of what it meant to be on the other end of the law in the ghetto.

At the corner of Menomenee and Clark, several straight young people were sitting on their doorsteps to jeer at the Yippies. The cops beat them, too, and took them by the backs of the necks and jerked them onto the sidewalk. A photographer got a picture of a terrible beating here and a cop smashed his camera and beat the photographer unconscious. I saw a stocky cop spring out of the pavement swinging his club, smashing a media man's movie camera into two pieces, and the media man walked around in the street holding up the pieces for everybody to see, including other cameras, some of which were also smashed. Cops methodically beat one man, summoned an ambulance that was whirling its light out in the traffic jam, shoved the man into it, and rapped their clubs on the bumper to send it on its way. There were people caught in this charge, who had been in civil rights demonstrations in the South in the early Sixties, who said this was the time that they had feared for their lives.

The first missiles thrown Sunday night at cops were beer-cans, then a few rocks, more rocks, a bottle or two, more bottles. Yippies and New Left kids rolled cars into the side streets to block access for the cop attack patrols. The traffic-jam reached wildly north and south, and everywhere Yippies, working out in the traffic, were getting shocked drivers to honk in sympathy. One kid lofted a beer-can at a patrol car that was moving slowly; he led the car perfectly and the beer-can hit on the trunk and stayed there. The cops stopped the car and looked through their rear window at the beer-can on their trunk. They started to back up toward the corner at Wisconsin from which the can was thrown, but they were only two and the Yippies were many, so they thought better of it and drove away. There were kids picking up rocks and other kids telling them to put the rocks down.

At Clark and Wisconsin, a few of the "leaders"—those who trained parade marshalls and also some of the conventionally known and sought leaders—who had expected a confrontation of sorts in Chicago, were standing on a doorstep with their hands clipped together in front of their crotches as they stared balefully out at the streets, trying to look as uninvolved as possible. "Beautiful, beautiful," one was saying, but they didn't know how the thing had been delivered or what was happening. They had even directly advised against violent action, and had been denounced for it. Their leadership was that, in all the play and put-on of publicity before the Convention, they had contributed to the development of a consciousness of a politics of confrontation and social disruption. An anarchist saw his dream come true though he was only a spectator of the dream; the middle-class man saw his nightmare. A radioman, moving up and down the street, apparently a friend of Tom Hayden, stuck his mike up the stairs and asked Hayden to make some comments. Hayden, not at all interested in making a statement, leaned down urgently, chopping with his hand, and said, "Hey, man, turn the mike off, turn the mike off." Hayden, along with Rubin, was a man the Chicago cops deemed a crucial leader and they would have sent them both to the bottom of the Chicago River, if they had thought they could get away with it. The radioman turned the mike off. Hayden said,

"Is it off?" The radioman said yes. Hayden said, "Man, *what's going on down there?*" The radioman could only say that what was going on was going on everywhere.

The "leaders"? The real leaders were out in the streets, the leaders were the men at your elbow when anything was happening. The leaders were everywhere. In the way that Tolstoy tells it in *War and Peace*, the cops and the City and Daley were Napoleonic in that they were haunted by a necessitous vision of a few essential leaders, while the Yippies and the demonstrators were like Kutusov, the Russian general, who knew that it was the spirit of battle that decided the outcome, and the spirit of battle summons forth the necessary men in any responsive situation. The good general stands aside and does not presume upon the spirit of battle. In Chicago, it went further, into an inexorable, deadly serious, rambunctious movement that knew its own power, and the conventional leaders became spectators before the lesson. Some of these leaders were those who tried to stop the tall boy with the VC flag. Many were frightened, and only a few were ready to go with it. "Beautiful, beautiful," it was said, as if watching an electrical storm, but one with a lesson in it, patterns of a direction that already knew its own course.

The action stretched through the streets over an area of many blocks, south to Division Street and then southeast to the Michigan Avenue Bridge, and petered out in the dark morning hours. Yippies and demonstrators sought pads to crash: in the Movement centers (places for organizing activities and services for New Left and Yippies), in private homes, in the crash-pads in Old Town, in churches. Wherever they slept, the edges and depths of their sleep were permeated by relentless excitement, and they might well wake up with cops walking among them to find and take someone away.

Behind the iron fences of the garden in the Movement center and first-aid station of The Theater on Wells Street —home of the original Second City Players—Yippies were packed, some actually sleeping on the flat extension of the roof. Broken heads were being bandaged. A few were holding the gates shut and looking out through the bars to screen those who wanted to come in—trying to keep plainclothesmen out. A numb caution, in the face of the cop fury, now deadened many people's feeling. But the tall actor was sitting tilted back on a chair by the gate, aglow, in good humor, similar to the feeling of Julian Bond and his delegates when they knew they had won. "Schultz!" he cried out when he saw me. "He's all right, let him in." Haggard, numb, bearded faces were looking through the iron bars of the gate out at the street, as if fearing a supernatural invasion—cops, in short. Only the actor, leaning back in his chair, laughed at the stars. I gave him a sort of salute, not without awe and a touch of dismay.

On the Logan statue. Monday August 26. Grant Park opposite the Conrad Hilton Hotel. Photo by Nina Boal.

monday: the beast and the hunt

Grant Park: Boys Capture Union General

Monday, the delegates in the Hilton woke to find in their morning papers that those cops, who guarded the entrances to the Hotel with a hard lack of courtesy, were, in that place northwards called Lincoln Park, cracking the heads of kids and beating newsmen, too. If newsmen were being beaten, the uneasy implication was that anyone could become a target. The Chicago cop, in his skyblue short-sleeved shirt and skyblue helmet, was already the most constant image in all of the activities of Convention Week. Monday afternoon, the delegates could watch, on the other side of the street a bit south of the Hilton in Grant Park, on the man-made rounded green hill on which stands the statue of Union General John A. Logan on horseback, another pedagogical spectacle with their own eyes. In a scene as dramatically visual as the Boston Tea Party, demonstrators took the hill and climbed on top of the statue carrying the red flag and the Viet Cong flag. The tall boy who carried

94

the VC flag in Lincoln Park the night before was in the forefront here, too, reckless as ever.

It is interesting that this action came at the end of a march that started faraway in Lincoln Park and plodded through the Loop to the main police headquarters at 1121 South State Street in protest over the arrest of Tom Hayden that afternoon. Participants describe the march as strictly controlled by Mobe marshalls who, with a portable speaker, were obedient to the cops, and the ineffectuality in the feeling of the march became depressing and dreary. When the cops told them they could proceed on only half the sidewalk, they obediently proceeded on only half the sidewalk. The "law" could arrest them, beat them at will, and here they were obeying the "law." Many marchers were yelling at the Mobe marshalls: "Fuck the marshalls! Marshalls are pigs!" The dissent among the marchers was strong. The naked hollowness of the permitted forms of protest, the ineffectuality, the miserable submission, disposed people toward rebellious action in which there might be the feeling of dignity.

It was when the march dragged itself into Grant Park that it was awakened by the injection of young, reckless energy, and it shook off the Mobe marshalls and headed for the Logan statue. The rebellious feeling was directed as much against the conventional, public leaders of the movement as against the arbitrary law enforced by the cops. In the beginning of the week, the catalytic people for the rebellious actions were usually quite young, often in their mid-teens, with little or no experience in previous demonstrations. That was true of the older catalytic people, too: No previous experience. Their only forms for action were mythological ones, school-book heroics, theatrics, such as carrying a flag to turn a re-

treat into confrontation or riding an equestrian statue
shouting protest slogans. The conventional planning and
anticipation of protest by such publicly well-known leaders as Hayden, Hoffman, Rubin and David Dellinger of
Mobe had failed. They did not comprehend the failed
situation into which came new energy. They either stood
aside, marvelled, or actually tried to dampen the energy.
It is only because the media are incapable of thinking or
perceiving outside of celebrity consciousness that they
continued to regard these men as the leaders. No doubt it
would have dynamited the minds of the American public
if they had not been able to assign cause to celebrity
figures of good and evil.

While the demonstrators were taking the hill and
climbing on the Logan statue, photographers were everywhere, taking pictures. The cops did not feel so free
about smashing cameras in front of the Hilton. As a result, some of the most dramatic photographs of Convention Week came from the scene on the hill and at the
statue. Cops were pulling kids off the statue and order-
ing others to climb down.

One boy's arm, catching in the scabbard of the statue,
was broken when the cops pulled and kicked him off.
One cop, up on the statue, kicked the boy's head while
the boy was being pulled down. Another cop, standing
on the stirrups at about the same time, struck with his
fist at the boy's groin. When the cops had first ordered
the boy to get off the statue, he had been reluctant to
come down because he was terrified of the way the cops
were treating people around the foot of the statue. He
was yelling, "You're breaking my arm!"—and sure
enough they broke his arm. The City went directly to
the Cook County Grand Jury, without bothering about
a preliminary hearing, and the boy was indicted on a

felony charge of aggravated assault, for supposedly kicking the cop in the shoulder when he was being dragged off the statue.

He was David Lee Edmundsen, 17 years old, not yet out of high school, and he had come to Chicago to work with the NDPEA—a group from Alabama challenging the regular Democratic delegation. I talked with him, when he got a continuance on his case at the Criminal Courts building several weeks later; he showed me then that the nerve to his thumb was gone and there was a metal plate in his arm. It was likely that he was no longer physically qualified for induction into the Army, having ridden with Logan in the Park. The cop who had pulled him off the statue, a stocky red-headed walking side of beef, in plainclothes in the courtroom, used the VC flag that he had taken from the scene, wrapped around its piece of cheap slat lumber, as a cane in the courtroom— smiling, smiling constantly toward Edmundsen and whoever might be sitting with him. Edmundsen was short and slight, and straight and courteous in his manner as only a Southern kid can be straight. The VC flag was apparently important material evidence. On Monday morning of Convention Week, Edmundsen had reported to the NDPEA in the Hilton to do leafletting, but was told that there were plenty of people out working, so, being opposed to the Vietnam War, he became involved in the demonstration, exuberantly.

Kids climb on statues in Chicago parks in all seasons. In Lincoln Park, they sit in the lap of Hans Christian Andersen and in the lap of the Great Emancipator, and cops on three-wheeler motorcycles chug past them without comment. They ride behind generals, among them Union General John A. Logan. The cops, following orders, were making new law again, pulling and kicking

kids off the statue of Logan, and so provided the delegates and the public with a scene in which the images
were almost of school-book heroics. Chicago cops, in a
confrontation, almost never stand with their arms folded.
I have wondered what would have happened if the cops
had stood on the other side of Michigan Avenue, protecting the environs of the Hilton, with their arms
folded, and, as the kids on the statue yelled their protest, called back, "Ride 'em, cowboy!", "Look at the
bronco-busters!" But that is not satisfying for men who
walk with arms deliberately ready at their sides, and not
satisfying to their superiors, either, who would sense uneasiness in their positions if they did not take their jobs
with awful seriousness.

Instead, the delegates trooped through the ever-
present arrogant police security to the Convention at
the Amphitheatre where the fight over the seating of
Julian Bond's Georgia delegation impended, with their
heads full of bees about the police violence and the self-
righteous outrage of the newspapers about reporters
being beaten. David Lee Edmundsen was interviewed
on national television, and then lay in a hospital for several days. Network newscasters and commentators in
general found a ready-made vendetta and poured forth
their criticism of Chicago as a "police state," causing
Mayor Daley to blow his cool, and show that his hand
was heavy as a ham and his skin suckling soft. He asked
them why they didn't protest the security at the Republican Convention in Miami and why they accused him
of police state tactics. And well he might wonder why
the Republican Convention was exempted—written off
is the better phrase—and why some people had such
hope for the Democratic Party that they were willing
to wreck its Convention in order to make rebirth, re-

newal, or even transformation possible, by getting rid of established figures who would lose out in this election and by forcing changes where the Party might actually be governed internally by democratic process down to the precinct level.

Later Monday afternoon—after the capture of the hill and the Logan statue—I saw in the main lobby of the Hilton a tall Negro New Left leader, whom I recognized from a meeting the week before, moving with nervous speed, with news messenger's credentials hanging around his neck. I knew that the New Left people were assembling credentials of different kinds to get into the Hilton and the Amphitheatre to perform rather clever sorts of observation and pranksterish sabotage. So I followed him, at a good distance, as he moved from room to room, place to place, sitting here, standing there, pretending to read a newspaper whose pages he flipped too quickly and too loudly, never sitting or standing long in one place, always moving nervously, perhaps dropping those chemical stink pellets on the carpets that gave the Hilton the smell that so many remember, perhaps just cruising and listening and looking around. He could have been more artful, and it did seem unwise to pick him, who might be easily recognized, for the job. Humphrey was supposed to arrive in the Hotel soon, and when the Negro New Left leader ended up near the balconies over the front entrance, I thought perhaps more important theater was in the offing. A tear gas bomb. Anything. Fantasy upon fantasy upon fantasy everywhere in this Convention. A gigantic sort of learning by role-playing. I was enjoying the game, although I soon got a distaste for it, probably because I would rather at that moment have been doing his job. I was the everlasting witness—snoop sometimes seemed the better

word—throughout the Convention. And snooping on the
ambiguous acts of people with whom you are more than
sympathetic, in the name of some kind of further truth,
does not always jibe with one's personal inclinations. I
quit following him, and never found out what he was
up to if anything, certainly nothing that made the news
or the scuttlebutt.

I wanted to be out of the Hilton, out of the feverish
air jammed with people in fake straw hats, away from
rumor upon rumor, all of the imagery and most of the
rumors prefabricated, hold-over imagery and hold-over
emotions with no soul held over with it, if there ever
was any. It could have been a merchandising show, or
a 1940's musical. In the Hilton snack bar, I'd listened to
a white waitress and a black clean-up man talking about
their feet tenderly—"I'll watch out for your feet, too"—
because of all the long hours they were working. Around
them were delegates and political staff and media-men
rapidly eating hamburgers, tuna fish, bacon-lettuce-and
tomato—the sandwiches that Americans eat from coast
to coast and border to border. I wanted to be in Lincoln
Park where fantasies were being made and broken moment by moment. We are building boats in bottles, Mc-
Carthy had said, speaking of his difficulties at a press
conference in the Hilton. In Lincoln Park kids were
breaking bottles. In Lincoln Park Tom Hayden was arrested that afternoon. The cops were not so stupid as
to make a Ché Guevara style martyr out of him, but
they were stupid enough to arrest him, took him right
out from under a tree where he was sitting, for "letting
the air out of a tire on a squad car," something like that.
They explained that they had wanted to arrest him before but hadn't dared when he was "inciting" a couple
of hundred people in the Park. The cops' arrest of him

did provide incitement, firing up the anger of the Yippies and New Left kids in the Park. They were more ready than ever for the night. So were the cops.

Lincoln Park: The Barricade

The Convention opened in the Amphitheatre that night with a keynote address by Senator Daniel K. Inouye of Hawaii in which the Yippies and demonstrators were accused with the phrase: "What trees do they plant?" The Senator always stood sideways to the cameras so that he did not reveal that he'd lost an arm in World War II.

As the 11 PM curfew approached, the number of people in Lincoln Park was larger than the night before. By now, there was increasing interplay between Lincoln Park and Grant Park in front of the Hilton downtown; Yippies and demonstrators moved back and forth with the action, keeping the city rocking on its feet. In the large caucusing group, which sat in the dark on the grass under the trees on the eastern slope in the "Valley" in Lincoln Park, with only dots of light here and there, one person after another used the portable speaker. Some of them pleaded that we *have* to get organized, we have to agree on *something, anything;* but there was no sort of organization that would catch the consent of even a large number. A few of the voices that wanted organization were desperate, causing a laugh here and there. But mostly those who called themselves Yippies, and the SDS kids, and others who had decided to join the action, were going to let happen what would happen. The portable speaker was usually held by one man on top of his head, while persons behind him used the trailing mike, and the blandness of his face under the speaker was striking. Voices were saying that to engage the cops in this way you need weapons to equal them; and some said for people to put down their rocks; and others said no, and the ones with rocks held onto them anyway. What the cops would do was unknown, and the fear of them was intense. In other groups, the drums were going without cease in the dark under the trees, keeping expectancy stable, holding people in the Park. Quick incidents had occurred throughout the day between the police and the kids—arrests, shovings, beatings, cops on three-wheelers in wedges riding at people to terrorize them, a helicopter coming bamety-bam close overhead.

And yet at other times during the day, the cops would approach, giving the V sign like a white flag, to talk, usually picking the obviously young hippies, in beads and scroungy levis and long hair, not the SDS kids, who might also wear levis and long hair. But there was a more recognizable pride in the SDS kids' manner and simpler dress—a touch of the elitist, the cavalryman— that set them apart, and they were more articulate and not at all willing to let the cops have a big brother attitude. Sometimes the very young teen-agers were positively eager to hear the cops try to straighten them out, giving them a chance to straighten the cops out. In one instance, a white-haired, crew-cut cop drove his squad car onto the grass giving the V sign through the window and came within a foot of running over a kid sleeping on the ground on the right hand side of the car. A couple of long-haired Yippies came up eagerly to the car and there was the usual discussion of beards, long hair, the War, and responsibility. With some indignation, I pointed out to the cop how close he had come to the kid sleeping on the grass, and the cop as he drove away waved his hand at me, as if I, in my straight suit, were the one whom he really despised. Yippie kids even joined in the cops' game of catch with a softball, at the south end of the contested area near LaSalle Street, where many cops lounged during the day in collapsible lawn chairs and puzzled over the leaflets and literature —free love, anti-war, anti-capitalist, drug freedom, etcetera—being handed out in the Park, with their blue helmets resting on the grass beside them. "See you at 11 o'clock, kid."

Early in the evening a young fellow, dressed darkly, as if he were a visitant from the river Styx, came up to the main group carrying an American flag—the kind of flag that might stand on a pole in a classroom. He made a speech to the kids, who at first did not know what to make of him, saying *we* are the ones who stand for what this flag stands for, and he wanted the Yippies to carry the flag in the demonstrations during the coming night.

The kids stirred uneasily in the face of this sentimental gambit, muttering, "No, no, that's not where it's at"; then stronger voices told the fellow to "Burn it, burn it!" He was put down and disappeared. The American flag would become important on Wednesday afternoon, as Americans in Chicago worked their way through troubles of identity that started in the first grade. I remember that when I was in the Army in Korea, wherever I saw the American flag flying, I knew there was food and warmth beneath it for *me* and for any other American soldier, while hungry people, their skin grey with the cold, might be clinging to the very fence around it. The feeling of such near absolute Roman power is both strong and bereft—the way a cop would keep beating and beating a helpless person. What if we pledged allegiance to a skull in our classrooms?

There was a stillness when 11 PM came and passed— the time whispered here and there—a stillness in the

belly on the beat of the drums. A few people left the
caucusing group and went to Clark Street, frightened
and angered at the lack of organization and saying so.
The main body was in agreement only on staying in the
Park and confronting the cops: the courage of those
damned by their own acute sense of the ridiculous necessity of history. It was not the confrontation that they
would choose, but it was the one thrust upon them.
Leave the Park and, in Yeats' phrase, "admit that you
turned aside." When would the skirmish line of cops
sweep the Park? How would the cops be armed? What
would the cops do?

The embankment along Stockton Drive in the Park
was packed with people, as if at a football game. This
was another major group, and these were not so much
spectators as peripheral and potential participants, who
most of all did not wish to meet the cops head-on in the
dark. That drifting and milling back and forth in fear
and fascination began between the embankment people
and the caucusing group and other small groups. And
the waiting for the cops stalled on the point of screaming. Joints and little pipes were being passed, most
brotherly, and no one cared if a plainclothesman should
see and bust them. Pot would quiet the moths of fear
whirling about the flame in the soul, bring ease and com-
panionship, good sexual aggression, and if you had to
die you might as well be high. Scouts came back to the
caucusing group saying that the cops were massed northeast along the road behind the Zoo. Attention focused
in that direction.

And then, at the end of the caucusing group deepest
in the Park, a few kids suddenly began building a barricade out of whatever was available. When the barricade
became visually noticeable, visually possible, it took

over, became the point of enthusiastic effort, and the solemn, damned feeling was swept away. The media were helpful here, too, giving light to work by, and of course the image was most satisfying to them. The barricade itself was made of picnic tables, trash baskets, and anything else that could be rolled or carried into place. It was wide open to attack on both flanks, and any cop who grabbed hold of it would have torn right through it. On one side, it joined a snow fence that could have been easily flattened by the cops, and on the other side it stretched up to where it stopped several yards south of the Garibaldi statue. The recent Paris student revolts and images from older revolutions—Soviet barricades in Petersburg—were instrumental in bringing forth this barricade.

Kids massed behind it, constantly yelling in the direction of the cops across 50 yards of grass. In the middle and on top of the barricade, with media lights glaring upon it from all sides, was the core group, flying the black flag on a tall pole, a red flag, and VC flags. The red flag and VC flags seemed out of place, but the black flag—the flag of anarchy—rolled with a smooth, sensual authority. Kids out in front of the barricade kept up a constant harassment of the unmarked cop cars that came up close, breaking a few windows with rocks. The tall Chicago actor was working this night, too, and I saw him go into the core group on top the barricade, his voice exultant, no longer taunting, with the cry of "*Revolution!*" "Slim," the kids had called him, but now they were saying, "Hey, man, what's your name?" The cops used their bullhorn to announce that anyone in the Park was in violation of the law, but the cops did not do anything. And the more the cops waited, the louder became the noise behind the barricade, drums, voices. Tom Sawyer

would have envied this barricade, this impressive stage-
set. And yet it was not even a worthy stage-set, since no
director would let his audience see the flanks wide open
to attack or that the barricade could not withstand bullets or the jerk from a stout arm. But the feelings behind
the barricade were deadly—the fear, the hate, the exul-
tation. The flimsiness of the barricade and the sort of
feelings behind it intensified the fear for anyone with
eyes to see. Trash fires smoldered along the barricade,
and there was one good blaze where someone set fire
to a picnic table. Burning down your own barricade,
your own stage-set, but the sight of fire gave strong feeling to the scene. When would the cops attack? Continual
fear and fascination surged back and forth in the crowd
behind the barricade. People were carried by the crowd-
feeling, the strength of the sea was in it. If you were
not yelling your head off or throwing something to keep
your energy going, the waiting was unbearable. Someone would yell, "They're coming!" and the crowd would
surge away in retreat, look back over its shoulder, slow
down, pause, and return as if pulled. The crowd could
be surging away from one flank and pulsing forward at
the other, like waves moving back and forth on a rocky
beach. Then, as if someone had noticed when a surge in
retreat started, the drums and the beating on trash cans
mounted higher, summoning in rhythm and volume,
pulling the crowd back to the barricade, lifting courage,
stilling fear, answering ancient calls. The drums summoned, and people moved to the summoning.

Over the barricade we watched the cops march down
the road on the other side of the meadow and then stand
in ranks in formation watching us. Expectancy jumped
high every time the cops moved. Now they were at last
in full view—an attack would at least end the waiting—

and then they moved in formation farther south on the road again, and again just stood there watching us. Where among them were the cops who said, "See you at 11, kid."?

A black boy suddenly stopped among the trees, as if hit with revelation, and screamed: "Black brothers! Black brothers! Get out of this mother-fucking park! Them are *white* cops! They'll kill you, black brothers, they'll *kill* you, if they catch you in this mother-fucking park!" Many of the black brothers knew the truth of it and they were, as soon as he finished, already in motion to get out of the Park, except for a black Yippie who always stayed with whites anyway, and a few other black students and younger kids. The whites were daring the confrontation, while blacks felt good reason to avoid it. The black boy's fear, however, gave a fillip to the deadly feeling of the potential of the violence.

Then came a weird sound approaching through the trees behind us: Allen Ginsberg, in full black beard, joyfully leading a group Omming for all they were worth, his powerful voice shaking his loose body, his face aglow with the expectancy of bringing peace to everyone, kids and cops. *Om*, he had explained, discovered by the Hindus, was the fundamental sound of the universe, and the wholehearted use of it, sounded on varying notes for a full breath to each note, would bring peace and good feeling. The poet and his group moved into the center of the barricade, where the flags flew, where the media lights blazed and all the newsmen tonight wore helmets. Ginsberg was always welcomed and he stepped on top of the barricade as if being accepted into his glory, where Om would still the anger of the kids, and the attacking cops would, irresistibly, sit down on the grass and Om peacefully, too. For a time, the Omming up and down the barricade became huge, vibrating across the grass to where the cops stood in formation, watching, listening. I tried the Omming myself, and it did—as Ginsberg would say in Grant Park Wednesday—help quiet the butterflies in the belly. But Ginsberg was quite serious about the more messianic use of Om. Common sense would have told him that it wouldn't work, but that was exactly why he tried it, out of his immense common sense, and common sense was not working anywhere during Convention Week. And the cops—those working men over there new to the middle class, new to a salaried job with a pension and other benefits, with their laughter and puzzlement over the leaflets handed out in the Park —were simply waiting to do their job. The cop bullhorn announced again that the Park was closed and anyone present in the Park was in violation of the law: "Move out, NOW." But time passed and the cops still did not make a move.

Chants were coming from behind the barricade in barrages—"Hell, no, we won't go!" "Stay in the Park! Parks belong to people!" "Dump the Hump!" A few kids were assiduously and almost pickily strengthening the barricade in places, and thereby strengthening the *fantasy* of the barricade, because it was really a rehearsal in the American mind. Then a short, slight, skinny New Left spokesman, who had to lift both his face and his voice, walked the length of the barricade, behind it, asking the Yippies and students to cool it and saying that it looked like the cops were going to let them stay and sleep in the Park this night. If he was right, what a victory, and you could almost believe it. It seemed so reasonable, as if he really expected the Enemy to be "reasonable." Yet almost any time that anyone tried to anticipate the movement and events of Convention Week, he was wrong.

If the City had made that decision, to let the kids stay and sleep in the Park, it would have worked the night before. The feeling this night was that there was going to be a confrontation if the kids had to back the cops into the water. But the cops must be waiting for something. Orders? Equipment? Or were they just trying to wear people down, exhaust them? When, *when*, were the cops coming? Maybe they *would* let people stay and sleep in the Park.

I was standing on a rise behind the main crowd, when I noticed a vehicle stop by the fieldhouse on the asphalt path, a couple of hundred yards behind the barricade. I noticed it because of a flicker of light, either of car lights turned off, or light going on and off inside the car. Then the patrol car with two cops in it came gliding with its lights out down the asphalt path toward the center of the barricade. It turned its lights on as it came up to the crowd behind the barricade, slowed to a creep, but kept moving forward. The squad car eased through the people, who were screaming at it. It pushed one girl up against a trash basket that was part of the barricade, pinning her there, terrified.

If the cop's job was to push a hole through the barricade, he had to run over her to do it. It is not possible to tell even from the reports of people who were right against the car—I was about 50 feet away—whether the first rock was thrown before the girl was pinned or after; but in any case they all agree that it was because of the pinning of the girl that the main stoning occurred. From where I saw it, the indignant fury of the kids hovered, and then the first rock was thrown at the back of the cop car. A pause. A realization. And then another rock. And then, from all sides, rocks were hurled at the car, to show the cops that other people can practice escalation, too.

Every window in that car was smashed, safety glass scattering like cocktail ice. A fellow had the driver by the neck and was making a good attempt to pull him out the window. The motor stopped with a jerk because of a slipped clutch. The car was a sitting duck. A mass of kids, in exultant hysteria, were throwing rocks down hard on the car. It was amazing to me that the cops did not use their pistols, except they probably knew that if they did they would certainly be stoned to death. The driver got the motor started and gunned the car in jerky lunges along the barricade, miraculously not running over anyone, around the left flank below the Garibaldi statue, and across the no-man's-land of grass to where the other cops were massed in formation, furious and frightened at the way the car was being stoned. They would use this as an excuse for the greater violence tonight. Did they really think that if they felt so angry and protective toward brother cops, that others, such as demonstrators and Yippies, would not feel the same way toward their brothers and sisters? Either this is self-righteous naiveté —regressive high school team feeling, which needs to be steeped in somebody's realism—or it means we are close to an internal state of war, where the enemy is always more beast or devil, never quite human. Two black kids, about 15 or 16 years old, danced past me in a sort of agony of physical glee. "Man, they fucked that car up! Man-n, they fucked—that—car—*up!*" They were really impressed with what the white brothers had done to that cop car. The high fury of victorious feeling towered now behind the barricade. If the cops assaulted the barricade head-on, around the flanks, or from the rear, there was going to be a terrible battle, a slaughter, rocks, clubs—why not guns? Somewhere there was someone Omming for peace.

The reaction from demonstrators, observers, and Lincoln Park citizens to the cop car coming from behind to test the barricade was so intense—they thought it was an obvious and profoundly dangerous provocation that could only result in what happened or worse, triggering *yet* worse events—that the police said they knew nothing about the cop car, it was not ordered to do that, etcetera.

The Walker Report, which gives a deferential amount of space to police testimony at very crucial points, says, without question or reasoning: "At about 12:20 AM, a single squad car approached the people behind the barricade. The two officers in the car had encountered a traffic jam at the Eugenie Triangle en route to a call at Wisconsin and Lincoln Avenues. They detoured through the park to reach their destination and proceeded north along a sidewalk leading up to the Garibaldi statue. The deputy chief leading the police in the park knew nothing about the car until he saw it approaching the barricade. The vehicle's lights were turned off and it was travelling between 10 and 20 miles per hour."

Let's investigate the plausibility of these statements. If the squad car were merely taking a roundabout route to get to Wisconsin and Lincoln, why were its lights turned out? Also, I saw the squad car stop on the asphalt path near the fieldhouse, stay there a few moments before it came on down the path, allowing the two cops plenty of time to see vividly what was before them. But the thing that really tickles the funnybone is *the roundabout route.* They really had to be high, those cops. They had to be Keystone Kops, to boot. If they were seriously headed for the corner of Wisconsin and Lincoln, it would have been fastest for them to double back to North Avenue and then go north on Wells Street. If they insisted on

going through the Park, the next fastest way, and most
obvious, would be north on Stockton Drive to the Dickens Street exit where they could double back south to
their destination. Or, if their call was most urgent, they
could park in the Park on Stockton Drive opposite Wisconsin and run two blocks. Or they could have taken the
center sidewalk in the valley of the Park and wound
around the Lagoon and through the Farm in the Zoo to
the Dickens Street exit. Faster than the way they chose
—you must remember Chicago police pride themselves
on their speed in answering calls—they could have
turned on their blue lights (and they turn them on for
any reason, such as going through stoplights where ordinary citizens must wait) and screamed around LaSalle
Street to the Outer Drive and north to the Fullerton
Parkway Exit and around the Park and down, once again,
to the source of their call, Lincoln and Wisconsin. But
no, *no*, they chose, if we are to believe the police and
The Walker Report, *to drive over a curb at Stockton
Drive, to this asphalt path which leads them down to
Cannon Drive, behind the Zoo, where Cannon Drive is
one-way going south* and there were plenty of police
waiting there to ticket them for a moving violation. In
brief, they chose absolutely the worst way to get to
Lincoln and Wisconsin. They had to be high. The idea
that they were taking a roundabout route to Lincoln
and Wisconsin is ridiculous. The suggestion in The
Walker Report is that the squad car also did not know
what was ahead of it. Then why did they stop by the
fieldhouse, in unmistakable view of the barricade and a
couple of thousand people, where police and media
lights blazed? They crept forward, with their lights out,
because of curiosity, I suppose. Then they reached the
crowd, turned on their lights, nosed into the crowd,

nosed up to the barricade, simply because they had to get to Lincoln and Wisconsin *some* way, one supposes. The Walker Report also says: "There are accounts of an 18- or 19-year-old girl screaming hysterically as she was momentarily trapped between the right side of the car and the barricade." The Deputy Chief of Police is credited, by his own words, with "knowing" nothing of the squad car coming from behind the barricade, but there are merely "accounts" of the girl trapped against the barricade by the car. Read pages 111–112 in The Walker Report. It seems so precise, so exact, and yet it amounts to a step-by-step exoneration of the Deputy Chief. Whenever the event will reveal a major police and City decision, rather than "riotous" action, the oddest and most thorough twisting happens in The Walker Report's presentation. Now you see it, now you don't. No, sir, the pea is under the other shell. See.

In front of the barricade, the cops were behind trucks with batteries of light that made the scene bright as Hell. The kids were furious about the police car, and the cops were furious about the stoning of it. Then something bounced on the ground about 20 feet away from me, crawling around by itself and sending out a straight grey stream. For a second, I could not figure out what was that thing crawling around on the ground. A kid danced up to it—amid cries of "Throw it back at the pigs!"— grabbed it, dropped it, shaking his hand as if burned, kicked at the tear-gas canister. And now tear-gas canisters were plummeting everywhere behind the barricade, through the trees. A huge cloud of gas rolled over the barricade, and cops with gas masks on came over the barricade in an assault wave, with shotguns and rifles and using the butts as clubs on anyone in sight, knocking people down and standing on them with a foot in

the small of the back or in the belly and hitting them
with the butts of their weapons, just beginning to take
their revenge for the smashed cop car and what it por-
tended. A McCormick Theological Seminary student got
one of the worst brain concussions of the week. "Gas!
Gas!" was the cry, as if poisonous snakes had been loosed
in the area. But the gas gave everyone not caught in the
cops' first assault moral permission to desert the field
where a mass slaughter impended. Tear-gas showed
itself to be an ambiguous form of de-escalation.

Thousands streamed across the Park toward Clark
Street, and panic started, headlong running, the sudden
threat of being trampled by your own people. A pretty
black chick beside me sang out, "Walk, don't run!" And I
boomed, *"Walk, don't run!"* and I boomed it again, and
I liked the way she glanced at me, as others took up the
cry, and the panic slowed to a steady, fast, efficient walk
for thousands. It was always a good feeling, connection,
control, pride, to walk, not run.

The tear-gas was catching up with us, a sharp menthol
sort of burning on the cheeks and burning in the eyes,
but though some people ran from it, most of us kept on
just walking. It was the students, once events were
started, who were sensitive to the ways of spontaneously
controlling crowds, either in action or saving lives. Now
the tear-gas began really burning, making the eyes twist
tightly closed, and if you rubbed it the burning got
worse, as if your eyeballs were being rolled in fire. The
medics—the doctors and nurses of the Medical Committee for Human Rights and the kids who were turned into
medics overnight, sometimes with crayoned red crosses
on the white band around their sleeves—were shouting,
"Keep your eyes open! Let it tear away! Water! Wash
your eyes with water!" The information on how to handle

tear-gas passed rapidly and with a warm feeling from one person to another. I went up to a park fountain, soaked my handkerchief, and used it as a mask. The gas drifted over Old Town, and the citizens came out of their houses, coughing and gritting their eyes, angrily.

Now, with people drifting up and down the streets, in a feeling that was almost peaceful, nothing more could happen unless contact was kept between cops and kids. People were moving in search of this contact. Get the gas out of your eyes and out of your lungs: then, back into confrontation. I went to the corner of Wells Street and North Avenue, and then back toward the Park, walking east on Eugenie toward LaSalle through groups of people retreating at a fast stroll in the direction from which I came.

Up ahead, at the large intersection of LaSalle, Clark and Eugenie surged a confusion of cops and kids, a bottle or two arcing through the air, and suddenly I was in the middle of a no-man's-land in a confrontation between cops and demonstrators—the mass of kids straightening across Eugenie behind me, and a line of cops with shotguns and pistols levelled in front of me. "Give us a target!" the cops were yelling, in absolute fury. "Come on! Come on!" they enticed, "*Give us a target!*" The kids began chanting, "Hell, no, we won't go! Hell, no, we won't go!" A huge cop, with a blue-shirted avalanche of a belly, was waving his pistol back and forth and waved it at me, and I stopped as if photographed in flight and made no motion either way, until he went past me and I was left behind the line of cops. The kids backed up grudging every step, chanting, "Streets belong to the people!" SDS kids, and other students, were in the forefront here, keeping a taut distance and connection with the line of cops. They threw bottles, rocks, and firecrackers at the cops: it took a form of historical courage to throw such things with guns pointing at you. The cops charged, and some kids ran away screaming because the cops seemed ready to fire.

Now the cops began methodically to confront the mass of Yippies and students in a four block area of Old Town with the corner of North and Wells as the center, blocking off all the intersections and alleys.

In the parking lot in Lincoln Park, cops were slashing the tires on all cars with McCarthy bumper stickers. Some 30 cars. Reporters saw it, reported it, and their papers would not publish it. The Walker Report says that the cops were slashing tires, but it does not mention the McCarthy stickers. The editors of Chicago newspapers seemed to feel that their reporters were often hallucinating. Cops are cops, not political activists, and why put any more bees in the ears of the liberal delegates? There was also the uneasy certainty that the cops were acting under orders, implicit or otherwise—lieutenants and captains in white shirts and many sergeants were much in evidence. That could mean that Mayor Daley was possessed by more than a small grudge against the McCarthy liberals, and Chicago papers generally award the Mayor the better part of valor. Plenty of bees were homing after the ears of the liberal delegates anyway.

At the corner of LaSalle and Eugenie, a group of ministers, most with medic armbands, petitioned the cops for permission to cross the no-man's-land and join the kids. These ministers—mostly from churches in the Lincoln Park area—wanted to act as a buffer between the kids and the cops; but the buffer role was tenuous and dissolved as soon as action began. Instead, the ministers found themselves acting as chaplains, medics, and support troops for the young warriors. A sergeant gave them permission to cross over, one at a time, darting along the sidewalk to where they could stand up and face the guns, too. On the whole, however, the presence of ministers incensed the cops. Any straight witness flipped the switch on the cops' guilty rage. Also, the police knew that the ministers' churches were being used as Movement centers by the kids.

In front of the Dodge showroom at the corner of LaSalle and Eugenie, a cop shoved me from behind with his club. I thought I would just try it once and I said, "I'm a reporter, officer." *"That's* nice," he said, shoving me hard again in the back and rapping the back of my head. I didn't react. I was committed to being an eye of history, and no cop was going to knock me out of it.

It was because reporters and photographers felt, in their naive arrogance, that they possessed special rights and asserted them that they were beaten so badly. You take a picture of a cop wrecking a kid's balls with his club, and you expect to walk away and publish the picture. Now that is silly. You expect the cop to respect you and say "Sir" to you and protect you and let you walk away and write things that he himself will feel to be disparaging. Very silly. No, sir, all groups in our sectarian, pluralistic society have ways of protecting their own, and cops are no different. Conjure a different society, my friend, and maybe you will be treated differently. *"Move,"* the cop said, and I moved south on LaSalle Street, into no-man's-land, trying to stay with the NBC men, who looked official but were no more comfortable than I was with all the guns around. I noted only that the cop had shoved and rapped me simply because I said that I was a reporter, doing us a favor by showing that there was no special status: only whether you are for or against. The ministers, too, had found that there was no special status: only for or against.

Just before I reached the corner of LaSalle and Eugenie, *Chicago Daily News* reporter John Linstead had been beaten badly by cops and carried away to a hospital. During the day, the Mayor's office had asked the newspapers and TV media why they were so upset, saying that there were 6,000 newsmen in Chicago for Convention Week and that only 17 had been beaten in Lincoln Park Sunday night. More were being beaten tonight. Six thousand newsmen in Lincoln Park would have been a hell of a scene, outnumbering the demonstrators about 3 to 1. A high percentage—perhaps 25% of the reporters and photographers in Lincoln Park—were beaten, not counting cameras smashed. But what got permanently under the skin of the reporters was that their editors refused to print, or drastically re-designed, what they saw.

The handling of news during Convention Week—and the stark debacle of the retrenchment in total favor of the Mayor in the week afterward—put immense energy into the disaffection among some Chicago reporters, and they found an angel who was also angry, who is unwilling to let his name be known. (It is interesting that we call the man with the enabling bread an emissary from heaven, from a life other than the earthly.) The disaffected reporters formed the Association of Working Press, and began to publish a monthly review (thriving at the time of this writing) called *Chicago Journalism Review.* In the first issue, the reporters say that during Convention Week there came a series of confrontations —that is the right word—between the reporters and their editors. They also reported that several newsmen

saw cops slashing tires of cars with McCarthy bumper
stickers in Lincoln Park Monday night. The reporters
were not unaware before Convention Week of news
priorities that dissatisfied them: of slanting, of news
withheld, of news not sought and not appreciated, of
certain political figures being baited and others let go
scot-free, and of misleading emphases in news stories.
In general, the reporters writing for the *Chicago Journalism Review* show, in the context of a story with which
they are familiar, how various forces and considerations
affect the presentation of a story in our newspapers. It is
one thing, for instance, to hear in the abstract that a
newspaper's commitment to its advertisers affects the
news; it is another thing entirely to see it described con-
cretely: the difference between seeing police violence
on TV and getting a club on your head. *Chicago
Journalism Review* reporters state that their purpose is
to improve the quality of news handling on the daily
papers where they earn their bread; they have received
support from powerful places in American journalism,
such as *The Columbia Journalism Review,* and they are
still working on their regular papers, though one of them
describes his relationship with his editors as somewhat
tense. To use Chicago Police Deputy Superintendent
James M. Rochford's phrase in a different context, "it remains to be seen" whether the relationship will endure.
Increasingly, in American life, there are reporters, editors, teachers, media-men, medical students, and many
others who are trying to work both inside and outside the
established institutions. This is especially so in communications fields. Whether they will eventually have to break
out or submit, or whether the established structures will
permit their own intentions to be rationalized to a point
that will satisfy most dissent, or whether such rational-

ization will only excite higher demands, also "remains to
be seen."

The cops were herding us away from the parking lot
just south of the Dodge showroom on LaSalle Street.
The NBC men were wearing helmets. I was sick with
seeing that the kids were being boxed into a trap. A
chauffeured car drove up. Out of the back seat right in
front of me a portly man eased himself, wearing a dark
blue blouse with a major's oak leaf on his shoulders. It
was ominous seeing him come to watch or take command. Cops stationed themselves with shotguns in front
of the parking lot on the other side of the street. Kids
were behind the cars and in the gangways that led to
Wells Street at the deep end of the parking lot. They
threw bottles and firecrackers at the cops. Now and then
a kid came dancing out between the cars, scared, scared,
scared of being shot, surrendering, and the cops would
make him spread himself out for frisking and approach
him with the shotgun levelled and then shove, push, kick
him. Then, on the east side of LaSalle, cops told the
newsmen to move down the street, far down the street,
and the newsmen didn't want to move. "*Move!*" came
the command with a flourish of clubs. The cops were
making sure that there would not be any witnesses, except their own, who could see into the parking lot. It
seemed that they wanted the chance to be able to shoot.
And then at a command, the cops moved into the parking lot with shotguns at ready. At the angle from which
I saw it from down the street, they disappeared quickly
in the lanes between the cars. Moments of sick waiting
passed. There was a loud report. Shotgun? Firecracker?
More like a big firecracker. Still, the shotguns were short-
barreled. Yippies were brought dancing out between the
cars with their hands up, and cops hurried them along

with the butts of their guns. "I'm coming, sir, I'm *coming*," one kid was crying, weeping in terror, learning something about his social expectations, too.

Most of the kids were in the trap in the four block area and every street around that area was being sealed by cops. At Wells and North, the kids were massed, holding the streets. But a great many kids were outside the trap, and the word was being whispered up and down the sidewalks, "The Hilton, the Hilton"—always said as if it were a code phrase, a charade of a code phrase, like "the frost is on the pumpkin." Cyclists were whispering, "The Hilton," from their bikes to those on the sidewalks, as they cruised slowly. It meant: create a new, another activity, keep the City on the jump. But most stayed here to find what the cops would do with their fellows in the trap.

The cops gassed the trapped area, and waded into the gas in attack lines, clubbing. When the gas cleared, the kids were on the sidewalks, jammed there, and the cops were blowing their whistles and whacking cars with their clubs since they thought that was necessary to keep traffic moving. It was here that the sergeant said that if his men would only quit blowing their whistles and take it easy, these people would go away. Here it was also that Cleveland Mayor Carl B. Stokes, seeking to cop some prestige by upstaging Daley, came to show how a politician should move among the restless people to quiet them. He was greeted by unceremonious verbal rejection by the kids and he beat it back to his car.

The kids were almost benign, packed on the sidewalks, as if with the peace of achievement, watching these strange, violent, blue-shirted men, and wondering perhaps why the cops felt so unsatisfied. Cops were chasing groups of Yippies up and down the streets from

Fullerton to Division—a twelve block area—and citizens, weeping and choking with the gas, looked out the
windows of their houses and high-rises at the wild beatings in the streets.

Mobile street and find-your-own-action tactics were
quickly developed by Yippies and students, escalating
in response to the police escalation. Small groups would
ambush a lone cop car with rocks, break every window,
and the car would flee, its occupants frightened for their
lives. Yippies would also flee because in a couple of minutes the reprisal would come—an attack unit of cops
with shotguns and rifles, tires and voices screaming—
summoned by a 10–1 call: Officer in Danger. The kids
who threw the rocks would already be gone, but the
cops would catch any likely kid and administer justice
then and there. In one such reprisal that I saw Tuesday
night at the corner of Lincoln and Armitage Avenues,
the cops ganged up on one lone kid in the Augustana
Hospital parking lot, and beat and kicked him, clubbed
him with the butts of their weapons, until the few Lincoln Park residents keeping their uneasy distance were
looking around for rocks, too. It was Monday night that
some cops started shooting, supposedly into the air, although sometimes it seemed that they were aiming but
missed. Gunfire added considerable fever to the general
feeling in the area. A brick would come through the window of a cop car, and the cops would whirl, firing away.

And always, there were the Yippie-Mobe-student cyclists calmly keeping in touch with various actions—the
wounded, the arrests, the whereabouts of the cops. I
don't believe the cops ever got hip to the cyclists, who
would roll coolly past, within a few feet of an action,
again and again. Angry Lincoln Park citizens, also exhilarated by the revolutionary presence that you breathed

with the tear-gas in the air, were helping, housing, feeding, hiding, and ministering to the young rebels who confronted the police in the streets and parks. The focus of immediate danger gave the clearest sense that life is now or never, us or them. But outside Lincoln Park, Chicago citizens not on the receiving end of clubs and gas, were not so clear in their feelings, and in their anger or uncertainty they tended to support the cops.

One Lincoln Park minister tells of one of his parishioners, an elderly lady, who decried his turning the church into an SDS Movement center. She too supported the cops, despite everything she said she had seen on TV, until one night when she saw cops beating kids right in front of her house. She felt the beating was manifestly unnecessary and she went out to tell the cops to stop and they stuck their clubs in her belly and shoved her away. Even age, if it were a disapproving witness, was dealt justice summarily. She was radicalized overnight.

A veteran Chicago newsman who witnessed Monday night in Lincoln Park said it was "the most vicious behavior on the part of police" he had seen in 25 years of reporting; his paper, the *Chicago Daily News*, would quote him the next day, for the delegates and the out-of-towners to see.

Monday night, Hugh M. Hefner emerged for a stroll from his mansion on State Parkway—where electronic controls give him any time of day or season or satisfaction he wishes—and was whacked on the rear-end by a club. All the news and images on TV were not as effective, educationally, as a poke in the belly, a whack on the rear-end, gas in the eyes and lungs, a club on the head. Hefner held a press conference the next day and indicated that he intended to use all the forces of the

Playboy empire to explore, promote, and support positions of protest, to develop a new politics. He made good
on his promise almost immediately by making it financially possible for the American Civil Liberties Union to
publish *Law and Disorder,* its wide-selling compendium
on police violence during Convention Week.

Movement centers in Lincoln Park were harassed with
tear-gas and stink bombs, raided, and during the next
day police stopped kids on residential streets and beat,
harassed, and terrified them in broad, work-a-day daylight. In The Theater on Wells Street, citizens allied with
the Yippies were monitoring police calls on a shortwave
set, figuring out their signals, and getting to the point
where they could tell where the cops were going and
what they were going to do. I believe it was Rommel
who said that American soldiers know less but learn
faster than any others in the world. It is an observation
of ambiguous portent, since Americans are involved in
so many different and contradictory things nowadays.

Grant Park: Awakening in Front of the Hilton

"The Hilton."

"The Hilton."

But the scene in front of the Hilton—the sleepland
and playland of the delegates—where demonstrators in
Grant Park used a powerful portable speaker to awaken
the sensibilities in the Hotel across the street, was almost
the Isle of Innisfree compared to Lincoln Park. In Lincoln Park, there was the rock-beat, born of cyclones of
consciousness, and in front of the Hilton there were folk
songs, with a wan, poignant line in them, born of sad-
ness and gentleness. I should have at least a penny for
every time during Convention Week I heard "This Land
Is Your Land," "The War Is Over," and other select pro-

test songs, such as "We Shall Overcome." But many of
the kids who sang folk songs in front of the Hilton were
no strangers to Lincoln Park, shuttling between conti-
nents, a new one and an old one, jetting through changes.
The strong interplay of events and feelings, tactics and
attitudes, was beginning. Lincoln Park was heating up
the energy of the daring and the will in Grant Park
facing the Hilton. News was coming to the Hilton of
what was happening in Lincoln Park, and the speaker
announced to the Hotel, the street, and everyone present
that cops were breaking into private homes in Lincoln
Park and taking kids away.

But the cops in front of the Hilton were much more
well behaved. They glanced with laughter among themselves. The Yippies and demonstrators dared the cops to
clear Grant Park the way they were clearing Lincoln
Park. Once this night, the cops had tried to clear it because all city park areas were supposed to be closed at
11 PM. Rocks were thrown at the cops, there was shoving, clubbing, pushing. The Yippies and students made
it quite clear that the cops would have to do under the
windows of the Hilton and Humphrey's suite what they
did in Lincoln Park. The cops ceased, and this bit of
Grant Park became known as the "liberated area." And
each night in this area a number of the kids did sleep in
a Chicago park long after the 11 PM curfew.

If the Massacre of Michigan Avenue had happened
this night, instead of Wednesday evening, the Convention might well have been moved to another city and
perhaps, only perhaps, a different nomination might have
come about. But that would have been too simple, like
changing jobs but doing the same work in the hope that
it would, somehow, change your life. No, the reasoning
in the movement of events in Convention Week was far

more stern, thorough in its intentions, exact, as if a man with his hand on the throttle felt another invisible force close over his hand and insist upon its own speed and timing.

From the "liberated area," the demonstrators' speaker asked Hilton residents to blink their room lights in sympathy, and maybe 6 or 7 rooms—all on the 15th floor, McCarthy Headquarters—answered the call. One other window blinked on the 6th or 7th floor, and one lone corner window in the Sheraton-Blackstone Hotel located on the southeast corner of the block north of the Hilton. When the same call went out from the speaker on Wednesday night—after a doomsday roll-call of two more days of street confrontations and cracked skulls and violent arrests—the whole front side of the Hilton would be blinking in answer, and the 15th floor would look as if it were signalling jubilantly out to sea.

The bees were going mad in the bonnets of the liberals on the floor of the Convention at the Amphitheatre. The entire regular Georgia delegation had been seated and the Julian Bond delegation excluded, and the liberals, already stung by the police presence and action, wanted the regular Georgia delegation unseated. "Throw them out!" they were crying, "Throw them out!" jumping on their seats. But Bond would have to wait until Tuesday night—when Hughes' compromise plan would finally be passed—to take his seat.

Individuals at the Convention also understood the hunger of the media for strong visual images, with much confirming fantasy potential for the viewer, who would be excited on his way to the kitchen to open another can of beer. A California delegate—a Negro in African dress with an animals' tooth necklace—stood up and held up his delegate's credentials, trying to burn them, à la draft card burners, with a cigarette hanging calmly from one corner of his mouth. It made front pages and newscasts everywhere. Actually, he only singed the plastic-coated card.

By 2:45 AM the Convention was out of hand in pandemonium protest, and the liberals would not let the regulars do their work of stifling democratic process except on prime time TV the next day. A minister did not get the chance to give the benediction for the Convention. Mayor Daley signalled for the Convention to be adjourned rather than destroyed, letting everyone see that he was perhaps what those in the streets said he was, Head Hog in the Hoghouse.

To every question about the violence in Lincoln Park, the Mayor reacted as if it were the prick of a herdsman. His cops had done everything right—ask Professor Janowitz and the Department of Sociology at the University of Chicago—and now everything was going wrong. Lincoln Park was doing its work.

The Ritual and the Hunt

Monday night a dynamic pattern became clear, the interplay between the "theatrical" preparation in the Park—the carrying of the flag, the barricade, and the cross on Tuesday night to come—and "the hunt" that finally swept back and forth in the streets. First, there would be the theatrical image and situation in the Park—the magic-making ritual—that would gather and hold the forces and lift up the energy and keep expectancy high and stable until the Beast was invoked and the police attacked. Then came the quick mass retreat to the streets, to advantageous ground, where the next phase, "the hunt," began. The kids were the "hunters," and the cops the Beast. The instinct of the Beast, of course, is to run away unless it is cornered and then it attacks to defend itself. The cops were cornered by the kids. Up against their impossible orders, the cops attacked. The cops, too, tried to see themselves as "the hunters" and the kids as the Beast.

Not so long ago, men hunted for food, and yet, necessarily, in order to be as strongly productive as possible, our hunting urge is empowered separately from the need for food, and so we hunt for the gorgeous sport of it, too. Men ambushed animals or ran in groups on the savannahs to stone an animal to death—the ancient situation in which leadership constantly shifted, signals were obeyed from different people, according to the authority of the perception of the needs of the moment, through voice and the signals of the arms. It was here in the streets around Lincoln Park, in the ancient situation, that the kids sought confrontation again and again with the police, astonishing many observers with what seemed to be foolhardy daring. It was here that the spontaneous leadership of group energy sprang up hard and quick in shifting situations. There was great sport for the kids in the streets, serious sport, dangerous, sado-masochistic sport, and the cops occasionally understood the role of the Beast that was pressed upon them. But few understood that the event was seriously about survival.

The deep wrecking rage, touched off by the blocking of political access, uncovered the ancient aggression, the ancient game, the ancient purpose, and turned them inside out for a perverse but highly effective performance in the theater of Chicago, with guaranteed audience participation. Think of the wide sky far over your head and think beyond the buildings that block the plunge of our sight in the city, of standing upon the earth and seeing from horizon to horizon, the space and swing of our ancient soul. The importance that is masked in every revolution is whether it is about survival, one way or another, and if it is not about survival—with the undeniable urgency of spirit that can be both reckless and patient for all the necessary time—the revolution will be less than it could be, will perhaps fail.

The dawn filled the sky over the Lake in the east, against the deep dark blue in the west over the Amphitheatre, with stars dying in the blue. The next day was upon us.

Sunday August 25. Lincoln Park. Photo by Dan Morrill.

tuesday: the demands of revolution

McCarthy Meets California

Tuesday was chilly, the temperature in the 50's, as if the air were cooled by the same fear that causes blood to withdraw and leave hands clammy. Tuesday, many middle-aged delegates woke in the Hilton frightened of the young people in the streets, whom they imagined as scatological avengers; while citizens of Lincoln Park were frightened of their cops, who were also avengers— of the wounded guarantees of social mobility. Liberal peace-plank delegates jumped to seize more reason for their indignation in the police repression and the street warfare in Lincoln Park. They felt the repression was directed specifically against anyone opposed to the War in Vietnam. Tires were slashed on cars with McCarthy stickers, McCarthy people were harassed in the streets, and at least one kid, passing out McCarthy leaflets on the "Free Hayden" march the day before, was singled out by an officer in a white shirt (meaning a lieutenant

131

or captain), and asked to take a walk; he was arrested, harassed, sadistically beaten in the police station.

News of other incidents was flying about, seeking a roost, and the scuttlebutt, always rife with fantasy, was often more honest and more informative than any other form of news. It all put piss and vinegar, spine, strength and energy into the indignation of the liberals who would close the Convention in a near-riot Tuesday night. The papers showed pictures of the Czechs marching through Wenceslas Square, and told of Czechs piling Soviet leaflets at the foot of the statue of the Good King and burning them, with signs showing the way to Moscow, telling the bewildered Russian soldiers to go home, much as Asians chant GI GO HOME. There were newsmen in the Hilton and in Lincoln Park who had been in Prague when the Russians invaded a few days before, who did not find the situation in Chicago much different and they said so. This affirmed Yippies and demonstrators and gave an unexpected sense of dignity along with ready propaganda comparisons. Other politicians were glad to feel themselves absolved of responsibility for what was happening in Chicago because the Russians, too, had similar troubles with youth, as if youth belonged in the category of seismic disturbances.

There had been so many arrests and quasi-arrests in Lincoln Park the night before that it was becoming known that arrest meant physical harassment of all kinds and beating on the way to the station and in the station. There are reports of a seminary student who was pushed into the back of a cop car, worked over for a half hour, and then the car was driven across the City, where the student was worked over again and then dumped. No official arrest. Kids began to feel that if they could run fast enough, dodge about, break loose from a cop's hold, they might escape arrest and be free of police-station justice. You sought arrest in the non-violent way with the knowledge that it might be the stupidest thing you had ever done.

Tuesday, the aides in McCarthy headquarters—which was always a disorganized jam of tired, enthusiastic people seeking concrete reasons for being there—were worrying how the street violence would affect their candidate's prospects, positively or negatively. Out in front of the Hilton, at all times, the cops faced the demonstrators in Grant Park, either from across the street, or directly on the sidewalk in front of the "liberated area." Demonstrators and curious straight people went back and forth around the ends of the cop lines. Exchange of opinion and feeling was beginning.

And on Tuesday, Humphrey, McGovern and McCarthy spoke to the caucus of California delegates, who were supposedly seeking an emotional allegiance to supplant what they had felt for the assassinated Robert F. Kennedy—those wide eyes of the man lying on the floor with a .22 bullet in his brain, asking the people not to move him, please don't move me, for the last thin chance might be in not shifting the bullet. It was because of the blue-and-white McCarthy flowers printed on the backs of leather jackets in Lincoln Park and the McCarthy buttons on lapels and because the Chicago police had already singled out McCarthy supporters for harassment, and because the man puzzled me with his determination to live in the mind of an assassin, that I sat down in the newsroom in the basement of the Hilton before three TV sets and watched the three suitors serenade the largest of the state delegations—the widowed treasure of California.

Vice President Humphrey was a sweaty man staying

cool in front of the California delegates in the LaSalle
Hotel, where the caucus occurred. In a good drizzle, his
make-up would make a mess of his suit. Senator Mc-
Govern endeared himself to the delegates—smiling con-
tinually with a shaky amiability, as if the bottom of his
face were about to fall off, or as if he were thinking of
those who were truly great—by declaring that the Vietnam War was "their war," meaning the Saigon regime;
he seemed to imply that they did not deserve our aid
mainly because they were losing.

Senator McCarthy said that his own position on the
war was well-known, and that was all he said. If he
thought his abruptness was witty, he mis-guessed his
audience. He received polite, almost disappointed but
still hopeful recognition from these delegates who
wanted a passionate wooing and who undoubtedly
were not able to free themselves from the memory that
he started to come on strong in the California primary
against Bobby Kennedy. He ceased such foolishness
directly after Kennedy was killed, when it seemed that
for a time he wanted to quit entirely. Then he came
back to the use of a cool and careful wit, aimed at those
who might follow it. But now the California delegates
felt themselves up for grabs: Jesse Unruh, their Chairman, did not appear to be sewing them up for bargaining, and they were a sentimental lot, bless them, so it did
seem that passion or sheer wilful demagoguery along the
right anti-war lines could sweep them into one of the
three pockets. The man to do it was McCarthy, and the
moment came, near the end, when it seemed that he
needed only to tip the table and let all the chips run
into his lap. A sudden caution came upon the man, and
he was more cool, more hunched, as he faced the moment that he must have felt himself facing many times.

He said well what he had to say but with a cool bitterness, as if he were more aware of that moment than of the delegates, as if he felt that he himself held the string on a trigger somewhere and could feel when it was getting too taut, as if he knew someone was watching him on a TV set with a phone nearby.

Lincoln Park Citizens Meet Their Police Commander

Citizens of Lincoln Park—artists, clergy, lawyers, and others—formed themselves into an Emergency Committee and went to talk to their police, particularly to Commander Clarence E. Braasch, head of the 18th District, which includes the Lincoln Park area. The citizens wanted to let the Yippies sleep in the Park and they wanted to take the responsibility of patrolling the Park themselves, telling the police that they would call them if it seemed necessary. But the meeting with the Commander was helpless. He too had his orders. You'll have to talk with my superior and the superior above him who will have to talk with the Mayor, that was exactly what he was quoted as saying, and exactly the way many of the cops put it. When the Commander was asked about police violence, he was concerned and asked for names and numbers. The first thing on the mind of anyone being wildly clubbed, of course, was to struggle up close and get the name and number of the cop. But the Commander was also told that many of his cops, apparently under the orders of immediate superiors, were taking off their nameplates and badges. The Commander said that that was mightily illegal, and he would appreciate information that would help him find the offenders. He did try to say that most of the gratuitous violence was perpetrated by the Task Force cops, who came from downtown, not by his own 18th District patrolmen. Responsibility, somehow, was always out of reach. He spoke of the cops' fear of rocks and bottles. "We even heard that they are going to throw flaming spears," he said, and when the citizens laughed he smiled, having discovered the put-on was funny. Even if the Yippies did throw flaming spears, and some were capable of such theater, it was a put-on. It was a part of the rightness of the week that such put-ons hit home. The citizens, disturbed by their helplessness, asked if the police could at least mitigate their efforts, such as walking slower in the sweeps. They left the meeting with the feeling that the Commander was much like the Colonel in the film *The Battle of Algiers:* an intelligent, game-playing professional to the core, a man who coolly enjoyed his job. This attitude was unsettling to upper middle-class citizens who were accustomed at least to being indulged.

After Convention Week, these citizens directly affected by the violence in Lincoln Park—or drawn into it—would form a group called the Lincoln Park Town Meeting— sparked by theater director Paul Sills and chaired initially by the composer William Russo—with their first aim being to restrain and control the local police from committing peace-breaking acts, and to force the police, insofar as possible, to live up to the slogan stencilled on the sides of their vehicles: We Serve and Protect. (The slogan tends to remind one of the Air Force motto: Peace is Our Profession.) The citizens would organize police observer groups, and a community review board that would take upon itself the hard job of reviewing actual cases of police harassments and police shootings, attempting to instill in the cops, however slowly, that they are accountable and perhaps culpable for what they do. The citizens would apply the Nuremberg principle—which is always handy for being used self-righteously, what's sauce for the accused is not necessarily sauce for us—that even if the cops were acting under orders from their commanders, and their commanders under orders from the Mayor, they were nevertheless personally guilty. This also is troublesome because the City has shown itself quite ready to try to absolve itself by suspending and/or indicting a few low-ranking cops. At the Town Meeting—held in The Theater on Wells Street—a few policemen, including their Commander, would show up to suggest that they were much misunderstood men of good will, and also to keep track of how strong the group was becoming. At the same time, most members of the Town Meeting group were aware that the main problem is political control and intentions. Apart from its local implications, the group, even if aborted, may have unwittingly revealed a rough model for what would have to be the character of a political party containing the present components of the American revolt, in that, with considerable strain and no small emotional heat, it sustained a right-center-left combination of peoples—long hairs, short hairs, pot heads, jazz heads, classical heads, popular heads, country heads, etcetera—the right being what we traditionally call the liberals. Even, and one might even say especially, the American Left does not submit kindly to any grouping that departs from the sectarian. However, if we sought an historical parallel, we might remind ourselves that Eugene Debs' Socialist Party sustained such a combination in the years before World War I through much strain, heat and bitterness, until it allowed its own excellent comprehension of the American situation to be broken to pieces by the surprise of the Russian Revolution. Where is our own perception? Where the mirage?

The clergy, mostly from Lincoln Park, who had been present in teams Monday night, had been able to restrain some Yippies from throwing bottles or rocks, but they could not restrain the cops and were often clubbed, too. One cop was so indignant about meeting his priest face to face on the other side that he called up the parish office at St. Sebastian's Church the next day and said that he would not be a member of a church where the priest supported that unforgivable, dirty lot of kids in the streets. The violence was heating higher and spreading further every night, and if tonight surpassed Monday night, shooting would be general. The clergy and the citizens were impressed by the kids' collective, on-the-spot decision-making. The clergy began to conjure an effective way to participate, to give witness, to forestall or mitigate the violence in the Park. Their churches were now sanctuaries for the kids instead of Movement centers, all political workshops and mock counter-convention activity having been wiped out long ago Sunday night. The ministers finally decided, rather late, with no anticipation of how successful they were going to be, to hold a service right where the confrontation would likely occur in the Park. Tonight would be the Theater of Guilt and Redemption.

World War II Vets Meet War Resisters

The Yippies and a few SDS were gathered around small fires throughout the afternoon in what was called the "valley" of the Park, in the everlasting tread of the drums, in groups singing and dancing, passing a pipe or a joint, peanut butter and crackers, or just lying in the sun. One fellow leaned back against a tree reading a copy of Ché Guevara's *Reminiscences of the Cuban Revolution*. There was little sense of pleasure and lightness among those in the Park, only thoughts of the night to come, the continual expectation of pitched battle. The chill in the air waited in the shade, the temperature there in the 50's.

Many Yippies voiced strong feeling that they should arm themselves in an organized, effective way. Cool heads argued that there was no effective way, and the improvised ways could be suicidal in that they invited the cops to use their full firepower. There were the cops, and behind the cops were the Guardsmen, and behind the Guardsmen were the Federal troops waiting to be deployed. Now it was well known that 43 black GIs refused at Fort Hood, Texas, to come to Chicago with their units and be used against their black brothers: they too expected a ghetto uprising. The courage in the Park was turning hard and bitter with the awareness of the absurdity of the situation, to the point where a few cops spilling their blood on the grass or in the streets would be almost equalizing in satisfaction.

A little after 6 PM, kids suddenly showed up with armloads of ceramic building tile that they dumped on the ground around the trunk of a big tree that was more or less the center of the scattered groups. The cops had made bravery and territory the issues, but the cops were fully armed at all times, so it was a delicate game of escalation that the kids played, in which they must keep tension and threat alive and yet not provoke general shooting. Within a short time, almost every Yippie in the Park had four or five pieces of the building tile in his hands, chinking them. Then, quickly, the tiles in their hands, intended as weapons, were being used as a rhythm instrument—several hundred handfuls of the tile —and the rapid, rhythmic chink-chink-chinking rose weirdly over the grass and under the trees. Their faces

were deadpan as they looked around for the plainclothesmen who would report it to the police—gunslinger deadpan, oh, there were TV gunslingers riding through their
memories to pre-empt the expressions on their faces.
Plenty of rocks and bottles and firecrackers had been
used by Yippies in the previous nights, but this was the
first time that, in effect, weapons were issued from an
arsenal to the group as a whole. And the weapon, the
square piece of building tile, was something to think
about—hold it by the edge, sail it hard sidearm toward
the target, yes, it could maim, even kill, easily. The cops
were forever shouting in their charges, *"Kill, kill, kill!"*
And some of them would also yell, "Kill the fucking
commies!" or, "Kill the filthy fucking hippie bastards!"
That was their kind of theater. I could see the building
tile used against the cop skirmish line in the dark under
the trees. I could see it used against squad cars out in
the streets. Yes, it was a fine weapon, just the weapon
to provoke mass martyrdom. But also it was for the eyes
of the ever-present plainclothesmen: to make sure the
cops tonight would feel fear.

Around the edges of the main groups, with the eerie
rhythms of the chinking building tile, several conversations were going between Yippies and SDS and middle-
aged men who had come to the Park "to see for themselves" and to straighten kid brother out. Every conversation that I overheard was between a World War II
veteran, who had made it economically in some way, and
kids who were all born after that War was over. A large
proportion of the cops were also younger than these
World War II veterans: the cops were in their late 20's
and early 30's. The World War II veterans had been
intellectually disabled by the idea that they had fought
an honorable war. They possessed curiosity in only a

token sense, and they were easily offended. The kids showed good feeling and patience in talking with them, and this only offended the older men even more. In one conversation, two vets were answering a kid who was making a case for socialism. "Socialism," one vet said, "is taking one man's $10,000,000 and giving one dollar each to 10,000,000 people."

"No, man, *no*," the kid said.

"Well, it certainly is," the first vet said, and his red-haired buddy upheld him. "That's socialism. Distribute the wealth." The kid looked at the sky with that expression of confronting a mile-high, smooth wall. How to begin? Do you begin with a discussion of a potential design and program for direction of capital investment in a possible American socialism? Or do you take another tack, one of many? The kid took the usual route—that of social injustice, the War in Vietnam, poverty in the cities, etcetera—with all its pitfalls of clichés, too close to liberal rhetoric. Both vets began talking immediately about what they had fought for in World War II. The kid agreed that that war was a morally necessary and honorable war, but Vietnam was very different, he said. The vets were mightily justified by the kid's admission that their War was an honorable war, and they seemed to feel that this certified their competency to make many pronouncements. They had gone on to win other victories. They are car salesmen, insurance men, middle-level executives, owners of small businesses, who have fortified themselves in a place in American society worth $10,000 to $20,000 a year. And now they are told that it is built not upon rock, not upon good dirt, not even upon sand, but upon shit. They went away in a huff, as if ready to pick up nightsticks themselves.

"That is not what I worked for for 16 years."

"That is not what I fought for."

I heard that last statement several times during Convention Week: "That is not what I fought for." There was good feeling and a noticeable lack of resentment of parent figures in most of these kids who were talking to World War II vets. Many other kids in the Park were really off the wall, scattered, jerky, brains shot so ragged and turned into electronic braunschweiger, that they had no personal life left, and could only offer themselves on the altar of great events. The World War II vets felt that it was a generational duty to swallow whatever war was stuffed down your throat. They were profoundly offended that the kids would even question the Vietnam War, as if you separated yourself from decency by even exercising the question. They were not much different from the male delegate from South Carolina who suggested that to write a book was less than honorable—an interesting attitude, if you examine its communal pretensions. The veterans came to the Park "to see for themselves" only to verify what they had already concluded.

In another conversation, nearby, another World War II vet was trying to tell two kids that their violence was wrong and that in passive resistance there was dignity.

"*Dignity?*"

"Yes," he said, a little flustered.

"No, man, *no.*"

So it went in one conversation after another. The middle class had come out to justify itself. They wanted to find out "the real story," find it out "for themselves." They wanted to find that either the kids did not provoke the cops and the cops were unconscionable bullies, or that the kids were irredeemable anarchists. Their minds were not capable of coping with the fact that the cops *were* unconscionable bullies, and that the kids *did* provoke them.

Around a fire where only Yippies were present, the conversation was different, and if you were a little high it was possible to feel pleasure and humor. Peanut butter and crackers were being passed, and a black Yippie, prominent in the training of parade marshalls so long ago last week, was musing:

"This morning I had bacon, and ham, and sausage, and —"

"Man, that's all *pig!*"

"Well," he said, "at least it ain't still walking around."

They all laughed.

Tuesday evening Bobby Seale of the Black Panthers spoke to the assembled Yippie groups in Lincoln Park, and it is reported that he urged them to battle back and put the fear of God into the cops. That was no more than what many kids were saying. Seale came into town, spoke here and in Grant Park the next day, and was indicted by the Federal Grand Jury. Jerry Rubin also spoke, asking that the Yippies march and demonstrate in support of the black CTA workers' strike.

Three different marches went out of Lincoln Park that evening: a large march went north to the CTA car barns, comprised of demonstrators who wanted to show their sympathy for black bus drivers on strike for equal participation in their union; another march went south on LaSalle petering out rapidly; and a third went down Michigan Avenue mostly along the sidewalks to Grant Park in front of the Hilton. The usual police violence did not attend these marches. Indeed, the march that went up Clark Street to the CTA car barns at Clark and Diversey spread over the area along the sidewalks and in the streets, with a lot of singing and playing of guitars.

These marches and the Anti-Birthday Party for Lyndon Johnson which the Yippies would hold that night in the Coliseum, drained most of the Yippie power out of Lincoln Park. The marchers and the Yippies at the Coliseum planned to return to Lincoln Park for the 11 PM confrontation; but the theatrical potential of the major territory had been left untended for the time being, though all parties, even those who came to seize it, were unaware that this had happened.

LBJ Birthday Party and Anti-Birthday Party

Tuesday night the Democratic Party was throwing a birthday party for President Lyndon Johnson at Soldier's Field, and Lyndon kept the Convention waiting for him until nearly the last minute. Tuesday night the Yippies were throwing an Anti-Birthday Party in the Coliseum, and great was their desire that Lyndon should come to Chicago. They won either way. If the President did not come, it meant they had scared him away, and if he did come, it would be throwing powder into the fire. Lyndon waited until the last minute, and Lyndon did not come to Chicago. At Soldier's Field there was "Happy Birthday" and "The Battle Hymn of the Republic" sung by Anita Bryant—"I always sing it for him at the White House"—and in the Coliseum there was no-dance rock, blasting your ear-drums into the center of your head, and the chant of "Fuck LBJ," while Lyndon's family guided Lyndon's hand to cut a cake in Texas.

Far south of Lincoln Park, south of the Loop, a few blocks south of the Hilton on Wabash, the Coliseum may have been two-thirds filled, maybe three or four thousand people, I don't care to play the numbers game. The rock band was trying to blast the walls down, to create a moment of floating upheaval in space and time by sheer assault. Leaders, singers, writers, poets, TV "actors" —such as David Dellinger, Abbie Hoffman, Phil Ochs, William Burroughs, Allen Ginsberg, and Jean Genet, with Grove Press Editor Richard Seaver as his interpreter—addressed the audience.

Genet always received a welcome stronger than that given to other writers, and yet he was the most ironical in his appreciation of the Yippies, even saying at one point in Lincoln Park, after telling the Yippies how terrific they were, that the ones he really loved were these others over here, who also dressed unconventionally, the cops. His remark got a laugh, of course, with all of its implications: the sexual implication; the implication that the Yippies were also in uniform with their beads and long hair; and the implication that the cops, most of them in the prime of life with high energy, bellies and all, were the important agents of history, the *sine qua non*. The ironies of the remark never stop. The man never relinquished being an artist, heavy and careful, as careful as McCarthy in a different way, with those eyes that could see three inches into stone, with his seeming calm, a touch haughty to an American eye. It was interesting to see ourselves against him, our flamboyance against his conservativeness, our flagrant satirical put-on against his irony; those who ride time or are trampled by it against personal containment in time, those who felt the sting and confusion of responsibility against a man responsible to his eye and his soul and what they might give.

There was Allen Ginsberg, disturbed by the reckless Yippie fury, sitting quietly on the edge of the stage doing a Yoga exercise while his statement on police brutality was read because he had temporarily lost his

voice due to the combination of mantra chanting and
tear-gas. There was William Burroughs, glancing at his
everlasting wristwatch, always timing something. And
Dave Dellinger, when he first came onto the stage, said,
"I bring you greetings from Norman Mailer," who was
sniffing the sights inside the Convention at the Amphitheatre—and there were cheers, for Mailer's fame for
The Armies of the Night was large among the kids. But
most of the artists were put off balance by the power
that leaped from one event to another and seemed beyond anybody's control. Several of the leaders were trying to make statements to cool the beautifully absurd
power and energy of the kids who called themselves
Yippies.

Phil Ochs, when he went through his thing of strum-
ming and talking to the audience, moving forward and
back almost jumpily, tried to say that he thought
there was a tendency on the part of many kids to over-
antagonize the police. It didn't make the slightest difference to the feelings of the audience. When he sang
"The War Is Over," they stood up on their chairs burning draft cards or any card that would serve, as if that
were the summons that he had given rather than a
cautionary one. Lighters and matches were snapping,
and the burning cards were held aloft in one hand with
the other hand up-thrust giving the V sign. One very
straight fellow, crewcut and all, in the back of the crowd
was burning his draft card, a solemn fumbling business
for him. Now he had it lit and he was looking around
almost pleadingly for recognition or for someone to
guide him in this jump into no-man's-land, a forlorn
moment as he stood there quite separate from the thun-
dering ecstasy in the Coliseum. He even held the card
up as if he were watching the black edge of the flame

drift down through the words and numbers. Then he sat and stared at the charred pieces between his feet, while the exultant, wrath-of-God feeling jumped to other moments of declarative theater.

When Abbie Hoffman invaded the stage and made a speech about marching on the Amphitheatre the next day, again everyone was roaring on their feet, flinging up the V sign. But Hoffman and Yippies used resolutions as just another theatrical weapon. They did not feel bound by them, and there was no guilt if they did not carry through with a resolution. The resolution might simply help as publicity to awaken feelings from all directions, and cause another different moment into which they could pour their energies. Keep the Man off-balance. When the authorities were off-balance, they were on the edge of being invaded by their fury and by the necessity to restrain it, because of the threat of loss of control. A delicate game, as delicate as that between an artist's personal intentions and the intentions of the thing itself that he is bringing into being.

Images from ancient dreams, dreams of truth and prophecy and false dreams, were breaking loose into the Coliseum: knights and old warrior ecstatics raising and clashing their swords for the battle to come. Mass ecstasy, with all its hammering heartbeat of righteous rage for self-sacrifice. Or more. Or less. "Peace, now." Sieg, heil. "Peace, now." Sieg, heil. "Peace, now." Sieg, heil. The feeling of music and poetry was gone from the chant as soon as it began, and the mechanical rhythm summoned the memory, the radiant faces of an all-demanding destiny. Territory was the name of the game. Room to live in. A life and death matter, as real as ground to grow food, or a madman's charade. *Peace, now!* There were bare fists, here in the Coliseum. Long, tatted hair. Tired, jubilant feet. Bodies sweaty with the days. Ruined faces, about to disappear behind the ever-lasting soft smile of acid. Brains so scattered they think the chair they're sitting on is also on top their heads. It was the rage born of deliberate sexual deprivation if you were a Hebrew warrior ecstatic, and now born of the deprivation of play, not deliberate, but deliberately accepted. There was the building tile used by the hand-fuls as a rhythm instrument in Lincoln Park. I could visualize the skirmish line of cops, the Yippies in the shadows ahead of it or in the cloud of gas before they succumbed, the pieces of tile hurled hard sidearm, cops wounded or killed, and then cops firing at the hundreds of people. "Fuck LBJ! Fuck LBJ! Fuck LBJ!" Like the reversal of ceremony in the Black Mass, the birthday song was meant to poison cake all the way through Texas, joyful, this verbal arsenic.

The unconscious wisdom that ruled Convention Week was especially discreet in holding the Anti-Birthday Party in the Coliseum. If it had been held in Lincoln Park, where the energy could leap immediately into action, there would have been a massacre, enough mar-tyrs for decades to come. I drove north to the Park ex-pecting it. Even by this time I had not yet learned not to anticipate anything that might happen.

Deep in the Park, on the slope under trees near where the barricade was raised the night before, was a tall, crude cross, and around it a number of people were sit-ting and standing, singing hymns.

Attack at the Foot of the Cross

In the time that most of the Yippies were out of the Park doing things in other parts of the city, the Lincoln

Park clergymen had usurped the potential theatrical moment. They had come to the Park to give a service, carrying the cross from a neighborhood church (the Church of the Three Crosses at Sedgwick and Wisconsin), to give witness, to mitigate the violence. Kids helped them carry the cross and were both nonplussed and glad to see them. Other kids were suspicious, because they saw the movement of events being deflected if no other visual image were raised to supersede the commanding cross and the service. Many citizens sitting and standing around the cross were as angry at Yippie violence as they were at cop violence. Unity of all participants only came about under direct cop attack.

The service began with a small number of people, and then the number of people by 11 PM curfew in and around the area of the cross was perhaps a couple of thousand, though most of them were simply waiting for the cops. Only those within a short radius of the cross could clearly hear the service and the discussion over the portable speaker. But they could *see* the cross. Where was the building tile? It was not to be seen. Songs and hymns were moaned out of a feeling of impending loss, helplessness, even a need for absolution. People who did not wish to be so closely involved were massed back on Clark Street alongside the Park and on the embankment by Stockton Drive inside the Park. But there was no will in the Park to create an alternative image or event. The feeling in the Park agreed with the ministers and the cross. People waited for the cops, restlessly. There were no catalytic people. The actor may have been there but he was not to be seen, and the boy who carried the flag Sunday night was not to be seen. Enough American writers were present around that cross that the cops

could have wiped out a large portion of that literature
which they use as an excuse to keep some of their bud-
dies employed on the vice squad.

The usual debate began rapping over the speaker
about what should be done. But no heart was in it. It
was personal statement, personal witness, accusation,
why I'm here, the revivalist weeping rail without the
revivalist vigor, and no girls made pregnant in the
bushes. It was all serious, for those making the statements and those hearing them, but not serious in the way
that the students and the Yippies had tried to work out
some resolution of effort in the two days previous. They
tried to sing "We Shall Overcome," but it was a dead
loss for these kids who regard non-violence as just another flicker of the serpent's tongue. A girl with glasses,
dressed incredibly in Army fatigues, who played a strong
part wherever she was present, grabbed the mike and
said they shouldn't let themselves be seduced by this
We-Shall-Overcome shit—"It didn't work back then [in
the early Sixties civil-rights movement in the South] and
it isn't going to work now"—and she said that the ministers were trying to cool the revolution and *fuck* the
ministers. A few kids, within hearing of the cross, agreed
with her, but it was not the sort of agreement that could
call upon present energy, not the way the boy cried fuck
the marshalls Sunday night and only a few agreed with
him, yet they carried the night because it agreed with
the under-moving energy. "We are free, too," a minister
said. "We are free in Jesus Christ." A Yippie standing
beside me fluttered his lips with an astonished exhala-
tion. What the minister said was out of the most radical
of modern theological training, yet, in the context, it
sounded so medieval it freaked the scene. "Will the lady

who lost her wallet please come to the cross?" There was the bland face of the kid holding the speaker on his head. "Will Mary come to the foot of the cross where John is waiting for her?" The ministers made the most of the cohesive power in little moments and favors. A kid made a statement about people over 30, with a bitchy fervor, as if the masochistic catering of adults to him were as essential as the air he breathed, and a middle-aged woman, close to tears, came to the mike to answer the statement angrily. The cross. The cross. You kneel and meet before it, you pray, cry, confess, and even if you use the cross to absolve and free yourself for action, it is off center from action, and the large cross shifted attention in Lincoln Park off center, willingly. Another smaller barricade was constructed this night, but it could not supplant the cross as the central image. In fact, though the ministers were trying to move the kids' energy into more pacific directions and wanted to act as a buffer between the kids and the cops, the demonstrators unconsciously used the ministers as a way of holding a large group in the Park for the confrontation with the cops after 11 PM.

Very few newsmen were present among the demonstrators in the Park this night. Writers and underground newspaper reporters were there, but the four major Chicago dailies, so outraged Sunday and Monday, had, in a conference with police and city administrators, capitulated. The cops told them plainly, and euphemistically, that if the newsmen wanted "protection" then they should stay *behind* police lines rather than among the demonstrators and Yippies *in front* of police lines. Now the media were in back of the police skirmish line that was forming a few hundred yards northeast of the cross.

If you stayed behind police lines, you saw little or nothing of what happened, as media and citizen observers would shortly find out.

Gas was coming. At the very least, there would be gas. The people in the group around the cross were resolving to steel themselves to sit through the gas and the cop attack and be arrested or beaten right there. "This is our park. We will not be moved," a minister said. Directions were given over the speaker for using a handkerchief, preferably wet, to cover your nose and face. I had already soaked my handkerchief at a water fountain when I came into the Park and was carrying it in a wad in my coat pocket. Gas we could expect. A student told me astutely that the group would not sit through it. I said that I had learned at last not to anticipate anything. By this time, the principle was established in everyone's deepest mind of not being bound by resolutions but going with the movement of whatever was happening. This in itself was an advance for the American revolt. A few years ago, the group around the cross might have sat through what was coming.

Most of the Yippies, students, and others who chose to be at the point of confrontation were not paying much attention to the affair at the cross, other than letting it be the main visual image, but were on their feet, waiting, watching, moving, or scouting for the cop attack. Once again, from Clark Street and the embankment by Stockton Drive to the groups deep in the Park, that milling and shifting back and forth was working, at the behest of fear and fascination. I glanced around to see if building tile was in anyone's hands, and none of it was visible. The cross was moved to a position adjoining the barricade, a maintenance of centrality by absorption on the part of the cross.

From the cop lines, huge batteries of lights on Fire Department vehicles sprayed a stark glare over the Park. Every shadow was a hundred miles long. The cops made the usual bullhorn announcement that the Park was closed and anybody in the Park was in violation. There was little yelling or throwing of things at the cops this night, so the energy of fear had to go in a different direction. Some of the people around the cross hugged each other hard, reminiscent of movies and books where people, about to be wiped out, turn to each other in sudden love and pity.

Then the canisters, lobbed from tear-gas guns, came crashing through the trees, broken branches falling too, into the group around the cross and all over the Park. The cops claimed to have learned a lesson: that tear-gas, in the present shape of situations, was a most effective and satisfying form of attack that was also de-escalation. Americans have such marvelous equipment for putting into effect the lessons we learn. A Sanitation Department truck drove up and down spraying out an enormous cloud of gas that would roll with the slight movement of air and make the Park uninhabitable for some time. The Yippies and students did not want the fight to be in the Park. They wanted it to be in the streets. It was only necessary to stay in the Park for the triggering confrontation. They were Green Mountain Boys now, and they were not going to stand up on open ground in suicidal lines. I looked back over my shoulder and there in the cloud of tear-gas with the brilliant lights behind it was the cross and the group sitting around it praying and singing, and, spreading rapidly away from the image of the cross, away from the brilliant cloud of gas, were thousands of fleeing figures. It was out of *The Book of Revelations*, Hieronymous Bosch, the Hell of

Breughel. The people in the Park were in the ages of
guilt and redemption, small hope of the latter, but the
skirmish line of cops came from a later imagery. Three
deep, with gas masks, tear-gas guns, clubs, shotguns,
rifles, Mace cans, they stepped through the cloud, as if
they were picking up their feet and moving off the pages
of science fiction comic books, invaders from an insect
planet. They did move more slowly this night, in the
Park, giving people a chance to clear out, and perhaps
the entreaties of the clergy and the citizens that afternoon had had that much effect.

The people in the group around the cross did not sit
through the attack. With all that purposeful waiting, the
containment of adrenalin energy, there were moments
of near hysteria; then they went in all directions, some
plunging right through the cop lines, through the gas
thick as milk. People in other parts of the Park, several
standing on the bridge over the lagoon, were seen by
cops but not told to clear out. Apparently the curfew
law, which seemed so rigid, was flexible, depending on
where you were and who you were. Individual cops
could make the interpretation, and the crime was to
identify yourself with the area of confrontation.

The cross. The cross. A few clergymen went back the
next day to find it, but it had been dragged away. They
said that the local Police Commander was "over-solici-
tous" in trying to help them. The cross could not be
found. Imagine a bunch of Irish Catholic cops tearing
it to pieces!

The imagery of Sunday night and Monday night was
out of school-book heroics and modern revolutions,
Yankee Doodle and student barricades. But the cross,
the cross. The cross agreed with a feeling among the
people in the Park even if the kids only cruised past it

to cock an ear now and then. Make no mistake, the acts of the revolt in the streets during Convention Week were done to make the Democratic Party pay for its betrayal, to call it to account for its 1964 program and therefore its possibility. It happened in Chicago. Not Miami. In pointing this out Mayor Daley was correct. The passion for blood vengeance was so strong in the streets that several New Left people questioned if it all added up to what they would define as political acts, focused, with future intents. Nobody who felt personally responsible could be sure, since no man knows what cometh or that he is doing the right thing. The fear of responsibility was being felt Tuesday night for having initiated the energy, the impulse, that became the driving force of a turning point in history. It was an anticipated responsibility, and therefore more frightening, the deep, dim feeling in the Park of a need for personal and collective salvation, of confession and absolution, a cleansing and readying.

Escaping the tear-gas, thousands of kids joyously hit the streets, as if made free, with the find-your-own-action, find-your-own cop tactics at which they were becoming more skilled each night. There was no standing up in lines in the open in the street, as there had been Sunday and Monday and would be again Wednesday and Thursday. First, the action shifted northward out of the drift of the gas, small bands pounding down the streets overturning trash baskets and setting fire to them, doing anything to attract the cops and then stoning the cop cars. If the scared cops fled, radioing a 10–1 (Officer in Danger) call, the kids might flee, too, or if they felt the situation to be advantageous, they would wait for the attack unit, three squad cars with heavily armed cops, and hail it with stones and the cops would start

wildly shooting into the air. Cop sweeps of Lincoln Park
and Old Town were swift and vicious, but the further
action went from Clark and LaSalle Streets, the more
vulnerable the cops became and the more violent. A few
hundred cops were threatened with being split into
smaller and smaller units, faced with fast hard quasi-
guerrilla warfare.

Kids from white gangs, intrigued by the opportunities
for their kind of play and for vengeance upon the cops,
were more present tonight. The potential for involving
large sectors of youth was apparent. The right game was
there. But other kids were also out on the streets trying
to get into the game from a different angle—West Side
"Wallacite" working-class short hairs, looking for long
hairs to beat up. They got the surprise of their life when
they found that the cops not only did not want their
help but made no distinction between them and the
other kids.

Tactically, Tuesday night was the most daring in the
streets, an advance that was unsettling in its implications. The rebels were wholly within their situation and
using it, and, for a time, the images of Ché Guevara and
other revolutions were benignly distant. There was so
little window-breaking and looting, the cops being accepted as nearly the sole representative of state power,
that there appeared to be a basic awareness that real
estate is only auxiliary to modern property and power.
That engagement with the cops might be or become a
diversion from challenging real political power, was an
idea not entertained.

These were not kids who felt immediate material deprivation. They were ready to take on corporate-political
power at its base. Their attitude was doubly wise in that
window-smashing and looting would have alienated the

very citizens from whom they received support in the way of sanctuary, hiding places, food, first-aid, and general help. Citizens accompanied wounded kids to hospitals saying that the bloodied heads came from "household accidents," to avoid arrest as "demonstrators." Other areas of Chicago might not have been so helpful, since artists and liberals form a significant component of the Lincoln Park population. Other people sat behind wall-to-wall glass on the cliff edge of their high-rise apartments and watched the beating and chasing in the streets below.

Demonstrators Meet Guardsmen Brothers

Many kids began moving from Lincoln Park to the scene in front of the Hilton, where you could stroll around police lines, from the Hotel to the demonstrators and back again. The numbers of the demonstrators were small, and the proposed march to the Amphitheatre was coming up tomorrow, but the news from Lincoln Park gave energy and pitch of expectancy to the feeling that, out of sheer daring, the thing sought would still be accomplished in Chicago.

At the Amphitheatre, the Julian Bond delegation was finally seated according to Hughes' compromise plan, half the votes to the regulars and half to the Bond delegation. Hale Boggs read the majority report of the Platform Committee in support of the War in Vietnam, written by the Administration in Washington—LBJ all the way—and the peace-plank delegates stampeded all attempts of Daley and Humphrey regulars to sew up debate and vote on the war plank that night. The liberals played catch with the Convention over the heads of the regulars, and Daley made his famous, furious throat-cutting gesture for Carl Albert, the Chairman, to adjourn the Convention, once again without a benediction. Yes, the liberals would make the Party debate the war issue on prime-time TV tomorrow before the nation, too. Many of the liberal delegates, when they returned to the Hilton, crossed the cop lines and spoke through the demonstrators' portable speaker to their fellows and all other listeners in the Hilton. "We're with you," was the gist of it.

Out of Lincoln Park came the draft and the fuel for the fiery enthusiasm building up in Grant Park. With a fine instinct, the cops were trying to nail the kids coming down the streets that led from Lincoln Park to the Loop and to Grant Park. The cops stayed in front of the increasing mass of people in Grant Park, not about to do what they did nightly and daily in Lincoln Park, but facing the energy that they helped to create there.

The demonstrators' powerful portable speaker bombarded the Hilton, heard all the way up its 25 floors, the upper floors hearing it faintly as if they were floating over a source of siren song, with all of the chants, the songs, the statements, the declarations from the full spectrum of the Convention Week revolt, from Black Panther leaders through Yippie and Mobe speakers to McCarthy delegates. Delegates woke in the Hilton finding themselves helplessly humming, "This Land Is Your Land." Julian Bond asked over the speaker for room lights to be blinked in sympathy, and room lights were blinking up and down the 25 floors, many of the 15th floor McCarthy headquarters windows winking almost in unison. The plain jubilance in the unrelenting power of the demonstrators' verbal assault made the Hotel listen.

Then there was sudden and growing fear as, for the first time, National Guard vehicles, among them the jeeps enclosed in barbwire frameworks, moved into the side streets by Grant Park and around the Hilton. It was the visual image of ARMY that made everyone feel a cold and unfamiliar threat. In fact, the Guardsmen were relieving the cops, who had been on duty for more than 12 hours. But there were other differences: the Guardsmen were the same age as the demonstrators and in their baggy fatigues they were wholly without the physical glow and relish and assertion of the cops. The cops marched away in easy cadence; the demonstrators cheered, for no cop could claim that he had been on his job longer than these kids today. The Guardsmen slopped into position, with rifles and the bayonets that were also a new point of apprehension.

Brigadier General Richard T. Dunn climbed on top of the hood of his jeep and tried to use a bullhorn to tell the demonstrators that they could do what they wanted to do and the Guard was here only to keep order. He could not make himself heard clearly against the force of the other speaker, over which the demonstrators were saying that they hoped no violence was intended. The Brigadier General said that that was exactly the way he felt about it, no violence, indicating that he differed from the cops and whoever gave them orders. He was non-plussed by his inability to use his bullhorn effectively against the speaker, and the demonstrators were beginning to enjoy it. "Come over and use our speaker," they said. "All right," Dunn said, "I'll use your speaker," clambering down off the hood of the jeep and crossing through the lines to the portable speaker. It was a theatrical moment in which Dunn's paternalistic attitude and the basic stand-pat attitude of the Guard was declared. Dunn stood to win much in the minds of those watching with a display of willingness to personally mitigate the in-

tensity of feelings. As soon as he tried to use the demonstrators' speaker, he was drowned out by singing and
chants. They would not let him get away with it. Their
enthusiasm that he sought to mitigate had been won
with blood. There was more confusion and a few smiles
among the young Guardsmen. The Brigadier General
finally had to use a police car's loudspeakers to say what
he had to say. At one point during Convention Week,
Dunn said that he regarded the kids in the streets no
differently from the way he regarded his own children,
maybe they just needed to have been spanked when
they were growing up, he said. *Children:* these kids who
had sat in their minds on the arctic porches of red suns,
and slid through the arteries of their arms to find what
ticked in their fingertips. The police commanders looked
upon the situation as revolutionary, and played that side
of the game. Dunn saw it as mere adolescent rebellion
and dissent. The cops were more immediately interesting, but the Guard may have been a more awful presage
of things to come.

A few scuffles occurred Tuesday night in front of the
Hilton, now well into Wednesday morning, between
Guardsmen and demonstrators, mainly between black
Guardsmen and sentimental demonstrators. Some of the
young black Guardsmen made it plain that they didn't
want any brotherly integration talk. The black Guardsman could hardly feel fairly approached if the demonstrators with their repetitive sentimentality picked him
out for solicitation rather than the white Guardsman
standing beside him. It is said that Dunn then ordered
that black soldiers were not to be used in lines directly
facing demonstrators. Imbued with the ideology of gas
and anonymous pressure, he wanted as little flesh-to-

flesh or weapon-to-flesh contact between soldiers and demonstrators as possible.

Until dawn, the demonstrators kept the front of the Hilton hovering in a revelatory fever between sleep and waking. "Dump the Hump, Dump the Hump." "Peace, now, peace, now." "Join us, join us." The knell of November was there for Humphrey to hear, and McCarthy, reportedly confused and upset, could be thinking, "No, this isn't what I meant at all."

Lincoln Park—now become the Atlantis of the Left—had done its work.

wednesday: war

Vietnam War Plank

On Wednesday morning, newspapers reported that
McCarthy had said Tuesday that he would lose the
nomination. It seemed to be the stoic report of a man
who always knew where he was. But the timing of it
was eager, 24 hours early, as if he needed to stay in control of something, his feelings perhaps, his life perhaps,
as if he were making absolutely sure about something.
His aides denied that he had said it, of course, not wish-
ing to take steam out of the debate on the Vietnam War
issue due that afternoon, but he certainly managed to
forestall any irrational upheaval of support for his candidacy. The workers in McCarthy headquarters were
irritated and depressed, and they wondered why their
candidate should so suddenly and purposefully, and
with such unrelieved cynical stoicism, withdraw himself from being the support of their passion and their
energy. But they were not giving up, and they waited
for the debate on the War issue and for the nomination

163

vote. For the demonstrators in the streets and parks, on the other hand, the play and by-play of the Convention evoked only muted feeling now, though the debate on issues was sharply important. It was as if you were trying to make sense of reflections in a display window past which you were running for your life. But the implications of the action in the streets and parks were jumping into the heads of the delegates in the Hilton and the Amphitheatre.

Wednesday afternoon, the National Mobilization to End the War in Vietnam held the only planned event, from the demonstrators' point of view, of Convention Week: the rally around the bandshell in Grant Park for the march to the Amphitheatre to protest United States involvement in the Vietnam War. There was a permit for the rally. There was no permit for a march. The Mobe had sued the City for a permit to march to the Amphitheatre, but Federal District Judge William J. Lynch— get the name—a former law partner of Mayor Daley, denied them, ("being unable," in his judgment, "to find that the Park District and City of Chicago have acted arbitrarily"). The Mobe was granted finally a permit for the rally within a circumscribed area around the bandshell and *that* permit was not delivered until late Tuesday—the day before the rally. The alternative routes of march proposed by the City were considered wholly ineffectual by the Mobe, and rightly so. The City—and that means the Mayor (who is supposed to possess direct control of two-thirds of the votes on the City Council)— created one situation after another in which brave and dedicated men were dared to go home calling themselves cowards. Bravery, the right to exist in your own mind, was once again the issue.

Wednesday was a blue and beautiful day, as blue as

nearby Lake Michigan. Black cops had been detailed to hand out leaflets saying that there was no permit for a march, to everyone entering the rally area. There must have been smart people on the police force who detailed black cops to hand out these leaflets. White cops would have been shunned. Demonstrators found their sentimentality exposed when they expected a leaflet handed out by a black cop to be something other than a warning that there was no permit for a march. "Read it, *read* it," the black cops were saying, with a modest enthusiasm, as if they were enjoying the game. "Join us, *join* us, brother," the demonstrators said, after reading the warning, bantering with the black cops. "Read it and believe it," a black cop said in return. In those skyblue shirts and skyblue helmets, the police were lined up in force on Columbus Drive, looking in upon us in the bandshell. The feeling of the Lincoln Park battles was simmering in everyone.

Yes, the feeling of Lincoln Park was there, as if it had forced the City to grant the permit for the rally, and might yet force the City to let the march go to the Amphitheatre at the last minute. But the City, as we have seen, gave permits only under pressure and at the last minute. The police let the demonstrators stay in Grant Park opposite the Hilton all night because the demonstrators made it clear that the cops would have to crack heads with general violence under the eyes of the delegates, candidates, and notables in the Hilton. The Park District gave the permit for this rally at the last minute. The law was obviously expedient and arbitrary, and was to be met on that basis. The law was arrogant, grudging, and insistently and defensively self-righteous, to the point of existing in a condition of pent rage. The law might give in, throw the crumb of permission at the last

minute, and it might not. Demonstrators, Yippies, and
the Mobe parade marshalls, who had trained in Lincoln
Park, were saying here and there in the bandshell area
that there would be a march to the Amphitheatre anyway, and they were making plans for it. The plans varied
from motorcycle sorties to peaceable foot marches and
vigils. It was the talk of men who must, in their minds,
plant a stake in their future to keep a sense of direction
and movement in the present, even if the stake is mostly
illusory.

The rally was boxed on three sides by cops and Guardsmen. The Guardsmen were lined up south of the bandshell area, and demonstrators were trying as usual to
talk to the young Guardsmen as brothers. At the beginning, the feeling in the bandshell area was festive above
the quiet simmer of fear-expectancy in the belly, festive
in the way that peace marches assemble and the way
that people come to the bandshell area and sit on
blankets on the grass and picnic while listening to music.
The crowd was as diverse as that which might be assembled on Judgment Day. People were meeting friends
that they hadn't seen for a long time as they usually do
at peace marches. I stood in one place and met five people that I had not seen in years. Ice cream trucks out
on Columbus Drive were selling Good Humor bars as
fast as the attendants could pass the bars from hand to
hand and make change. A Yippie with an Indian head-
band with FUCK lettered in the center of it was stuffing
a Dreamsicle into his mouth. There were plenty of
straight people in this crowd who strongly disapproved
of Yippies and particularly the Yippie inclination toward
confrontation. No matter, they would find that their flesh
was just as offensive to cops as the flesh of longhairs
with weird clothes and love beads and FUCK on their

foreheads. But the straight peace-marching types intended to keep control of the demonstrations away from the kids who were fresh from the training of Lincoln Park.

Look over this crowd and see all the flags flying haphazardly—red flags, black flags, Viet Cong flags—and then look up a way into the sky at the regulation flagpole west of the bandshell benches, the American flag.

A lot of the kids have learned to expect anything at anytime, and they already have vaseline smeared on their cheeks, here and there an actual gas mask, and helmets, World War I and British Army style helmets, motorcycle helmets, American Army helmet liners, football helmets, and a few jackets thick enough to partially cushion a blow. People are massed in the benches before the bandshell, and milling around the edges of the crowd, watching the cops out on Columbus Drive.

Plainclothesmen are also moving in the crowd. A few of them I recognize from Lincoln Park, dressed in straight casual sport shirts and pants, wearing sunglasses and carrying cameras. They are husky, with the smooth physical presence, the smooth faces and the smooth unemotional smile, with the slight taunt in it, of sadists. But there are the other plainclothesmen, the ones with beards and hippie dress, such as Robert L. Pierson, the police undercover agent, who became Jerry Rubin's bodyguard. These are the ones to fear. Now and then one of them is found out and they are crazy, stupid, violent provocateurs—young men whose brains are cracked with guilt and anger that they cannot manage. Not that Yippies needed their help to bring off any confrontation, but they make most Yippies look like models of character stability.

We are here to listen to speeches, no one knowing what

will come after the speeches and no one to tell up from down, left from right, sheep from goats, sinners from the saved.

Then the cops made the move that was the first major provocation of Wednesday afternoon. A large number of cops—perhaps 100—moved at walking pace into the rally area, positioning themselves along the trees north of the flagpole and west of the bandshell. When they moved off Columbus Drive, a sucking sound of fear went through the western edge of the crowd. The 100 cops tried, in their cop way, to appear discreet along the trees, as if they grudged giving in to even an appearance of discretion. They refused, in their arrogant self-righteousness, to recognize that their immediate presence was an irritant that acted upon the soul the way Mace acts upon the body. More than a majority of the American people have, at the sight of a cop close enough to act upon them, feelings of unease, fear, anger, hatred. The cops' general reputation for lack of courtesy and arbitrariness, or outright sadism, is there in the feeling; and there is that damned pistol, that club, and that can of Mace on their belts.

Add to this the fury and indignation of the last three days and nights in Lincoln Park, and it can be seen why this move on the part of the cops into the rally area, was, at the very least, unwise. If they did it to gain a more advantageous position to protect the few of their own who'd been stationed near the crowd since the rally began, it would have been wiser to withdraw the few. The Mobe leaders and parade marshalls, who were everywhere in the crowd, were making it plain that they intended actively to keep the rally peaceful, to the point of asking the many by now militant Yippies to go somewhere else. If the cops moved up along the trees to gain a more advantageous position to control the crowd, then it was deliberate provocation on the part of those who gave them their orders. The cops moved within taunting distance, within missile distance, close enough to be in emotional contact with the crowd, to be in contact with their own cop emotions. The blame for the events that follow, with absurd but powerful logic, rests squarely upon the conscious and unconscious mentality of the Police Department and the City Administration. The cops were acting and moving under orders. If they expected more of the demonstrators than they expected of themselves in the way of military discipline, then they were worse than stupid. Imagine David Dellinger barking orders over the microphone, and every peace-marcher, student and Yippie in the bandshell area snapping to, following the orders with precision. Yet the Mobe leaders and marshalls were perfectly capable of keeping control, *if* the cops would stay out of emotional contact. What the Mobe could not control whatsoever, was the actions of the cops themselves. Now watch the flagpole and remember Old Glory, Betsy Ross, the Pledge of Allegiance, and wish that American schools spent as much attention on instilling respect for civil rights and liberties as they spend on that piece of dyed cloth.

The Battle at the Bandshell

Speeches were being made over the microphone in the bandshell; but on the western edge of the crowd attention was given only sporadically to the speech-making: all eyes and ears were on the cops. If a cop so much as shifted his feet, or moved forward or back, it ticked the expectancy in the demonstrators.

Then the 100 cops shifted along the trees and moved several yards in the direction of the bandshell and closer to the edge of the crowd—and stood still again. Tension hardened in the bellies of those watching.

Kids with transistor radios were following the event at the Amphitheatre. The stranglehold of the political hogs in the Amphitheatre on the issue of the War would have its repercussion here in Grant Park. Among those demonstrators whom I heard talking the main motivation for what happened now came in response to the War issue—the majority report of the Platform Committee in support of the government's unending hysteria in Vietnam—being debated and voted at the Amphitheatre.

A fellow climbed upon the base of the flagpole, and started trying to lower the flag, and some were crying to tear it up, burn it, and others were saying to lower it to half mast. The kids were between the cops on one side and the Vietnam War on the other, both guaranteed to bring out the issues of righteous declaration and bravery. The fellow lowering the flag was a hippie, helmet and wild hair, and a few cops, who could probably recite the Pledge of Allegiance by heart but would credit the Bill of Rights to Chairman Mao, came forward out of the group of 100 cops to stop him. A flurry of pushing and shoving burst around the flagpole, and those nearest it say the kid was beaten unmercifully. I was about 100 feet away. The immediate reaction of the demonstrators was fury, spreading swiftly from the base of the flagpole. It happened instantaneously so it must have been in response to what the cops had done to the hippie. The kids were shouting PIG as if the word were a cannonshell; and there was a brief throwing of things, anything they could pick up—paper, boxes, pieces of board, a few rocks of whatever variety, paper flowers, real flowers, anything. One fellow, out of his skull with fury, picked up a wide open newspaper as if it were a deadly weapon and hurled it, and of course it went nowhere. The Mobe leaders and speakers in the bandshell were forced to pay attention to the flagpole. Dellinger was saying that the flag should be lowered to half-mast, and others were cautioning severely against responding to the cops. Many demonstrators were yelling for others to be careful what they were throwing because, in their rage, they were hitting their own people.

The confrontation eddied, and then a group of men—huskier than most Yippies or students, who are generally kept on the skinny side by lack of money and running from cops—stepped out of the crowd almost like a weird color guard, and began rapidly lowering the flag and raising another object that could have been a pair of red leotards slightly stuffed with something. Most of the people nearby, out of American schools all the way, were caught in feelings of shame and anger. Lowering the flag to half-mast would be enough. I repeat that the Yippies, who were daring enough to do the work of provocation themselves, did not need any police-assigned provocateurs or CIA assignees or what have you: nevertheless, throughout Convention Week the feeling was never stronger that the weird color guard was composed of plainclothesmen.

Cops came in a small group, and then a larger group, to clear the flagpole area, clubbing. Verbal abuse and material objects were thrown at them by the demonstrators. The confrontation sawed back and forth. Mobe leader Rennie Davis came to quiet the flagpole area, cool the demonstrators, and got badly clubbed by police who recognized him. Parade marshalls were moving back and forth, in and out, shouting for people to sit down, and the voice over the microphone was bellowing "*Sit down!*" A few objects, anything available to be

picked up, were being thrown at the police now and
then from all directions in the crowd, but it was certainly
not the rain of objects that The Walker Report tries to
lay upon the public mind. If 20 witnesses saw one object, The Walker Report writers seem to have reported
it as 20 objects, until they multiplied it into a "rain" of
objects on the police. Were The Walker Report authors
themselves eyewitnesses of these events? The Walker
Report says that the police say "cellophane bags of human excrement" were thrown at the cops here by the
flagpole. Could be. But I never saw such bags and I
stayed on the western edge of the crowd, near the flagpole, all afternoon.

I had gone earlier into the men's toilet in the park
building on the western edge of the area to soak my
handkerchief with water in expectation of gas. One cop
limped out of his group back toward Columbus Drive,
apparently hit by a piece of brick, and a cheer went up
from the nearest demonstrators. Churchmen and most
of the peace-marching types did not share such militant
enthusiasm of Yippies and many students. A smoke
bomb canister was tossed into the crowd by the police,
and a fellow with an oven glove on his hand threw it
back at the police. Cheers again. It unrolled its white
smoke by the trees north of the flagpole.

The cops were gathering in formation, whipping their
clubs in the air with sharp eagerness. Now the kids were
becoming raunchily imaginative with the obscene abuse
they gave the cops. Occasionally a sexy hippie chick
would flounce toward the police line, taunting the cops.
Cops are imaginative with obscenity, too, as anyone
who has been in a police station can testify, but cops
seemed more than usually sensitive to mother-wife obscenities, in the way of men who will take such abuse

with good humor from their own kind but are enraged
when it comes from people whom they specialize in
despising. Parade marshalls lined up holding hands to
keep the demonstrators back.

Then the cops rammed in a loose wedge into the bandshell area, wading into the crowd, clubbing, clubbing,
clubbing, overturning benches and leaving the wounded
to be trampled. They were met with rocks. Kids threw
themselves upon the cops, hand to hand fighting, while
others piled up benches in barricades and yet other
frightened demonstrators panicked and trampled each
other. For a moment, it looked as if the cops, chopping
people right and left with their clubs, were going to
drive a swath straight through the crowd to the other
side. But they were meeting direct resistance—a lot of it.
The kids from Lincoln Park had simply had it with pigs.
Dust floated up behind the cops, drifting over the agonized wounded, and a strange peacefulness followed a
few yards behind the cops. Then the cops, having administered their form of justice, having filled out the situation that they themselves initiated, withdrew slowly,
many of them wounded, albeit superficially.

The lowering of the flag and the baggies full of "excrement," these, not the few rocks and bricks and pieces
of concrete, were the reasons offered by the police and
police observers for the cop action. The flag. The flag.
All flags are dyed cloth. These are excuses, not reasons.
The cops moved in formation, and they moved under
orders. When they moved into the rally area they were
under orders. From this moment, there was that feeling
in the gut that people were going to get killed.

The Walker Report describes the police wedge that
rammed into the crowd in the following way: "They
came first in a relatively straight line. Then as the line

of marshalls broke in the face of the police advance, the officers waded into the crowd individually." Why the use of the word "individually"? What does it connote? Who is served by this word "individually"? Why not leave it at exactly what happened: that "the officers waded into the crowd"? The Walker Report also uses the word "individual" to describe the cops in the captions of the photographs of this event. There are other photographs in other publications that show the general shape of the attack more clearly. Let me tell you, that if they moved into the crowd "individually," *all*, or nearly all, of them moved into it "individually" in a rough wedge. It would seem that once again responsibility is being displaced, and that the accusation of superiors in the Police Department and the City Administration is being avoided. The Walker Report appears to be a careful set of signals from one power area to another, telling it to shape up or be shipped out, and implying that it would be preferable for them to shape up because it would be a tolerably bitter struggle to have to get rid of them. The signals are given as carefully as a judge gives signals to contending parties in a courtroom. Your present attitudes are not productive, the Report implies. The Walker Report was, in a grander sense, the gauntlet slapped down between a new area of American corporate-political power and an old area. At the same time, the Report seeks, not so subtly, to discredit the demonstrators. The new political area must amass public support—as must all such ambitions in American life—and give direction and tone to it, for public opinion in this country is a range never quite staked out: people are always waking up to find that their fences have been moved and they will have to think twice about moving them back. There will be more to say about this new political area, later. It, too, lost out temporarily in the struggle within the Democratic Party. *Smile* when you say that.

It all had happened so swiftly.

On a long walk-bridge that arches over Columbus Drive and the Outer Drive to the Field Museum, curious onlookers and Guardsmen were leaning on the railing watching the events at the flagpole. Kids were twisting on the ground and moaning with their scalps split and blood pouring. The police made no effort to get them medical aid; it was students who called ambulances, and MCHR doctors and medics who treated the wounded. A Fire Department ambulance crew arrived. City hospitals were telling demonstrators not to bring their wounded to the regular hospital emergency rooms because cops were waiting at the door to jam the wounded into paddy wagons. The cops stormed into improvised hospitals—such as the Church Federation on Michigan Avenue—and jerked transfusion needles out of arms and, broken bones or no broken bones, crammed the wounded into vans. This was witnessed by citizens both in improvised aid stations and in regular hospital emergency rooms. These are the attitudes of total and ruthless repression. And there were still New Left friends complaining that they saw no politics in all this ridiculous violence, no organization, no purpose, no plans, no focus. There were straight people in the crowd dazed with the realization that it was a given situation with a ruthless dynamic, with no organized choice and no personal choice—you could only move into or away from it. It existed and moved in and of itself, opening the gates in the complex sewer system of American rage that drains out of the above-ground status scramble, in which self-importance is measured only by the diminishment of another person or assured by benumbing equalization—hence, *rage*.

After the battle at the flagpole, the crowd hardly listened to the host of speakers who trooped one after another to the microphone. Everyone was waiting for what would happen with an attempted march out of the bandshell area to the Amphitheatre. Allen Ginsberg, with his voice still ruined and croaking from Omming and from tear-gas, tried to lead the crowd in Om to quiet the butterflies.

Then Carl Oglesby of SDS spoke, and as his voice loomed over the crowd, I remember thinking, "My, how the New Left has progressed: they have a speaker or two now." He used the old thing that the future will be ours, and the new society will be born out of the old, but most people were not sure whether they were witnessing a birth, an abortion, or a death in Chicago. But all the rhetoric coming from the speakers sounded odd and out of place and aside from this movement of events that would begin when it would begin and end when it would end.

The inevitability of birth or death was in that movement, and you could only give your attention to its practical details. Wet your handkerchief. Get a helmet. Pick up your rock. Put down your rock. Smear your cheeks with Vaseline. Tie your shoes. Sing your Om. Find a friend in whose presence you might feel better about spilling your blood. Or find a friend who will hit a cop over the head if the cop is hitting you. Wait. Wait. The fucking speech-making will never end. They're trying to dull us. Make us manageable. Hey, there, Guardsman, brother Guardsman, loan me your helmet. Helmet, fuck, loan me your rifle. *Fuck* marching to the Amphitheatre.

That will take goddamn forever. Let's storm the Hilton. There's a trip, man.

There was talk on the part of some Yippies of ambushing cops. A few of the other publicly known leaders were suggesting strong action because of the intense fear and indignation over the recent cop invasion of the bandshell area. A toughening urge to fight back was showing in many of the kids, and it was not just talk. The demonstrators might prepare to seek a cop actively and then not do anything about it, but if they were attacked by cops they would not just cower or run away, they would resist, fight back—as they had done during the violence around the flagpole. Absurd improvised weapons were made on the spot. Stakes, rudely sharpened out of bench slats, were made to stick in the ground, a fantasy borrowed from the reports of Viet Cong using sharpened bamboo stakes on trails in Vietnam to pierce unwary GIs. Nails were driven into one end of a slat so that it could be swung as a truly dangerous weapon. Any kid using such a weapon in a hand to hand fight with a cop knew that he stood an excellent chance of being shot. The kids had a fine sense for the unequal weaponry, and they seldom separated themselves into personal fighting with cops. That indicated a certain sense for revolution. They made it a confrontation all the way. And the cops, with impossible orders behind them, were forced to face this spontaneous group sense that helped bands of men survive long, long ago. The kids did not try to hide these improvised weapons. They brandished them and walked up and down with them, and were told by parade marshalls to get out of the march because of them. But the weapons were made as props to satisfy and bluff the fears and needs in the minds of the kids and to bluff and put-on the cops. These props worked, at least in the mind, to equalize the weaponry, satisfy a fantasy of blood vengeance, and apparently both irritated and deterred the cops and their commanders.

David Dellinger was using the microphone in the bandshell to promote the march that would attempt to leave Grant Park and go to the Amphitheatre. The message coming from the bandshell was insistent that those who wanted trouble, those who wanted to provoke and throw rocks at police, should stay out of the march, do what you need to do, brother, we're not putting you down, but do it somewhere else, this is a non-violent march. The march was organized by the statue at the south end of the area, and parade marshalls, with black bands around their biceps to show who they were, actively and thoroughly asked kids with rocks and other improvised weapons to leave the march. They did leave the march, a few slipping a "Fuck you" over their shoulders. The inevitable portable speaker was carried on the shoulder or on the head of one fellow, while others used the microphone behind him to give orders and directions in forming the march. The marshalls worked constantly, from the time this march was organized until it met the cops, to get control and exclude or govern the Yippie impulse. The Yippies left the march easily when asked, in some cases walked beside it using their sticks as staffs, because by now the Yippies and many of the students much preferred the fast, quasi-guerrilla warfare of the streets around Lincoln Park. It was Yippie actions that had filled the plans of the Mobe at last with people— people willing to attempt marches and demonstrations that were not permitted. Now the Mobe was trying to exclude the main attraction. Wednesday was the height of participation by out-of-towners, perhaps as many as

5,000, added to another 5,000 to 8,000 who came from Chicago and nearby places. In the March on the Pentagon in October 1967, there had been the weight of numbers and a single symbol toward which attention was addressed—and courage, to be sure. In Chicago, during Convention Week, the cops themselves became the focus, and just behind them were seen rising the misty evil presences of Mayor Daley and Hubert Humphrey, war-making puppeteers who were themselves puppets, their reactions controlled and directed by the demonstrators' flagrant, foolhardy courage.

The march, controlled by those men with the speaker who stepped backward in front of the front ranks, moved with the speed of cold glue and the fear of personal death to meet the line of cops on Columbus Drive. An ice-cream truck rolled along beside the march, doing a decent business, thank you, nickels and dimes. The lines of approximately eight demonstrators hooked arm in arm, their feeling of comradeship high, inched even slower as they approached and then stopped before the line of cops. The marchers were on the sidewalk and the grass, and media trucks waited beside them on Columbus Drive. Parade marshalls and Mobe leaders talked with the cops, who obviously did not feel threatened by the march they faced. It was announced over the speaker that the police sergeant said that he saw no reason why such an utterly non-violent march should not be allowed to continue but he needed the permission of his commander. The fellow using the speaker seemed to take heart from what the police sergeant said, and so did the marchers who heard it. The answer from the commander was that there was no permit for a march to the Amphitheatre.

Negotiations began, in a small Grant Park building,

between Mobe leader Sidney Peck and the police officials. It was a long time. It was long enough for the
orders to come from the source of all such orders in
Chicago: Mayor Daley, whose frequent use of a nearby
telephone in the Amphitheatre was noted by many observers. And the answer was no.

The lower ranks of cops here in Grant Park, having
just taken a lot of fighting back in the bandshell, seemed
to want to be relieved of their unrelenting orders and
the sergeant must have thought the non-violent march
would be a worthy excuse that would siphon away hostility. No one should know better than the cops on the
line what happened when they blocked all access. The
negotiations continued, the police commanders offering
ineffectual alternatives, and the humiliating feeling of
being worn down began to fester in the marchers. Groups
began drifting and milling here and there in Grant Park
along Columbus Drive, and some Yippie groups were
talking of going to the Amphitheatre by cars, by motorcycles, by any way that they could get there.

The National Guard stood in lines, with their military
equipment, on bridges from Grant Park to Michigan
Avenue. I saw some media men go through the Guard
line on the Balbo Drive bridge and I came up to the
same spot. A Corporal asked me, courteously, for my
credentials. I had credentials—colored cards for admission to all of the Convention committee hearings and for
the Hilton and a letter from the editor of *Evergreen
Review*. None of it was good enough. "We can only let
through members of the major press," the Corporal said.
I said something in anger. He said, "I'm sorry, sir. I have
my instructions."

I said, "Your instructions are absurd."

He said, in a tone that agreed with me, "I'm sorry, sir."

But beside him was a Private who felt differently, and the second my anger showed, the Private stirred as if poked, made a face, and bumped his M-1 butt at me, just to show that he would rather be a cop. The Corporal was either middle-class or getting a middle-class education. The Private was out of what we call working class, and if you ask me how I know that, I will have to say that I have been an American since I was born and I know it. The anger of some working-class whites at the presumptuousness of middle-class protestors and journalists was extreme. That Private would, indeed, rather have been a cop. I had to walk northwards to the Bridge just south of The Art Institute where the Guard granted exit to Michigan Avenue.

I decided to follow some of the Yippie groups to the Amphitheatre. As I moved farther away from Grant Park and the Hilton in my car, there was a huddled strangeness about the ordinary actions of the City, as if the people were figures on a screen and the sound was turned off and then the figures themselves realized the sound was off, and felt odd. Out at the Amphitheatre, it was so peaceful in the late afternoon—a spacious, grey emptiness behind the blue police barricades for all the protected blocks up to the building itself: an emptiness peopled with the blue of cops and their blue sawhorse barricades, bored cops, cops joking away the time of day, a coming of evening emptiness widening around the building, silent and grey as a prison, with red-white-and-blue banners and pennants racketing in every breeze. It was a building in which it was hard to feel that anything was happening, but in which more than 1,500 delegates were voting to continue the carnage in Vietnam and 1,000 were voting against it, losing and singing, mourning and yet with a joy of finding themselves. There was

a connection between this building and the demonstrators near the Hilton, a connection through the air,
breathed out of a transistor radio into the ears of kids
who might or might not go to Vietnam if called, but
were ready now to march to the Amphitheatre or meet
the cops and know why and why not. It was the connection that appeared to trigger the flagpole battle in
the bandshell in Grant Park.

No Yippies or demonstrators were near the Amphitheatre or riding the main streets toward it. The march
that could not occur was the compelling focus for
Wednesday afternoon and evening, and nothing could
detract from it, not even for bands of Yippies, who felt
the upwelling of power leave them as soon as they left
the environs of the Hilton and Grant Park. I drove back
to the Hilton; I had been gone about a half hour.

I parked the car in a garage in Wabash Avenue,
watching the black attendant come toward me blinking his eyes, twisting his head, smiling, and then I felt
my eyes burning. The march in Grant Park was being
gassed, gassed heavily, and it was drifting over the City.
The black attendant said nothing, only smiled. It was
sharp stuff and I was coughing as I crossed Wabash,
having a hard time keeping my eyes open. Then I got
the knack of it, blinking my eyes rapidly to keep the
tears flowing and pressing the damp handkerchief over
my mouth.

A working man in a white shirt, gassed while eating in the pancake grill on the corner of Wabash and
Balbo, burst out the door furiously and spotted a squad
car right there in the street in front of him. In all Convention Week, I never heard any Yippie, demonstrator,
or citizen curse cops with such incredible anger, utterly
lacking fear. A cop opened the door of the squad car

and stepped out to deal with him, hefting his club by
his side. That did it. It was not provocation that the cop
met. It was unmitigated righteous fury, as the man in
the white shirt dared the cop to lift that club and told
the cop that the City did not belong to him. The man's
anger triggered my anger and I came up to the curb
beside him and raged at the cop in the same way. A few
Yippies, dressed as if by Tom Sawyer for Halloween, as
witches and goblins and sad tramps, came up uneasily
yelling, "Pig, pig!" Pitiful provocation! The man in the
white shirt turned to a Yippie beside him and said, "I'm
with you! I'm *with* you!" Then other bystanders were
shouting at the two cops from both sides of the street.
The one cop had been uncertain from the moment he
stood up out of the car and met the force and tone of
the man's outspoken fury. There was no fear in it. There
was no fear in me. There was no obscenity of tone and
feeling, though the finest cussing was used. It was direct
accusation, from a man who was the cop's class peer
and who spoke the cop's language, and this cop could
not cope with it. Then the cop noticed more angry people
gathering at the corner and he might have been glad to
feel outnumbered; he slipped back into the car and it
moved east on Balbo to the Hilton. Then came the familiar sight, a cop line moving toward us, slowly, threat of
reprisal, but this did not deter the man in the white shirt,
who kept on shouting and pointing with his arm, "Look
at them! Ruining the city!"

The cop line stopped. I went past one end of it. They
glanced at me, but in a glassed-over way.

I was sure that the marchers were being slaughtered
in Grant Park and I was running, with a reporter who
said he was from New York, up the hump of the Balbo
bridge that arches from Michigan Avenue over the rail-

road tracks into Grant Park. The gas was thick and sharp; it burned on my cheeks and was savage in the eyes and burned the throat and really twisted the bronchials; it seemed thicker and more nauseous than the gas the two previous nights. But the damp handkerchief over my mouth, and the power of my rage, kept me pounding along at full speed anyway, above the gas effects. At the other end of the bridge ranged a group of Guardsmen wearing gas masks, and a couple of them were using tear-gas guns lobbing canisters into the Park, *pomp*, *pomp*, that turned end over end through the air and fell into a daytime hell of gas and stumbling groups of marchers and blue-shirted cops also wearing masks. Imagine the Fourth of July painted as Hell by Breughel.

A little Guardsman, with a converted flamethrower on his back, was sowing a steady cloud of gas, so thick you could hardly see the few furious demonstrators trying to break through the Guard lines. How the little Guardsman must have felt, spraying people literally as if they were weeds or bugs, while he looked like nothing more than an evil Jiminy Cricket himself, with the gas mask, the helmet, the green fatigues, sleeves tied at the wrists, gloves, pants tightly bloused in his boots so he wouldn't get any of his own gas. Other Guardsmen were ramming the demonstrators back with rifle butts. "You sons of bitches!" The New York reporter and I were both shouting. You have to consider the way men sound when they shout out of absolute rage. For a second, as we pounded down the slope of the bridge, it did seem, both to the Guardsmen and to me, that we were going to attack the fellow with the converted flamethrower. The Jiminy Cricket turned and calmly sprayed the thick grey stream right at us. The New York reporter caught it in the face, and he didn't have a handkerchief, and I ducked and headed toward the bridge railing. There was a feeling of competence in being able to duck tear-gas when it first spewed out, or dance around it or ahead of it and manage to keep going without benefit of a gas mask. We raged at the Guard until they were all looking at us through their gas masks and some of them made motions of starting after us, as if to say *"Git!"* while the Jiminy Cricket continued laying down the cloud in our direction. If we stayed we couldn't avoid succumbing to the gas, and I needed urgently to get inside the Park, so I ran back down the hump of the bridge to Michigan and headed north. During these few minutes Wednesday afternoon, several men in their middle 30's were running in a rage in the streets and on the bridges, all well-employed men, all possible veterans of the great silence of American history, the Korean War—almost, but not quite, hurling themselves upon the cops and the Guard, as if they felt they should be the protectors of the kids in the Park and were now too late. Over the Congress Bridge and over the intersection at Columbus Drive deep in the Park, people, small with distance, were splashing in the water of Buckingham Fountain to wash away the gas. Then I reached the bridge just south of The Art Institue.

The Battle at Michigan and Balbo

The marchers came over this bridge, where exit was granted, with eyes stinging, coughing; some doubled up in nauseous agony, and not knowing what would happen next, in hopelessness and up-for-grabs confusion. Then —in an accident that could not have been timed better by God—down there, stopped at the traffic lights at Jackson Boulevard and Michigan, were three pitiful mule-drawn wagons of a Southern Christian Leadership

Conference Poor People's March. It was a token march,
but of course it had a permit and the impression was
that it was going to the Amphitheatre. The situation was
recognized and the cry went up. The stream of people
coming across the bridge straightened out and they ran
cheering down to mass behind the mule-drawn wagons.
SCLC blacks, including the Reverend Ralph Abernathy,
stood on the wagons and waved for the demonstrators
to come on, and both kids and blacks were yelling, "Join
us! Join us!" and the people coming off the bridge suddenly were not feeling the tear-gas so much. The mules
shied and reared with all the noise and excitement, but
they were calmed and the SCLC leaders welcomed the
marchers. It is said that the SCLC wagon-train had a
permit to march around the Hilton and down Michigan,
but *not* to the Amphitheatre. I was standing beside the
lead wagon, and that was not the impression derived
from the quick conferences that occurred between the
kids with the portable speaker and the SCLC leaders.
You join our march, we'll join yours, brother, brother,
brother, brother. The feeling of everyone was that they
were now participants in a march with a permit that
could not be denied.

In a few minutes, the three mule-drawn wagons were
at the head of thousands moving down Michigan toward
the Hilton, chanting with incredible energy, "Dump the
Hump," "Peace, now," convinced that they were going
all the way to the Amphitheatre. McCarthy workers,
wearing black armbands in mourning for the defeated
peace plank, were coming off the sidewalks to join the
march. And, because this march had a permit, *the cops
were leading it.* The Pig had been fooled. Many of the
cops were laughing, and there was an unbelievable
camaraderie between demonstrators, cops on motor-

cycles, and the SCLC blacks. *The Pig had been fooled.*
But the cops stepping backwards about a 100 feet in
front of the wagon train were grim as they guided the
march. Their feeling was not the same as that of the
cops on motorcycles and the other cops, who, being
among the demonstrators, may well have felt that joking was valor's part now. On the west side of the march
on Michigan, a few cops, in what amounted to personal
hysteria, waded into the crowd clubbing. The portable
speaker stayed in front of the march moving forward
with that steady caution and tense sense of distance that
showed in the parade marshalls when they had a chance
to define a situation. "We're going to the Amphitheatre,"
the speaker said. The mules of the wagon train shied
and reared now and then at the sound of the powerful
speaker, so the speaker moved away from them and
seemed to become more muted. A mule rearing and a
man leaping up to catch the harness at the bit was a
new sight. Only a few people on this street, born before
World War II, might have gone to town in a mule-drawn
buckboard. Lines of cops waited in front of the Hilton.
They stopped the march at the Balbo-Michigan corner,
where TV cameras were mounted on the Hotel canopy,
ready to let the world watch everything that happened.

The cops had to safely separate the SCLC blacks from
the crowd before they could deal with the marchers.
If they treated these blacks, some of them famous, such
as Reverend Ralph Abernathy, the way they had been
treating Yippies and demonstrators the past three days,
there might be hell to pay in the ghetto. The April 1968
insurrection in the Chicago black community had been
triggered by the assassination of Reverend Dr. Martin
Luther King, Jr. The demonstrators were loud and jubilant in yelling their appreciation and support to the

Negroes on the wagons, and at first the feeling was returned in kind. But now at the corner of Balbo and
Michigan, with plenty of cops in front of the Hotel, the
Negroes became uncertain, their smiles became more
forced in meeting the huge jubilance of the marchers,
and perhaps the near absence of black faces in the crowd
was also unsettling to them. The gas was still in the air,
and though it was not affecting the demonstrators, a
one-armed Negro man on the seat of the lead wagon
was nearly overcome, as if he didn't know what was
happening to him. The woman beside him caught him
and dabbed at his eyes, and kids on the street tried to
offer water and advice—keep your eyes open, breathe
through a wet handkerchief—but the uncertainty was
there in the Negroes and it was growing, with the huge-
ness and loudness of the crowd and the pressure of
the cops.

Dellinger and other Mobe leaders were talking with
Police Deputy Superintendent James M. Rochford—not
that anyone could see that such talk had anything to do
with what was happening. Dellinger and the Mobe had
no control over the marchers now, and the cops had no
control over their orders. An order to clear the streets,
for instance, was an impossible order in this situation.
All rational, on-the-spot control ended when the non-
violent march was denied in Grant Park. The cop commanders self-righteously offered ineffectual alternatives
again, such as peaceful demonstration in Grant Park opposite the Hilton, and persisted in not understanding
the absolute insistence on the part of the marchers of
heading for the Amphitheatre. It said that the "permit
controversy" was finished and over long before this time.
It was not finished in the minds of the marchers, and

the City had a reputation for granting permits at the last minute.

The huge crowd, in a jam of thousands, milled on that corner and stretched for more than a block north, covering the wide street and overflowing into side streets and adjacent areas of Grant Park. I was standing near the curb on the northwest corner of Balbo and Michigan by the Sheraton-Blackstone Hotel. A cop on a three-wheeler, in the middle of the crowd, was right beside me. He was bantering and laughing with the demonstrators. It was the exuberance of enemies who suddenly find themselves in a moment of comradeship. A cop on foot came past, asking, with a courtesy that I had not heard in a long time from a cop, for people to get up on the sidewalk. I stepped up on the curb and so did most of the people there, and then, as usually happens, as soon as the cop was gone we slipped into the street again. The crowd was too large for such control. An SCLC leader began making a speech over a bullhorn to the demonstrator brothers, saying that the Poor People's March agreed and sympathized on the issues of war and poverty and racism, but he indicated that the two marches should now go their different ways. Shortly afterwards, the mule-drawn wagons were separated one by one from the marchers and the cops moved in behind the wagons to keep the demonstrators from following the protection of the blacks' presence.

I left the corner of Balbo and Michigan and went through the police lines to go to the newsroom in the basement of the Hilton to see on the TV how the nomination proceedings were going at the Amphitheatre. The Walker Report says that at this point the cops were restricting entrance to the Hotel to only those with hotel

keys. I did not have a hotel key, only my press credentials, and I was permitted by the cops to enter the
Hilton. If ever I wanted to believe that I have a guardian angel, I now have reason to believe it, because I left
that corner of Balbo and Michigan just a few minutes
before all hell broke loose, the Massacre of Michigan
Avenue, the famous 17 minutes on TV, and the place
where I was standing near the Sheraton-Blackstone
caught some of the worst of it. When I told my wife
about it, "That's a guardian angel," she said, for, though
I did not know it, she was watching the entire scene
from a 15th floor window of the Hilton. She had been
working in the McCarthy campaign for weeks. I could
imagine Anne leaning out the window there, with the
McCarthy straw hat pushed back on her head, her pianist
fingers holding the sill, her British voice much softened
by eight years in America.

What happened now on that corner is one of the few
major street-and-park events of Convention Week that
I did not directly observe. Now I have an opportunity
to compare the impressions and testimony of other people. It is said in The Walker Report that the mood of the
crowd was "increasingly ugly" and another witness says
in the Report that this seemed to be a crowd that had
come to fight. The mood of the crowd up to the point
when it was pushed back by the police from following
the mule-train was joyful. Camaraderie. Demonstrators,
mule-train blacks, bystanders, and a number of cops participated in this feeling. Other reporters say that there
was a lot of "joking" at this corner. I left the intersection
to go into the newsroom in the basement of the Hilton
because the mood of the crowd was far from ugly at its
center near the point of the impending attack. The police
say—and The Walker Report devotes a good deal of

space to police testimony at this point—that they were pelted with a veritable barrage of missiles, the things that demonstrators throw. If so, none of it happened within the range of my sight. The crowd, of course, was wide, long, and packed, north a block or so on Michigan, on Balbo between the Hilton and the Sheraton-Blackstone, and on the edges of Grant Park on the east side of Michigan. Anything could be happening on its periphery where I could not see, and so many things were thrown by demonstrators at different times during the week that anyone would feel that he could get away with saying something was thrown at any point. But my wife, watching from the 15th floor of the Hilton, with a wide view of the intersection, saw no missiles thrown, nothing significant or numerous enough to catch her eye. And The Walker Report itself says, in one sentence that must surely qualify as the folk-joke understatement of the year: "The films fail to show any barrage of missiles at this time, although some may have been thrown."

Demonstrators on Michigan, after they were denied in their attempt to follow the mule-train, began sitting down in the street and on the sidewalks in protest. The police say that they were "faced" with this sort of thing, as if a sit-down were in the same category as being faced with a raging bull or an armed attack. The mood of the crowd was changing. They had felt so legitimized and happy with the legal mule-train and the felt assurance of marching to the Amphitheatre. Now they were feeling denied, trapped, and angry. A police bus unloaded cops at the corner of Wabash and Balbo, a block west. They moved in lines east on Balbo with a big van behind them, obviously ready to make arrests. The police commander of the Balbo unit says they were met with chants of "Hell, no, we won't go," and then a barrage of missiles. My wife, in her eagles' nest view on the 15th floor, directly above Balbo, saw no such thing. She saw lines of police, one, two, then three lines, moving east on Balbo at walking speed, then walking faster, and then simply charging into the crowd clubbing crazily, line after line of them. Norman Mailer, four floors above my wife, reports pretty much the same thing in his book *Miami and the Siege of Chicago*. ". . . they [the cops] cut through the intersection at Michigan and Balbo like a razor cutting a channel through a head of hair . . ." The Walker Report, after giving the police testimony on this moment, says, in another of its understatements, "The many films and video tapes of this time period present a picture which does not correspond completely with the police view." Other observers say the police did begin to make a few arrests before they charged in lines into the crowd.

Arrests, however, were secondary to administering violent punishment on the spot and whether anyone was arrested—and plenty were stuffed into vans—was rather arbitrary. Many were clubbed to the ground and left there to be beaten again; to be helpless was an invitation to further beating. One fellow reports seeing a cop stuffing a demonstrator into a van that was already overcrowded, and the cop kept trying to slam the door shut and the door would not close, bumping against people, and the cop kept on trying to close the door, as if it were a refrigerator door not closing because it was bumping on something. Cops were attacking on Michigan and on Balbo, from south and north, east and west, with no exit for the crowd. They crammed people up against the window of the Haymarket Restaurant on that corner of the Hilton, and a window gave way and the cops leaped through the window, chasing people into the restaurant and into the lobby of the hotel. The cops went absolutely crazy raging wild, defeated, in executing their orders.

Deputy Superintendent James Rochford is reported to have been so upset by the violence of his men that he was jumping on them and trying to pull them off demonstrators, shouting, "For Christ's sake, stop it. Stop it, damn it, stop it." The poor Deputy Superintendent. He didn't really mean to have all of this violence happen. That at least is the implication that many people want to draw from this report, thereby exonerating the police commanders and the City up to the Mayor. This is, in the tongue of all folk, *bullshit*. It amounts to saying that all these cops lined up by personal decision, and then moved forward in formation by personal decision, and then, at the dictates of personal conscience and emotion, attacked the crowd, in wave after wave in unison. Perhaps Rochford had learned how to be an actor for the media, too.

The alleged breakdown of police discipline such as the Rochford episode is supposed to illustrate, has caused much heated comment among sympathetic critics of police action during Convention Week. There was no breakdown in police discipline during Convention Week or at any other time. Police discipline, on its own terms, was superb, something to get frightened about. If the orders were to club and maim, they clubbed and maimed. If the orders were to keep the clubs sheathed, they kept the clubs sheathed. If the orders during the black insurrection in April 1968 were shoot to kill, they shot to kill. If the orders were shoot in the air, they shot in the air. In addition, there is always in military and police situations a latitude called the spirit of application, where the real hopes of the men in power

are expressed, the meeting point of guilt, rage, fear, reactions to symbols, personal courage and personal vengeance. Perhaps Rochford was truly shocked at the rage
of his men in obeying their orders.

Mayor Daley made it clear as early as April 1968 that
he not only trusted this latitude, but counted upon high
energy pouring into it.

In April 1968, during the insurrection in Chicago's
black ghetto areas sparked by the assassination of Martin
Luther King, Jr., Mayor Daley gave in public his "shoot-
to-kill all arsonists and shoot-to-maim all looters" order,
specifying that anyone with a Molotov cocktail in his
hand should be killed and that all of these decisions
were left to the discretion of the policeman on the scene.
The Mayor was criticizing the "restraint" of the Police
Department up to this moment in the April riots. In most
street actions, there were always a number of cops who
did not use their clubs, just as a very significant percentage of soldiers do not fire their weapons in combat
actions. After the Mayor's order, the cops did shoot to
kill, perhaps to win and keep his approval. They also
clubbed and gassed a largely white march at the East
Chicago Avenue Armory protesting police action during the April insurrection. The Mayor had to bear up
against a hard wind of public criticism and condemna-
tion for this order, and Police Superintendent James B.
Conlisk Jr. became his fall guy, appearing on TV to take
the criticism. Later in April, the yearly Peace March,
which was drearily peaceful and obedient, was wildly
and methodically clubbed and driven out of the Civic
Center Plaza. Blacks were shot, whites were clubbed.
More criticism came at the City, and a protest march a
week later was permitted to move peaceably. The only
difference with Convention Week was that the Mayor

had learned not to make his orders public. A month after Convention Week, the largest protest march in Chicago's history, herded in good humor by the police, went down Michigan Avenue to Grant Park, peaceably.

With impossible orders and impossible emotions, the cops lunged out on Balbo and Michigan, as if from a broken dam, just the way they had been acting in Lincoln Park for three nights. And the public is asked to believe that there was a breakdown in police discipline. The only breakdown, so far as the City was concerned, was that the TV cameras mounted on the entrance canopy of the Hilton recorded the event and then the film was played before the nation. The cameramen were lucky they were not on the sidewalk, within range of an "undisciplined" cop, or their cameras and that famous 17 minutes of film might have gone the way of cameras and film in Lincoln Park. The Mayor faced strong accusations in the Convention itself, and from nationwide media, so he covered himself with the rhetoric of "overreaction" on the part of individual cops. The cops were the fall guys. They should be used to it.

I came up out of the basement newsroom of the Hilton, as if out of a diving bell in which there was no awareness of the storm above it, only the dull pleasure of watching underwater specimens, the politicos at the Amphitheatre, nose up to the TV screen. People were moving fast in the lobby of the Hilton with the intensity of needing a place to hide in their faces. By the elevators a few cops were switching their thighs with their clubs and looking around heatedly and eagerly. A media-man ran right into me, bearing the canister of film, and yelling, "I am going to get this on national TV! They can't get away with this! I am going to get it on national TV!" I asked him what was happening, and he looked at me,

unbelieving, and said that they were just beating people
everywhere outside. He spoke in the voice of a man who
simply could not find appropriate words for the magnitude of what was happening. He continued his dash
down the lobby and he did get it on TV for the nation
to see.

There are some events of such sudden power, as in
Lincoln Park and in front of the Hilton, where the men
who actually gather the news, see it and feel it, are able
to ram it through the processes of selection onto the
screen or into the newspapers, before those in control
of the media have a chance to determine the political
necessities of how the thing *should* look. Media men and
reporters, in a great many cases, were witnesses in the
truest sense, and took an awful beating from the police
for it. After Convention Week, massive and energetic
whitewashing in favor of the City Administration became the order of the day, particularly in Chicago, on
the screen and in the papers, until The Walker Report
came into the vacuum of opposition to co-opt what had
happened by calling it "a police riot." The reporters and
media men on the streets were left chewing their radicalized feelings, and how they digest them will be
important.

On my right there was stunned turmoil in the Haymarket Restaurant where, moments before, the crowd
was pressed by cops against the glass, which shattered,
and the cops leaped through the window, chasing the
demonstrators. I went through the police line at the
Balbo entrance and onto the street, where a line of red-
faced cops were sweeping the street, crouching, asking
for trouble. The cop on the end of the line nearest me
was literally growling. The feeling of rage and fear in
the air gave an electrified sense of caution and clarity.

The street looked like a huge picnic had been hit by a surprise storm, debris everywhere, personal belongings, shoes, purse, papers, this and that. I came out on the street at the point where it is said in The Walker Report that the police had "gained control of the intersection."

Battles in the Loop and Lincoln Park

But righteous indignation and the joy of battle was the feeling surging from the demonstrators on the other side of Michigan Avenue in Grant Park. The cops were flushed with fury, but the kids were clear-faced with the feeling that they were right and they were winning. The cops were trying to get traffic moving, as if that would be most satisfying to them, when suddenly the kids came dancing out of Grant Park into Michigan and formed into a march facing south, with a portable speaker; quickly cops were facing them and the march backed up north on Michigan, with a line of Guardsmen behind the cops. The kids joyfully threatened to march to the Amphitheatre, but their purpose was to make sure that the cops kept contact. The march did not even begin to move south in the direction of the Amphitheatre.

The kids, once again standing up in lines in the street, were at last in a situation that they could manipulate. With a brilliant use of distance and provocation, rocks, bottles and firecrackers, with the march in the street and other demonstrators acting as agitators on the sidewalk, they backed up north on Michigan, gaining the exultant support of traffic stopped on the street and people crammed on the sidewalks. The agitators on the sidewalks shouted slogans, as if they were part of the crowd, "Peace, now," "Streets belong to the people," "Dump the Hump," etcetera. They did not attempt to disguise themselves as utterly innocent bystanders, and some-

times the ones on the sidewalk would openly talk with
the marchers in the street about whether one or the
other wanted to change places for awhile. It was an
effective gimmick, and the sympathy of the crowd on
the sidewalk was stimulated. The agitators moved north
on the sidewalk parallel to the march, leisurely, with
an easiness about them that was good to feel, an elite
cadre air. One touched the elbow of another and said,
"It's happening, man, it's happening." And the other
answered, "Beautiful, beautiful." Horns were honking
in sympathy up and down the street, and the crowd on
the sidewalk was shouting in sympathy. No one in Chicago was as calm, easy, good humored, accepting of
moment to moment, as these young men, who wore
jeans and khakis and long-sleeved shirts open at the
neck and rolled up at the elbows with a quiet flair. They
had the confident manner, the seeming stable center,
of men who have early passed several physical and spiritual risks and tests. There was also the feeling of more
profound risks to come for them, isolation and worse,
and their confidence was too easy for the shock of what
might be coming in the next few years. But once again
I was impressed with the lack of disguised neurotic
hatred. They had, strangely enough, been loved well
when they were children. If some American liberal parents want to take credit for that, let them. The raising
of happy, courageous, quick-minded children is surely
the very embodiment of the possibility of a fresh life,
simply because it asks some of the same qualities of the
parents here and now. You want to help your children,
then help yourself.

A police lieutenant walked a few steps in front of the
police line, systematically spraying arcs of Mace back
and forth at the front line of the demonstrators. From

behind this front line cherry bombs and firecrackers were lofted accurately into the police line, plus a few rocks and a few bottles. The police jumped a little, but not much. Their discipline was superb here also. A loaf of bread was hurled from deep in the march and came down in the police line, with general laughter from the sidewalk. The lieutenant pointed, not because of the bread, at a fellow in the front line of demonstrators, indicating that he wanted to arrest him. The lieutenant asked, as the fellow stepped forward, if he would let himself be arrested and the demonstrator said, yes, he would, and he was. A few more were arrested in this way. The lieutenant acted as if he were picking out the ones to be arrested for specific reasons, and it would be assumed that he would pick out those throwing things, but that was not so, because most of those throwing rocks and firecrackers were well behind the front line. He was simply trying, with this arbitrary harassment, to break the will of the marchers, whose discipline was excellent, too. Others moved up to take the places of those arrested in the front line.

Some of these marchers were Lincoln Park veterans, but the air of this group was different from the hippies turned Yippies. These had beards, long hair, yes, but tending toward the trimmed, and the levis and khakis and pieces of Army uniforms, had the suggestion that it was casual wear, a conscious choice and style of dress to be both comfortable and give an air to the work to be done. There were far more men than women, but there seemed to be a few more women present in this march than in most of the actions in the streets and parks.

In the beginning of the march, they had all been singing "My Country, 'Tis of Thee," and the song swelled for a minute or so. A few kids were clustered around a trash basket striking matches and trying to light the contents. They got a small fire going and rolled the basket into the street toward the cops, who kicked it aside and stamped out the burning paper. Nothing was happening yet, it was like two boxers circling each other at the start in the ring.

The cops stayed steady in their line, backed up by the Guardsmen, moving the demonstrators away from the Hilton, away from TV cameras. Then, except for the front line of demonstrators with the portable speaker, the mass of the marchers turned facing north, walking forward, calling for support from stopped cars and from people on the sidewalks and in the windows of the buildings along Michigan. Kids were jammed around the portable speaker to make it difficult for the cops to arrest them or disrupt their activities. The din of horns and voices became ecstatic, and the V sign was waved by uplifted arms all over the street, out of cars, out of windows, on the sidewalk. The people in one car definitely did not want to be participants, and a group of demonstrators with some difficulty, helped the car to turn around and go back north out of the scene. It was an act of deliberate courtesy that irritated the car's occupants; their faces were grim. A huge searchlight on the bed of a white truck was surrounded and nearly usurped by the marchers. The cops were picking off more demonstrators for arrest, and a few clubbings were happening.

Then the monitors using the portable speaker displayed an unforgivable ignorance of Chicago when they turned the march tightly down Jackson Boulevard toward State Street, into the blank chill of middle-class Chicago. They were winning on Michigan and winning big, because on Michigan were the young people and others concerned with the Convention. They could have kept the march together, in a mass, and gone the length of Michigan to the bridge, and it was tasty to think of that whole street tied up in that ecstatic din. Instead, the march split into several groups, on Michigan, Jackson and other streets, and the cops found the smaller groups more vulnerable. They attacked. In Lincoln Park, fast-footed small groups were often the best tactic, but here one huge mass group, in the public view of the Convention people on Michigan, would have been best. The main group, smaller now, began running on Jackson almost as soon as they turned, with cops rushing them from behind and clubbing and picking them off. A good and eerie imitation of the cries of the women in the movie *The Battle of Algiers* was done by the marchers, wailing hollowly in the Loop streets which were nearly empty of pedestrians. Groups were splitting off here and there, and the cops became much more active outside the range of the cameras. The main group, getting smaller, pounded north on Wabash Avenue and their chants were louder than ever, as if shouting in a huge barrel, for there were no receptive and responsive by-standers here. "Join us, join us," the marchers yelled, but the pedestrians looked and cringed with fear, distaste, or just plain surprise. The demonstrators ran out of the exuberant reality they enjoyed on Michigan Avenue into the nightmare neon caves of the Loop, as if out of the boisterous indulgence of the Beautiful People into the frigid unwelcome of the middle class, and their thoroughly indigenous style and discipline of confrontation was replaced by frantic imitations of a singular mannerism of a different revolution.

Kids were yelling to go to State Street where all the

people were, and I actually tried now to tell a few near me that this was an awful mistake. But their thinking seemed to be that anyone who had heard of Chicago knew of State Street and that was where it was at. The police sent a fire truck screaming off State Street driving within a couple of feet of the curb hell-for-leather, forcing demonstrators up on the sidewalk. It was lucky that the people in front of that truck were young and nimble of foot. They came onto State Street, appalled in that empty canyon of neon, and they stayed on the sidewalks. It was so chill, so blank, no emotional support anywhere —sudden terror before these cold bystander faces, cold but mightily energetic cops—and the demonstrators avoided the confrontation that would have occurred if they had tried to take State Street. They preferred, they were even willing, to shed their blood if there was a feeling of supportive warmth around them, but here there was no such warmth, not even in their own souls this moment. They were disorganized and dispersed.

Cops were guarding the subway entrances. Anyone who looked as if he were in his teens or early 20's would be shoved, clubbed, told to keep moving, and was not permitted exit or entrance to the subway stations. The cops wanted to cut off the lifeline between the downtown area and Lincoln Park, where there was trouble now, too. Cops responded to simple obscenity and verbal taunts with moments of furious attack. One cop, at State and Monroe, lunged for a heckler blindly and got instead another boy, wearing a helmet, who, with a worthy presence of mind, grabbed hold of the cop's club so that, hard as the cop pumped the stick, he could not effectively hit the boy on the head. The cop went into a helpless fury and bellowed in the boy's face for him to let go of the club, and the boy did not let go until he had made the cop realize that he was hitting the wrong man. The cop then pushed the boy away, smack into a news-stand, and left him alone. The other fellow, the heckler, was long gone.

A portion of the demonstrators—what might be called a reduced core of what was once a large group—ran east on Washington toward Michigan. They—perhaps 100 or so now—stayed mostly on the sidewalks and the only organization they could muster was to chant "Hell no, we won't go" and shout "Fuck the draft." Remember that the idiot carnage of the War in Vietnam was sup-ported by a strong majority vote at the Amphitheatre on Wednesday afternoon. Wednesday night the chant of "Fuck the draft" was more frequent than in the days before.

Traffic cops at corners calmly watched them go by, and it became one of those instances where, when the cops stayed away, the energy of the demonstrators dis-solved. They needed the focus of confrontation, and the police were usually generous in giving it. The demon-strators dashed across Michigan into the edge of Grant Park, where they began shouting for a "caucus." The cops stayed on the west side of Michigan, while the demonstrators caucused on a set of concrete steps lead-ing up from sidewalk level to the park. The initial vic-tory of this march had been dissipated in the Loop, and a few Yippies and more far-out demonstrators, possible veterans of Lincoln Park, made a disgusted wave of their arms and as they left the caucus, said they were heading for Lincoln Park. No hard feelings. Everybody do his thing.

One young woman, who led this caucus, was so sexy,

so joyful, so serious, that it addled the head and the belly
to watch and listen to her.   If a revolution had such
women,* how could it lose?

*Wherever SDS (Students for a Democratic Society), YSA (Young Socialists
Alliance), CADRE (Chicago Area Draft Resistance), and other student groups were
present in protest actions during Convention Week, women and men appeared to be
about equal in numbers.   Out of 668 recorded arrests during the five days of
Convention Week, the arrest ratio was about 1 female to 8 males.   In the Lincoln Park
actions, men appeared to outnumber women.   Of the 118 arrestees with previous arrest
records, only 8 were female.   In other areas and in other historical periods before and
after the 1960s, men have been statistically more inclined than women to physically
violent engagement.   This, combined with the fact that only 1 in 8 arrestees were
female, caused some Convention Week participants to speculate on the relationship of
gender to the propensity for violent engagement.   It also triggered a feeling among
those SDS women who would become the Weatherwomen in 1969 that New Left
women had been too passive and must nurture a disposition for more violent protest
and revolution.
   The arrest records open a statistical door to supporting or putting the lie to well pro-
moted media and political impressions concerning the protesters.   Impression: Most of
the protesters came from outside the state "into our living room" (a favorite of the
Mayor of Chicago).   **Fact: 52.6% of arrestees came from the Metropolitan area
of Chicago. Persons from 36 states, the District of Columbia, and five foreign
countries were also arrested.**
   Impression: Most of the protesters were "hard-core," with previous arrests.   **Fact:
Out of 668 persons arrested, 550 had no previous arrest records.**   Obviously
most of the protesters were motivated by their protest against the Viet Nam war.
   Impression: Most of the protesters were radical students.   **Fact: 32.6 percent of
those arrested were students, 43% were otherwise employed (teachers, ministers, social workers, other professionals, factory laborers, and so on) and 19.9
percent were unemployed. Some of the latter were among the 9.6 percent of
total arrestees under 17 years of age, many of whom were high school
students. A few arrestees had no employment status listed.**
   Impression: The protesters were in some way "terrorists trained in Cuba," armed
and dangerous.   **Fact: Fifty two persons possessed something that could be
called a weapon when arrested, mainly rocks and bricks (it's hard to call a
bottle or popcan a weapon, since the person can claim that he or she had just
finished drinking the contents), and nine with knives, two with guns, two
machetes, and one bayonet.**   You could have found more guns in a random
search of 668 people on any American street or downtown area.   Also, if a cop
arrested a disguised undercover agent with a concealed handgun, the initial
report would have listed the weapon as carried by a protester.   If 1 in 6 protesters were undercover agents, as Army Intelligence claimed on a CBS program
in 1978, it's likely that several agents were arrested as protesters.   A female
undercover agent admitted on the witness stand at the Chicago Conspiracy
Trial that she had carried a handgun in her purse when she went

On Michigan Avenue, then, the caucus among the demonstrators was over, nothing was decided, because there was nothing to decide except to go back where it was at, in front of the Hilton or in Lincoln Park. A fellow had climbed astride one of the lions in front of The Art Institute, yelling "Fuck, fuck, fuck," at the cops. And the girl, with her loose and wonderful hair held back by a kerchief, and her hands folded between her knees, looked, alert and yet dreamily, out into the street.

Many incidents had occurred throughout the Loop. Cops attacked small groups of kids, with no apparent intent to arrest them, just beat them. Kids put their shoulders against squad cars and paddy wagons and swayed and bounced them with the cops inside. Kids were lighting fires in trash cans, and one kid picked up a bottle to throw while others made him put it down and break it on the sidewalk at his feet. There was the fake Green Beret, who attacked demonstrators and who was aided and defended by the cops who gathered

among the protesters in Lincoln Park. Other undercover agents were deep in jail before they found a way to declare their status undetected. Apparently the debates in the underground newspapers, as in the widely circulated Berkeley Barb and The Seed, about the prospects of violence and bringing or not bringing guns to Chicago had a salutary effect.

The one media and government impression supported by the arrest statistics was that most of the protesters were young. **Nearly 75% of those arrested were 25 years of age or younger, male, and tended to be residents of Metropolitan Chicago with no previous arrest record.** If we could extrapolate figures for those under the age of 30, the proportion would be even higher.

Of the 118 who had been previously arrested, 39 had been arrested only on misdemeanor charges for protest actions. Other arrestees had been previously arrested for protest actions combined with felonies, narcotics (usually marijuana), vagrancy, "rogue and vagabond," and counterfeiting and larceny. No figures were given for how many had been involved in the latter two crimes. Narcotics, vagrancy, and "rogue and vagabond" were charges frequently used to harass New Left protesters and hippies.

People usually avoided arrest by whatever means possible, until Thursday night when they would line up at 18th St. and Michigan Ave. clamoring for arrest. In most cases, as we've seen in our story, the authorities preferred "street justice" to the time-consuming complications of arrest.

around him and someone he was beating, as if making an impromptu gladiators' arena. The Walker Report says that he was a deserter from the Army. Cops on three-wheeler motorcycles were chasing people on sidewalks and pinioning them on walls. Lord God, the guilt that was being raged out in these streets! And yet the scale and intensity of it was not equal to that of Lincoln Park. There was always the feeling that, just around the corner, a camera might be coming your way, though certainly some people wanted to give the cameras interesting pictures.

I moved over to State Street where people were running in opposite directions, and it was hard to see why. A group of America's writers were running hotly north while I was running south. I saw Studs Terkel—author of *Division Street U.S.A.* and a famous radio interviewer for Chicago's WFMT—and we exchanged greetings. Studs asked me if I wanted to meet Bill Styron, and I said, "Later, Studs, later," and I flew south and he flew north. Then I came hiking from Wabash east on Balbo toward the Hilton, with holes in my shoes, my feet feeling scroungy; the sidewalk was wearing through my socks and brushing my bare soles. I couldn't take the time during the day to get the shoes fixed, or go home to change, for fear of missing something in the streets. Soldiers, demonstrators, reporters, cops, and writers-turned-journalists are always advised to take care of their feet. You have to walk a lot, and run hard now and then. Our friends on the savannahs 200,000 years ago had good, springy grass under their calloused feet. Look at those demonstrators over there, wearing good boots, fast sneakers, they know how to take care of their feet. Then, as I approached the Balbo entrance to the Hilton, where a line of cops permitted entry to only those who could display a hotel key, something happened that enabled me to be unaware of my feet for another few hours. A kid, who claimed that he worked in the Hilton, but did not have a hotel key, was facing the cops and being insistent about getting back to his job. Suddenly one cop, tall, heavy, and blond, grabbed him by the shirt front and shoved him out from under the public area of the marquée, brushing me, and jammed him into the alcove of the wall. "Don't give me anymore of your lip! I've got my orders, *buddy!* I'll break your fucking neck! I'll—break—your—fucking—neck!"

"Yes, sir," the kid was trying to say, without much success, because his head was being rattled against the building. The next moment a tall, distinguished, silver-haired Seagram's whisky ad sort of man was denied entrance at the same place because he didn't have a hotel key. He understood and congratulated the cops, "I think you boys are doing a *fine* job." And the cop who had denied him and was ready to shove him with his club, laughed uncontrollably with working-class disdain.

The Nation Faces the Demonstrators

Out in front of the Hilton banks of lights glared on the scene, with the demonstrators across the street in Grant Park under the trees facing Guardsmen and cops and National Guard vehicles parked everywhere in the streets, paper and other debris underfoot, people of all kinds on the sidewalks, and the lights so strong that it seemed they must burst into flame, or turn everything else to flame, any second. Streetsweepers growled up and down the streets around the Hilton, cleaning up. Literally, Mayor Daley was having the streets tidied for the delegates who would be coming back to the Hotel from the Amphitheatre. Blue, the streetsweepers were blue, the convention was blue, the sawhorses of the police barricade along the sidewalk were blue, the cops were blue. Then the portable speaker in Grant Park boomed, with an unexpected solemnity only slightly touched with the sardonic, telling everybody within hearing, "Look at Mayor Daley's streetsweepers cleaning the blood off the streets." It was a shock, as if being waked suddenly, to hear it, not because there was blood on the streets—blood was on many streets in Chicago— but because it gave a sudden sense of past and future to come: it meant that the thing *had happened* a few hours before. Throughout Convention Week you could come upon the scene of an action a few minutes after the action ended and no one would be saying anything about it, as if everyone hovered moment to moment without immediate memory, waiting for the next thing to happen, with eerie readiness in time.

On the sidewalks around the Hilton and Grant Park, delegates, politicians, news people, bystanders, black people, white people, were seeking out the demonstrators, asking them questions, talking with them, in a large exchange of opinion and feeling. A few days before, if a demonstrator had approached a politician to talk, the politician would have turned away. Now the politicians were seeking out the demonstrators. If ever anyone needed a concrete justification for the idea that violence can bring about the meeting of peoples, it was here. Two extremely well-dressed men who had the Seagram's manner and Seagram's silver hair, were talking with one demonstrator who possessed a well-trimmed full beard and a fine presence. They asked him finally what his program would be. He said, without a trace of being put up against it by the request for a detailed social program, "I am not a politician, but I am ready to co-operate with the politician who is ready to do what needs to be done in this country. I ask you, sir, not to underestimate the percentage of young people in this country who feel the way I do." He said it twice.

The demonstrators, when approached, entered into these conversations with energy, seriousness, and wit. It was too much to hope that the latter two qualities would show on the other side, too. The other side seemed to be standing on the self-righteousness of being forced to talk, though they were the ones seeking out the demonstrators. "It may seem slow, but things are changing. Why, I remember. . . ." That must have been said almost as many times as cops yelling, "I've got my orders!" The demonstrators were remarkably polite but tough with the "slow but changing" attitude. Eight years of the Vietnam War was slow, all right. The building of livable cities, livable education, was certainly slow, too, no argument about that. *What*, the politicians were asked, was the advantage in being "slow?" We are going to be buried in a blizzard of 25 feet of "slow." The politicians could not answer without being embarassed and hemming and hawing about political pluralism, but the demonstrators said that no amount of pluralism justified injustice. "Two wrongs do not make a right," said the politicians, hanging their minds out for the world to see, as if the demonstrators were the ones walking around with pistols on their hips and wielding clubs, a comparison so blunt that it was a stereotype, too. In response, a demonstrator spilled out a list of "wrong" actions that made a right, starting, of course, with the American Revolutionary War. The older people talked eternally about World War II, always implying that if they fought in that war the demonstrators were morally bound to fight in Vietnam, and the demonstrators answered again and again that World War II and Vietnam were not analogous, that they were not going to fight in an unjust War in Vietnam, they were going to fight a just war right here in Chicago and force the Democratic Party to take account of itself. It would seem that these conversations emphasized the generation gap that we hear about so generously, but the kids were pushing some new information and new attitudes into dull minds. These politicians were alternate delegates, a few were men in the entourages of important figures in the Democratic Party, a couple of nationally syndicated columnists, newspaper editors, etcetera. These were minds that did not know what to do if they had to do something besides shake hands or not shake hands. And there was no shaking of hands between these people and the demonstrators, no conversation was started or closed in that manner.

Not all conversations were between demonstrators and politicians of radically different ages. A fellow about 30, dressed according to the ads in the most fashionable of men's magazines, talked with three much younger kids who wore lumberjack shirts. It was a conversation about what do you want to be and what do you want to do. He wanted to be a millionaire and that was what he was doing, he said, and that was what he intended to be. He was forceful and angry, and it took the one kid in a plaid lumberjack shirt, who was most eager to talk, aback; but the kid was hellbent on discovering something that was brotherly in the man. "I know why you want to be a millionaire," the kid said. "You want freedom. You want to do anything you want to do with your time." And the kid said it as if he could understand and appreciate such a motive, and he started to say that that in a different way, was what they all wanted: the freedom to do what they wanted to do with their time. But the man-who-would-be-a-millionaire said angrily that that was not his reason for wanting a million dollars, that bosses worked harder than workers, and strangely the kid agreed with him. "You want power," the kid said, and again tried to compare their motives favorably. The man-who-would-be-a-millionaire again said angrily that he did not want a million dollars to get power, he simply wanted a million dollars. Nevertheless, he was obviously compelled to seek out these kids and talk with them, for they had become figures against which the nation must justify itself.

There was a confused black caucus in back of the demonstrators in Grant Park confronting the Hilton. Tear gas hung harshly in the dark behind the demonstrators with the red glow of a fire here and there. A lot of the blacks were in African garb, dashikis, and one black voice yelled to his fellows, "I ain't going to help any white man do anything! I ain't even going to help any white man get his skull cracked!" It unsettled them that whites were letting loose such violence against each other. They may have puzzled why there had been so much violence and no one was yet killed. They were also rightly angered that their own consciences were pushing them to confront the implication, with all its potential for betrayal, that lines of allegiance other than color were nearly surfacing in American life.

But a brown man on the sidewalk directly in front of the Hilton turned to the brown woman beside him and said, quietly, "Actually, no one is safe."

McCarthy people were standing out of the Hilton and crossing the street to join the demonstrators in Grant Park; or, if they were not yet ready to cross the street, they stood on the sidewalk in all the play and byplay of talk, shifting back and forth with the movement of the men in blue helmets.

Earlier, the McCarthy aides had started a first-aid station on the 15th floor. A few McCarthy women, among them my wife, were in the lobby on the 15th floor tearing up sheets from the linen closet to be used as bandages, when the cops came out of the elevators and, pointing their clubs, asked the women if they were tearing up those sheets to be used as bandages, and the women, out of the fullness of their indignation, said, yes, they were tearing up those sheets to be used as bandages. The cops tried to find the wounded to take them away, but were in this case stopped by the McCarthy security guards and doctors. The Senator came down to the 15th floor to talk with the wounded, and if Czechslovakia did not ruffle his cool, this did, for he had read perhaps too much of Yeats, who had written lines of poetry in the fear that his hot poetic Gaelic patriotism might have inspired young men to fight and be killed or wounded both in the Easter 1916 Revolution against the British and in the Civil War among the Irish during the early 1920s. Scalps split. Real blood.

The McCarthy aides were divided about joining the demonstrators. The conservatives said cool it, while the majority wanted to hit the streets and go into the parks with the demonstrators. But they did not move until later that night when they were watching on TV the roll-call of the states, the voting for the nominees at the Amphitheatre. When Pennsylvania, where McCarthy had been clearly the popular choice in the primary, delivered their votes almost all for Humphrey, the McCarthy aides became morally certain that the "system" had sold them down the river and knew that their man had really and finally lost.

Even the most naive McCarthy supporter had no basis for even a fantasy hope now. They milled, as if waiting for something, and then one man shouted, "Let's go down to the Park where we belong!" Tolstoy makes much, in *War and Peace,* of the crucial role of the man who shouts, "Forward!" at the right moment in battle, in agreement with the spirit of battle, such as the boy yelling "Fuck the marshalls!" in Lincoln Park Sunday night. Remember the famous scene where Prince Andrey in *War and Peace* lifts the flag from the fallen color-bearer and turns a retreat into a charge and is then himself wounded and lying on his back, sees "the lofty, limitless sky," asking himself, "How is it that I did not see it before?" Much of Convention Week confrontation on Wednesday and Thursday was in terms of 19th century European battle, out in the open; and therefore, 19th century heroics were suddenly on display on streetcorners, in parks, in byways and alleys. The man who shouted, "Let's go down to the park where we belong!" was the catalytic speaker for the spirit of battle, and swiftly and generously the McCarthy aides went down the elevators, onto the streets below, joining the bravest people in Chicago.

This was a victory the New Left wanted, and they got it, delivered to them by the police and by the intransigence of the regular Democrats who could not cope with that most important of outside agitators, their own creation, the Vietnam War. The influx of McCarthy supporters handsomely swelled the numbers of the demonstrators late Wednesday night and Thursday afternoon and night. But it was of an importance yet to be calcu-

lated that this significant contingent of young Americans, who feel themselves to be the advance guard of a
new ruling elite in this country, went home with sharply
radicalized ideas and attitudes. They joined the demonstrators and yet they didn't join them. "I have to go home
and think about it," they said, and it was apparent that
they were already thinking about it as they said it.

In Grant Park facing the Hilton, the demonstrators
were following the roll-call of votes on transistor radios.
They cheered in the obvious places, where there were
votes for McCarthy or McGovern, and booed the mounting total for Humphrey. Humphrey was supposed to be
in the Hilton now, and there was talk of storming the
Hotel. Not very likely, but they would say anything to
keep the cops on their toes. The cops kept constant pressure on the crowd, and made small punitive expeditions
to pick off a demonstrator now and then. The parade
marshalls lined up and locked arms to face the cops.
When the portable speaker asked windows in the Hotel
to blink in sympathy, many windows up and down the
face of the hotel blinked, and the 15th floor (McCarthy
headquarters), with all its windows in near miraculous
unison, signalled jubilantly to the Park.

The appearance of the National Guard, with all its
Army paraphernalia and Army images, always unsettled
the demonstrators—fixed bayonets, trucks with machineguns, jeeps with barbwire covering—and yet once the
Guardsmen were in position, the situation generally relaxed. They had their orders, too. The cops would
consent, deeply, to be goaded individually, while the
Guardsmen were impersonal and usually rather huddled
beneath their helmets in their baggy fatigue uniforms.
Not fair game. The demonstrators always wanted to believe that the young Guardsmen were brothers, and many

of the Guardsmen were very willing to let them believe it. It is said that, in "riot control planning," the Guard is considered to be merely a back-up force for the police, as if that would soften and explain away the stark differences in cop and Guard approaches. But the plain fact is that the Guard took over and faced the same situations as the cops, and the situation changed because the Guard was present, not before they took positions. The difference in style of mind and explicit and implicit content of orders between cops and Guard was there to see. Cops were seldom restrained by their superiors from giving personal response to provocation, while the Guardsmen were usually restrained by nearby non-coms and officers. "You can listen to it, but don't answer back," some of the sergeants would say. But Thursday night the Guard would meet the full rage of the demonstrators, and their anonymity would be taxed into personal flare-ups of violence, as it could have been if they had been asked to perform the cops' duty from the beginning.

Out at the Amphitheatre, delegates were leaving the floor to see the film of the Michigan Avenue violence on TV sets in other rooms. First, they had heard, as Gerald Moore, a reporter for *Life* tells it, that the cops were "slaughtering" kids; and the people in the Amphitheatre didn't know if it meant clubbing or killing, the uncertainty magnifying their desolate fears and angers. Donald Peterson, head of the Wisconsin delegation, when his state was called for voting, told the Convention that "thousands" of kids were being beaten in the streets of Chicago and that the Convention should be adjourned and re-convened later in a different city. The liberal delegates were chanting, "Let's go home." Mayor Daley was chastised from all sides, with Senator Abraham Ribicoff of Connecticut accusing him of Gestapo tactics and Daley retorting with obscenity. The liberals were defeated on their issues and their candidates, but in their anger they spat the defeat back into the faces of the regulars. Delegate Allard Lowenstein, denied use of New York's microphone, tried to force his way to the podium to make a motion to adjourn because of the police violence in Chicago. The delegates chanting "Let's go home!" almost, but not quite, seized the spirit of battle in the Amphitheatre. The Democratic Party was sundered. Humphrey would never be able to recover sufficiently from the stigma of the Chicago violence and the way in which that violence enforced the defection of McCarthy-McGovern-Kennedy liberals. "Dump the Hump," the demonstrators were chanting in Grant Park, but when it was certain that Humphrey was the winner of the nomination, the feeling in the Park was more of melancholy consummation, as if it were known underneath that Humphrey, because of Chicago, could not win in November and so the turn had been given to the movement of American history. What turn? Why would the revolt invite a repression?

I drove north to Lincoln Park, the bassinet of the new republic, to see what further nails were being driven into the coffin of that which had gone before. I have already told in the beginning of this book of what happened in Lincoln Park that night: the National Guard sweeping an empty Park; the efforts of a citizens' group to ride as observers in police vehicles; and the cop attacks, more vicious than the attacks in the Loop, on any cluster of kids in the streets. A couple of cop cars and National Guard jeeps were stoned at the corner of LaSalle and Eugenie Streets. It is said that gang kids called "greasers" were the main participants in Lincoln Park this night, but the greaser kids had been present since Sunday night and their numbers on Wednesday night did not seem to be proportionately higher. The cops did not even have the excuse this night of driving people who were in violation of the Park curfew out of the Park. The cop actions on the streets of Old Town had the air of concerted vengeance missions, as if they were going to make the kids pay now for what the cops and the Mayor would have to pay in the months to come. After I witnessed the mass cop attack on the hundreds of kids at the corner of LaSalle and Eugenie, I drove back to the Hilton with the clear anger of revolution, Us or Them, in my fingertips on the steering wheel.

In Grant Park again, there was melancholy; and about 3 o'clock there came a sight that was hard to believe: the candlelight march of 300 delegates, singing old protest songs. Delegates, back from the Amphitheatre, were on the sidewalks and among the demonstrators, and the talk between them continued the meeting of people from groups that shunned each other only a few days ago. The Us or Them principle dissolved old divisions and shoved people into more natural alliances—natural because of the immediate, felt danger—and made it possible to see the shape and lines of a new, wide-spectrum political movement. Maybe. But many liberals, under the club, acted as revolutionaries in Chicago without ever becoming radical.

We must first look into the dream quality of the events in Chicago, and dreams are notoriously powered by wishes: wishes that carry us backward and cuddle us in corners away from ourselves and also wishes that open us and bring us forward. If the events of Chicago were a prophetic dream for this nation, which way does the wish of the dream take us?

Rally at the Logan statue before the march to 18th Street. Thursday August 29. Grant Park. Photo by Bill Hood.

thursday: exile

Morning

Late Thursday morning I came out the back door onto our third floor back porch, open to the sky above, the framework of the porch painted Chinese red and its chicken wire interlaced with the morning glories that I had raised every year for four years. The hot haze of smoke and exhaust was gone, no longer hanging in the air over the city. The sky was bright, warm northern blue, and so were the morning glories, with the touch of gold in their throats and the violet streaks in their big blue trumpets. The porch rose up toward the sky a-blaze in a breeze with leaves and flowers, among back porches looking at each other across the arena of an alley. It was "the lofty, limitless sky" that gave the wounded Prince Andrey in *War and Peace*, lying on his back and watching it out of clear daze, a new awareness. It was the stoned sky, so unusual for Chicago, that the Yippies and students lying on their backs in the parks were watching, too. It was the sky of huge coun-

219

tries with large frontiers—the United States, Russia, China—countries with the ambition of space and the point, ever sought, where space disappears into time and the immortality of the speed of light. It is the great daring, and perhaps the basic cop-out, the final narcissism, of our age that we have identified the space of our soul with the space of the universe. It was also the sky of places that I have loved, and that I return to in my mind, the islands along the coast of Japan, the mountains of Japan, the mountains of Mexico, and the old wooded mountains of the Ozarks of my boyhood. And yet it was simply the sky of that moment, and there were no words whatsoever in my mind as I came out onto the porch into the sunlight, with a feeling of strong peace, just the peace and sunlight of that moment, and the sense that a nightmare was not far behind and not far away.

The porch was also an unruly mess, a sandbox, with the sand spilling everywhere, a picnic table and its benches, an inflated rubberized swimming pool, and the unnumbered pieces of board and bricks and chairs and old toys that a five-year-old boy and his friends and little sister use to build anything under the sun. I had seen a blanket become an expressway that goes all the way to the moon, where there was, my son would tell you, a swimming pool. I stepped between all the broken things, that are whole and useful to a child, and looked at the morning glories. They bloom, close, and make seed in one day. Ordinarily I would count them—33 one day, 29 the next—and see how many were poised in the white spiral cone with the purple tip for the next morning. They are an important, occasional image in Oriental poetry, and they graced the windows of kitchens of the houses of my boyhood. Breakfast on a bright

morning, with a window full of morning glories nearby
is a memory of mine, with the mother, making the breakfast, who sometimes felt as easy as the light in the window. A famous Japanese haiku is about a woman who
comes in the morning to a well and sees, *oh,* a morning
glory wrapped around her bucket. Convention Week
had such evanescence and such shock, something of joy
and something to mourn, though a bloody head is not
quite a flower and tear-gas is not quite the air around
a Japanese well in the morning.

The week was not over—oh, no, we had yet to be
ground through the wringer of Thursday night's revelation—but something was over, and I already knew it.
The accomplishment was over, and the peace was a
feeling of a share in that accomplishment. Thursday
night might give the direction of the new turn. I stepped
among the broken things, in my white t-shirt and briefs,
fresh from bed, not mindful of the other backporches
across the alley, and then my five-year-old son came onto
the porch in a happy rush, to help me water the morning glories. We filled kitchen pans and pots at the sink
and carried them out to fill the flower pots to overflowing. Morning glories need big pots and much water.
"Lots of flowers, daddy," he said, looking at them, touch-
ing them, finding them, and sometimes a flower would
be caught closed in the chicken wire and we would carefully unfold it. I was startled when he talked suddenly
about "bad cops," and then I realized that he must have
seen some clips on TV of the Michigan-Balbo scene and
heard what the commentators were saying. I asked him
about it, and he said uh-huh, in that abstracted way of
children when they are trying to avoid some pain in a
realization, in a change in their view of things. Later
he would say that he didn't want us to live in Chicago

anymore, and when I asked him why he said in the same abstracted way, "bad cops." Now five-year-old Timmy is among the happiest of children, generally full of incredible energy and trust, but through no commission or omission of my part or his mother's, mainly through the TV and the neighborhood children, he believed in good cops and God. God, whom he called "Gor," lived in the sky and was "as strong as Superman." I once heard him and one of his friends comparing with high energy the merits and strengths of God and Superman. I also remember that I was once made a little uneasy when he spoke of cops as "good," but I made no correction at that time because children do want and need to believe in Officer Friendly. In its primary impulse, though, there is more truth than not in the child's need and view of "good guys" and "bad guys." The basic feeling is so strong and so vulnerable that every culture starts early to feed it appropriate images, and many of the images are given to deflect the child from certain realities. On TV, the good guys changed, before Timmy's eyes, into bad guys, and the children of the neighborhood talked about the bad cops. It was urgent that they make the ground firm under this change in the way they saw their world. There has been much discussion among little children in Lincoln Park about "hippies" and "cops." Finally, with no fact except that they might see a cop lolling quietly in a parked squad car, they decided that there were some good cops and a lot of bad cops.

Months later, in the early spring of 1969, while Timmy was romping through Lincoln Park with his kindergarten class, he got frightened because one of his teachers was a hippie with long hair and Timmy saw cops in the Park and was afraid the cops would beat the hippie and "beat the little children, too," as he put it. He was

filled with uneasy feelings about long-haired male hippies. It was positively disorienting during Convention
Week for these white children to see their supposed
protectors in blue with all their strength and weapons,
almost as strong as Superman, suddenly become bad
guys with all their strength and weapons. "Superman
kill them like *this*," Timmy said, swiping his hand sideways. Later yet, he would ask me, "Should little children be afraid if cops take them into their cars?" He was
hoping now that at least little children might be exempt
from cop violence. I told him I thought the cops would
be decent with "little children" because it is psychologi-
cally intolerable for these children to consider arbitrary
violence from Officer Friendly. I winced, though, with
the memory of the biblical delight in dashing out the
brains of the enemy's little ones. So the division of attitude on good guys and bad guys sank deep into the
American psyche, deeper than anyone might have
thought. TV is indeed powerful, and it suffers the little
children to sit very near it, to see, to see, sometimes
actually to *see*, and freedom is somebody else's breakfast food.

"Yes, Timmy," I said that Thursday morning, "they
were very bad," and to hell with my own view of the
inevitability of that week. "I know-w-w," he said. I sat
down on a chair and held him between my knees for
awhile. In a minute or so he would be yelling over the
porch railing jubilantly to a friend on the ground floor,
and they would never quite discuss "bad cops" with
the same loud relish with which they discuss "Gor" and
Superman.

TV makes my son's feeling about what happens in
the world ambiguous, to say the least. He explained to
me once how violence was done on TV, that the guns

shot "play-bullets" and these "play-bullets" hit in someone's belly and made "them roll over and over and over,"
but they were not really "kilt," not really hurt, not really
really, because there is pretend really and really really,
and the people hit with the "play-bullets" would get up
and be perfectly all right later. That was how he had it
worked out that people were not actually killed on TV.
He would, of course, not believe that film of fighting in
Vietnam showed really-really killing, either. He was
happy and energetic in explaining it to me, as if it resolved something. The first word that Timmy could
write was his name, and the second word was the two
letters TV, which he sketched with a black felt pen on
a plain oak block and showed to me asking me what
did it say. I said, "TV. It says TV, Timmy." He smiled,
and gave a little laugh, with a touch of awe that the
two letters said TV to anyone who could read. He is not
addicted to the TV hour after hour; he spends most of
his time in play of all kinds with his friends. If we make
a rule that he can watch only Captain Kangaroo and no
more TV during the day, he will stick willingly to the
rule and some days not watch any TV at all. Yet we can
see the presence of the tube with all its pictures in his
life. I remember again the elderly woman who was
strongly disapproving of the demonstrators and thought
they were in the wrong, despite what she saw on TV,
until she saw the cops beating up kids on the street in
front of her home and the beating, when she *saw* it, was
manifestly unjust. She tried to intervene, and the cops
poked their clubs in her belly and shoved her away. The
TV experience of Convention Week, despite the fact
that some of that film was stark in its imagery, only re-
inforced her previous fantasy, while the actual experience radicalized her. TV uses the whole watching world

for the production of visual material that turns the whole watching world into play-act, stimulation and reinforcement of fantasy, right left or center politically, with the remarkable illusion for the viewer that he is witnessing the events, though its imagery is plucked gaping from the dynamic that produced it. For Timmy, it was enough to see to be there, and to live ever afterward with bad, fearful feeling about cops and hippies. For adults, whose fantasies are well formed, there is no substitute for a club on the head or a good gassing, it would seem. May we expect such great benefits from mass repression? Or is the situation so bizarre that the feeding of fantasy and distortion is just as necessary as direct experience for empowering all the possible forces for change, the sharpening of contradictory intentions?

I stopped for a cup of coffee in a restaurant on Clark Street because, strangely enough, it was a relaxing place for both cops and demonstrators. The police command post for Lincoln Park was located just across the street in the Park's Cultural and Recreation buildings, and a church Movement center for the demonstrators was also only a couple of blocks away. It was a red-leatherette-luncheonette sort of restaurant that can be found in American towns and cities east, west, south, and north, very clean, serving the staples of the common American diet such as fried eggs, hamburgers, pork chops, hamburger steaks, etcetera. It was run by a Greek family with considerable personal and family exuberance, and they kept a Greek salad and a couple of Greek dishes on the menu, and a few Greek friends came there and occasionally spoke the language. Perhaps because of the family exuberance and tolerance, and the fact that they could make a decent cup of coffee, it was a pleasant place, not the usual bus-station anonymity, and they were cheerful toward people who merely wanted a cup of coffee and the privacy to read a book.

In most restaurants in the area a quite active chill is pressed against the latter sort of person. In another such restaurant down the street, where Abbie Hoffman was arrested for having FUCK on his forehead, the proprietor will evict anyone who wants to read a book, who does not "sit nice," and who does not spend enough money to justify, in the proprietor's estimation, the temporary occupancy of a booth or stool, no matter how empty the restaurant may be. I have had so many runins with that proprietor, and so have many people in the area, that I never go there, and I am sure that it was because of the proprietor that Hoffman was arrested there. If Hoffman had come into the other restaurant up the street, the FUCK on his forehead would certainly have caused a sensation, but with much more humor in it, and likely it would not have been considered sufficient reason for blowing the whistle. In fact, he would have been sitting on one side of the restaurant while the cops were sitting on the other side, and both would have been eating whatever they wanted off the menu and had the money to pay for.

Thursday about noon the cops were sitting on one side, jammed into booths by the front windows, and several demonstrators were sitting in booths on the other side. The cops were feeling good, and if the demonstrators were more subdued, it was only because their numbers were less and their style of life was also different, more cool. The word "police state" was used generously in Chicago and about Chicago, but the feeling in this restaurant was more that of a dressing room being used by two opposing teams, who did not speak much to each other, but were not afraid of saying whatever they felt, in whatever tone of voice, in their own group. They were not afraid of identifying themselves or of being over-heard. Yet, in the face of such openness, the cops sent plainclothesmen to mix with the demonstrators and gather "intelligence." A game was being played, with different constructions and misconstructions on both sides, with 'free' territory and 'tag' territory, 'free' times of day and 'tag' times of day, with real bloodied heads, real broken bones, real arrests, real sadistic harassment in the police stations, and the arbitrary, at-your-pleasure breaking of rules that were only dimly being worked out, and grudgingly. The many contradictory pressures of American life created the arena and made the partial game-construct necessary.

But perhaps the game was emerging from deeper dreams, wishes and needs, from an emergency in the national soul that carries its unshriven past with it.

For instance, when the Aztecs conquered most of the city-states of Mexico, or brought them to heel in a trib-ute relationship, in the century or so before the Spanish came, they found themselves—a war-built, war-oriented, war-organized, war-trained society—*without war.* The strains of this oddly successful situation were found to be intolerable, so between city-states, there came about a deadly game, the War of Flowers, the flowers being the warriors. Selected equal groups of warriors from two city-states would fight, usually through the daylight of one day, before spectators, actually taking prisoners, actually wounding combatants and (only occasionally) killing them in battle. Taking of prisoners was more im-portant than killing in battle because of the need for fresh, beating hearts for sacrifice to the sun. The whole point of prisoners taken in the game of the War of Flowers was to sacrifice them. This ingrained training

about taking prisoners helped make the Aztecs less than
wholly effective when the game changed and they faced
the Spaniards who came with a concept of total war.
The honored War of Flowers was important in keeping
limber the uneasy stability of the Aztec empire.

It has been pointed out and worried over by a number
of American historians that not exactly war, but the presence of the frontier and concepts of the frontier have
been an economic and emotional imperative in our national life. The frontier has to do with space and sense
of space, territory, empire, external and internal, to the
nation and the person. How close are Americans to creating games that emerge from the necessity of uncom-
prehended wishes in dreams, to keep supportable this
curse of the frontier? Games where social change might
be the very point. Let's see what the events of Thursday
may tell us.

In the restaurant, John Sack, who was doing the police
side of the story for *Esquire,* was interviewing a cop.
In another booth, I was talking with Paul Krassner,
editor of *The Realist* and a Yippie founder, and Anita
Hoffman, wife of Abbie Hoffman, and another woman.
Krassner was joking about the plainclothesman who
tailed him everywhere; and was telling the story how,
one stoned night at the turn of the year, the Yippies
came into being, a non-organization that proved immensely flexible. The cops were having their own conversation on the other side, enjoying themselves, too,
more physical pleasure on their side. There was the feeling of being in the home-stretch, only one more day
and night to go, and both sides thought they were winning, perhaps because each was playing a different
game. Then I gave Krassner and friends a ride to the
Hilton, where a similar sort of easiness played with the

cops on one side and demonstrators on the other, all
waiting for the day's activities to begin.

It was mostly Guardsmen, with some cops on the ends
of the lines, who faced the demonstrators on the east
side of Michigan Avenue in Grant Park on Thursday
afternoon. Around the ends of the lines, people crossed
back and forth between the Park and the Hotel. I
checked the Park where, although it was 2 PM, a lot
of Yippies and students were still wrapped up in blankets trying to get some sleep. A portable loudspeaker
croaked out a message now and then: "We're going to
march to the Amphitheatre . . ." I moved back toward
the Hilton where McCarthy was to speak in the Williford Room to his supporters. A few demonstrators
crossed around the cop line at Balbo with me, when one
cop made an angry move toward a demonstrator who,
without a quiver or change of pace, put out his hand as
if quieting a disturbed spirit and said: "Always leave
an exit, man. Always leave an exit." The cop really
snarled and turned red with the wisdom of it, because
that was exactly what the cops had not done the day
before. He shoved his club at the demonstrator but withdrew. Rules were being learned, grudgingly. We finished the crossing without trouble.

McCarthy Speaks and Speaks Again

In the Williford Room of the Hilton, McCarthy gave
to his workers the most witty, generous, and emotional
speech that anyone ever heard from him. Julian Bond
was at the podium with him. New York senatorial candidate Paul O'Dwyer and Governor Harold Hughes of
Iowa, I believe, were backing him up, too. With enormous self-conscious enthusiasm, the young McCarthy
workers were waving the sign that many of them had

only recently acquired: the V sign, peace sign, Yip sign, V for victory sign, sign of revolution. When they saw McCarthy coming down the jammed aisle, with his hand raised somewhat slyly, somewhat shyly, in the sign, too, they shook the walls with their cheering. If McCarthy at that moment had said that he would lead an immediate revolution, several thousand young men and women in Chicago would have followed him straight to wherever. But he had different leaders in mind for them, and it was announced that he would also speak to the demonstrators in Grant Park.

He said many wonderful things to his workers in the Williford Room, who, if they had in days previous begrudged him for not storming the ramparts of paradise, now loved him more than they had thought possible, for he was different. He was physically easier, looser, not tight before the crowd; he had lost the nomination and so he was freed from complex feelings about winning and from the ever-pressing sense of some danger that could have been waiting for him to win. He addressed his supporters with a quiet, flattering irony as "the government of the people in exile," and he said, in reference to the whole campaign and the immediate events in Chicago, "You have always been ahead of me . . ." and "I have been set free in many ways . . ." It was almost possible to believe that here was a man who had actually responded and changed in a dialogue with people, issues and events. He spoke of the future in the simple terms of working for the election of some peace candidates and of working for the general renewal of the Democratic Party from the precinct level up, taking advantage of the new rules changes that had been forced upon the Party by his people. But most important to the young workers in the room when they thundered out a cheer and waved the V sign, McCarthy waved the sign back at them, albeit self-consciously, and that caused the cheering to step higher in the air.

Most of the McCarthy supporters in the Williford Room crossed the street to Grant Park to wait for him there, after he paid his respects, courteous and perhaps poisonous, to a Minnesota caucus, where no doubt he was threatened, entreated, and importuned to give support to Humphrey who, being low in popular estimation, needed McCarthy's full support. Possibly the caucus offered him the vice-presidency, and probably he told them, kindly, to shove it, for they could think no further than November and he was already thinking far beyond that month, already making connections that would enable him to move and think into the next few years, necessarily over a few dead bodies. Oh, the vendettas that could be coming, for Humphrey had such need of McCarthy's support, crucial need, *sine qua non,* and yet McCarthy held a much longer lease on the future, at least two years before he might have to face a Humphrey vendetta in a Democratic senatorial contest in 1970 in Minnesota. It was necessary that Humphrey and presidential patronage be removed so that a new Democratic Party, out of the McCarthy base, might grow hard and fast, out of the rules changes, from the precinct level up. McCarthy could not have sold his base to Humphrey for any price less than Humphrey's immediate suicide after Inaugural Day, assuming McCarthy was Vice President. Yet McCarthy must also be careful of many regular Democratic bases of power, tenacious of life; so he would in the last days of the campaign give a qualified support to Humphrey, and if Humphrey won the election, McCarthy could claim large credit and keep a grudging hold within the regular

Party; and if Humphrey lost, McCarthy would not have
to take too much blame, and would not have to expose
his actual power, and would still keep hold within the
regular Party while making entrance in it for the new.
(Julian Bond was regularly associated with McCarthy,
and we have already speculated that the Richard
Hughes-Julian Bond event in the Credentials Committee was aimed toward 1972.)

If McCarthy had such foresight, such awareness and
estimation of potential political processes, no wonder
Mayor Daley, who loves a winner, could not lead his
Illinois delegation into McCarthy's camp, even though
he, too, must have been sure that Humphrey would lose.
Daley could not trust a man who could sense so accurately new combinations of power with which Daley
was more than uneasy, and he must have felt that only
a ruthless, cynical, patient monomaniac would build
that sort of power. During the months of the presidential campaign in the fall of 1968, Daley's precinct workers were out in the streets of Chicago blatantly showing
voters in areas where Wallace was strong, how they
could vote both for George Wallace for President and
the Daley ticket. Newspapers such as the *Chicago Daily
News* reported this activity and it makes one wonder
if even honest, venturesome reporting has any effect at
all on political consciousness. Certainly it must have
thorough, frequent follow-up over time.

On the other hand, McCarthy would have had different reasons for feeling unsafe in the Convention if
someone as important as Mayor Daley had come to his
support. McCarthy had the artist's and the revolutionary's feeling for the detail and the spirit, the restraint
and the build-up, of a grand scheme more sensed than
designed. Adept at using smoke-screens, he was, out of

the ambition and fear of moral outrage, at work on the future the day after the nomination went to Hubert Humphrey.

After his meeting with the Minnesota caucus, McCarthy would cross Michigan Avenue and talk with the demonstrators in Grant Park. It was to be an uneasy meeting between McCarthy and the demonstrators, under the trees where the grass was beaten brown and dusty and newspapers and leaflets were soft ghosts underfoot. I brought the news that McCarthy was coming to a group standing around Allen Ginsberg. Ginsberg, humbled and disturbed by the anger and the violence, and croaking from the gas and all that Omming that never influenced one cop, said, when he heard McCarthy was coming over, "Good, then we won't be gassed." Paul Krassner said, "Yes, we'll let McCarthy speak—if he'll take his pants off." Krassner later used the same joke over the megaphone to tell all the demonstrators that McCarthy was arriving soon. Abbie Hoffman, fresh from jail, told us he had told the cops while they were beating him, "We beat you, we beat you," laughing at them. He also said that the events of the last week ought to end all talk of drugs not making good revolutionaries and he spoke of all those "stoned kids" in Lincoln Park.

Julian Bond—in a blue shirt that seemed unbelievably clean and sharply pressed to anyone on this side of the line, but with his tie pulled neatly loose—was given an unmarred ovation when he stepped up to the speaker. Julian Bond and Dick Gregory spoke to introduce McCarthy, thus insuring a generally good reception.

A black limousine stopped near the demonstrators' portable speaker and McCarthy stepped out, a big man in a big suit. Surrounded by Secret Servicemen, he

crossed through the cop and Guard lines, approaching
the group around the speaker. He came giving the V
sign, but his fingers and his arm never seemed wholly
at ease in giving the sign. The rightness of everything
that happened that week showed when immediately he
was largely cheered, while at the same time other voices
abused him for his voting record in the Senate.

He began in Grant Park with the same line as in the
Williford Room: "I am happy to address the govern-
ment-of-the-people-in-exile." A few laughs came; but on
this side of the line he was standing against the tension,
not entirely welcomed, and his wit was not so clear. Immediately, a few hard-headed demonstrators, mostly
around the outer edge of the crowd, sent up the demanding, not-to-be-cheated cry, "*Revolution! Revolution!*" In addition, McCarthy had to force himself to
talk above the noise of a white helicopter beating round
and round overhead. He wanted to be liked on this side
of the line, and he continued trying to give much the
same speech that he had given in the Williford Room,
where it had been magical. He was mostly cheered in
Grant Park, too, but unabashed hostility was also hurled
at him. *Fuck, McCarthy! How did you vote on such-
and-such?* That last question angered him, and he started
to answer but was showered by several remarks at once.
When he said that he intended to work in the coming
campaign for the election of a few senators who could
change American foreign policy, a demonstrator standing in front of me yelled at him, "How about a revolution, baby?" McCarthy finished his speech stubbornly
—"We can seize control of the Democratic Party in
1972"—then left to his black limousine just a bit hastily,
amid cheers and abusive cries. There was a rightness
about everything.

At the same time, some of the New Left brothers tend to wish that history would be linear, the way their thinking is, and the way history never is: they did not even sense that McCarthy, in crossing the line to speak in Grant Park, was seeking to give a further twist to the dagger already sunk into the old Democratic Party. It was right that they were made uneasy by this strange man and his strange relationship to this country. Co-optation is only one of the many dangers that come from all sides, and often it is only in accepting the danger that anything begins to happen, such as the catalytic event in Lincoln Park Sunday night. McCarthy gave a most powerful legitimizing gesture for his followers to cross the line and enter the bizarre logic whereby history begins to make men and women of some. But some New Leftists, who had just proven themselves in the past few days to be strong by the impact of their actions, still felt themselves to be so weak that they could only conceive that he had crossed the line to put them in his pocket. There has been much comfort and nurture in the past few years on the Left in living before the mirror of weakness and alienation, but when you confess your strength, you step beyond the looking glass, where possibility is no longer affirmed by the mirror image and identity becomes declarative and dangerous. It was shouted that McCarthy ought to lead the march to the Amphitheatre that afternoon. And it would have been an event, to be sure, if McCarthy had led a march. But the same thing would have happened to him that happened to Dick Gregory and the delegates who did lead the march that night south on Michigan Avenue to 18th Street: they were whisked away cleanly and nonviolently in vans, and the thousands behind them crying "Take us, too!" were left to face the gas and whatever

else the Guard might do. It was right that the uneasy
meeting in Grant Park may have made McCarthy think
more palpably of the directions of the new potential
combination of power. It was also a shock to feel that
New Left thought, which had been the most promising
thought in this country in the past several years, had
undergone a sea-change, a change without changing,
becoming in some aspects a static fantasy, while the
country itself was on the move. So McCarthy, who was
physically imposing on this side of the line, in his big
suit, with his Secret Service men about him, stooped
into his long black limousine, giving a last V sign, under
the noses of the cops across the street, some of whom
may have remembered slashing the tires of McCarthy-
sticker cars in Lincoln Park.

McCarthy may have also hoped that his act of crossing the line would legitimize the demonstrators in such
a way that it would mitigate further police violence
against them and his supporters who were joining them.
But Friday morning the cops would raid his headquarters in the Hilton. The cops were the ones who
named accurately the potential participants in the new
American revolution, if only those named could believe
it and believe their company. That's the new party: the
"Who, me? Who, *them?*" party. In the constant presence of immediate, us-or-them danger under the club,
in a primitive and yet theatrical revolutionary situation,
it could hold together, grow, and win, in time.

But when the repressive forces put away the general
threat that gives survival focus and energy to a mass of
people, and turn to picking off people one by one—sub-
jecting several but not a majority of participants to
severe punishment in deliberately exemplary situations
—it is a different game and people try to survive in

different, less unified ways. During Convention Week the cops, oddly enough, took the place of personal conviction in that they subjected anyone present to indiscriminate threat. Remove the cops, and you remove the conviction of many people. It takes rooted belief for people to stay unified and to handle attempts to pick them off one by one; or it takes a personal or group interpretation of survival that makes one able to stand firm in the face of the object lesson. "Leaders" are indicted for "inciting" to riot; dissident students unlucky enough to be fingered are expelled; social and economic benefits enjoyed by many are withdrawn from a few; and the hardcore of rebels is invited to martyrdom, while the main body of participants are let go scot-free, even if they sign complicity-with-the-accused statements. The issues opened up by sudden forays to the Left are co-opted by interim groups—in the civil rights movements, in the universities, in peace and war, in national politics. It would seem that New Left leaders are often far more naive than their followers, who use the leaders to open up issues and then sacrifice them. The followers are more sly and perhaps more aware of final and finite possibilities. The sacrificial is one type of leadership situation. If people recognize without spelling it out—essential for the sleight of hand between our conscience and our intentions—that the sacrificial is the situation, then a scapegoat-martyr sort of personality will choose to be the "leader," for everyone deeply knows what is going to happen, and the more the leaders point out their fate, the more satisfying it is—kicks for everyone. People are so smart in these ways that we have to conceal the nakedness of our intelligence in order to enable it to be effective. The true martyr, the one about whose death the faith of people coheres, such as Malcolm X, is generally one who loves life so much that he would undo the logic of the dues if he could because of the integrity of his self and his commitment.

Surely these are cruel and untrue ways of looking at good men. Surely it is also a way that some men rationalize to make things nice in their consciences. But at the present time, the liberal wing of the Democratic Party is readying itself to co-opt—more vigorously than ever before—the issues of peace, civil rights, poverty, and electoral reform. They have no doubt already joined with the fellows whom we will call the technocratic liberals. Altogether they will, if they are wise, change the theater, closet the general danger, for it gives cause for the powerful visceral survival forms of alliances and organizations. They will find the price of, and make the concessions to, most of the groups that are co-opting the issues, and they will point out the remaining hard-core for silent, dead-end martyrdom. There is the odor of death and dank passivity about situations where people have let this happen to them: the full sick inch around the heart that comes with helplessly seeing comrades picked off.

Who is this technocratic liberal; who can have a man killed in the morning and make the most genial of concessions in the afternoon, then jingles the change in his pocket for those nearby to hear. The technocratic liberal may be found in his middle 30's or early 40's in technologically-advanced forms of business, in government agencies, in education, even in the military. He believes that the society and its problems can be ordered and resolved on levels as sophisticated as the technology itself, without changing its basic profit-oriented nature; he is not democratic and he is not fascistic: he simply believes in the imperative of what will profitably work, and he is willing to wait a long time, in the name of survival, for the full return on his investment. The United States is largely "middle-class," basically approving of the technocratic liberal's attitudes and intentions if packaged correctly; and there are plenty of left-liberals to give him advice, warning, even designs of survival. The personnel in communications fields, for example, who actually gather the information—in TV, newspapers, magazines, publishing houses, radio, etcetera— are generally far more hip and more eager than those in upper executive echelons; and they are useful, perhaps far more than they believe, for the technocrat. He can let them move far, far into fields of reality and promise, as bait, and then reel them in with a handsome catch.

The strategy of the technocratic liberal when he deals with liberal Leftists is similar to the kind of effort that Governor Hughes was trying to aid and abet with such energy and success in the Credentials Committee hearings. It is the kind of combination of forces—of Kennedy-McGovern-McCarthy-Fulbright people in the national Democratic Party combined with the new groups for organizing precincts and the groups that spring up to co-opt them, plus most importantly the class-minded, nation-minded, gentry technocrat in business, the new black politicians, the peace forces, along with certain segments of the old liberal coalition—that could quite possibly achieve control of the Democratic Party in 1972. The joker here is the rest of the world: the War in Vietnam; the attitude of the majority of the middle class toward the War; and the extremes of dissent and repressive action taken internally because of the War. The hope of the revolt is both that the country will change faster than its issues can be co-opted, and that the revolt will not leave those people, who are attracted by an issue but not ready for the big activist plunges, to be plucked by co-opting groups.

The technocratic liberal is a strong challenger for leadership and direction of the nation's material intentions and capabilities. The revolt cannot indulge itself solely in its love of apocalyptic haste and leave this far greater mass of people behind to be absorbed by technocratic co-optation. The revolt must have the tolerance and the respect to meet the response of people attracted by issues. When coupled with a profound interpretation of survival, it is the general and determined sense of destiny that makes a revolution.

The technocratic liberal, for one thing, believes that all social, political, economic and, if you will, *spiritual* problems can be broken down until a desired combination and solution is established, giving everyone his bit: his bit of the Gross National Product pie, his bit of the time pie, his bit of physical and free-speech freedom, his bit of style of life, his bit of the exercise of profound emotion, his *bit*.

One of the best descriptions of the technocratic liberal occurs in a report given by Carl Oglesby in *New Left Notes* (SDS) in the summer of 1968. Oglesby and other New Left leaders were approached by a group calling themselves Businessmen's International, largely composed of young vice-presidents of huge, globally operating corporations. Businessmen's International is a cover group for helping to further useful political developments for corporations, such as the chemical and electronic firms, who are rapidly buying into (and close to buying control of) their counterparts in other countries. Over the summer, there were three meetings between the New Left group and the Businessmen's International spokesmen. The BI men were seeking a working relationship with the New Left, saying they found it, from their point of view, the only viable political vehicle left in this country. Now, that is flattery. The New Left leaders—and Oglesby shows this with some humor—felt not a little anxious to find that the BI men agreed with virtually everything the New Left was trying to do: they agreed about Vietnam and the ghetto scene and, most distressing, they agreed with the general New Left analysis of the United States. Moreover, they agreed about the Pentagon, in whose growth they had played no small part, but which now had become a monster, outside their control, not only no longer useful to them but standing in the way of the much advanced aspirations of their firms: to create on a high technological level a global consumer economy dominated by these corporations. They no doubt also feel that they are capable of solving the troubles of population and food. In the past twenty years, their corporations have grown mightily, and as their European counterparts reached the crucial point in technological development—where huge capital investment was required to go further but was not available from any source except the American firms—the American corporations provided the capital, buying into their counterparts, and making deep inroads toward control. In both their immediate and their long-term aspirations, the firms behind Businessmen's International come into sharp contradiction with the military-industrial sector of our economy, which—as Juan Bosch, formerly of the Dominican Republic, points out in a recent issue of *Evergreen Review* (December 1968)—wages war in peripheral areas of our world, not to exploit those countries in the traditional sense of imperialism, but to make profits at home. The military-industrial sector is variously estimated at 10% to 15% of the Gross National

Product, a figure that has been alarming to many people, but which is perhaps smaller than that represented by the firms in BI. This sector does not now possess determining influence on the highest policy-making bodies of government, which represent sectors that gained their place and kept it in the Cold War after World War II. A struggle for power is underway between these sectors, for the point now is not to colonize or bury countries but to control and develop their economic apparatus in a global network. It means development in a sophisticated and thorough way. Both kinds of imperialism in our country—the Pentagon's and the technocratic liberal's—are clearly beyond Lenin's main description of imperialism. But if Lenin had foreseen the way in which electronic technology would make surplus-value go wild, giving the American firms an empyrean latitude in capital and time, he would have understood the implications quickly. The Russians understand it, and get more Piggish by the day, history wisping through their fingers. With the Pentagon on one side, where the training of the American Army contains more and more emphasis on control of "civil disturbance," the new political-economic technocrats saw that they needed troops, too; and then they saw that they had badly neglected their home fences, where the supposed political center was the fief of the military-industrial contestant. Thus, the political-economic technocrats sought the New Left.

They were mostly McCarthy men, Oglesby says, and they sought the wrecking of the Democratic Party in order to open it up. Although on the immediate issues of our time, the New Left leaders could find no disagreement with these men, they finally located the basic difference—and one can almost see them breathing a sigh—in that the BI men still regarded "labor as the measurement of value," whereas the New Leftists regard free time and free effort as the only human measurement of value. The BI men wanted to help the New Left, financially and in whatever other way was possible, to disrupt Chicago and the Democratic Convention. In the final conversation, they offered help and authorized activity, "up to and including burning the city down." What could they care about real estate? The New Left leaders, perhaps more flattered than they care to admit, were fascinated to discover the character of the new force represented by Businessmen's International, and also shocked that they had to dig deep to find their own historical identity. But the last proposal was more irresponsible than the grandest put-on by the most freaked-out drug-head. The New Left leaders cut off the talks and rushed into print their side of the story in order that it might not be used against them, while also informing their fellows of an important metamorphosis in a part of the area called the Establishment.

SDS participated in the scene in Chicago during Convention Week with the wooing of the McCarthy kids as their stated motive. Businessmen's International, in the talks with the New Left leaders, had also indicated its intense interest in winning the McCarthy troops. If the opening-up of the Democratic Party should mean the ascendancy to power of the technocratic liberals, it could be a matter for immense mourning, or it could be simply a necessary extension of our labyrinth.

It could be the way of preparing American life for socialization, which would then happen more as if we passed through the magical shiver of a magnetic field, into a baronial sort of socialization, hardly being able to tell the transformation of our lives from the mirage and crackle of the passage. But an American Armageddon

must be waiting around a corner somewhere in the life-
time of anyone under 40 now—since it is so generally
accepted that power is not changed or given up easily
and must be won by those able and worthy to do it.

At present, the technocrats are not in the public centers of power: but they are waiting and aching in the
wings. As a possible main agent for the technocratic
liberals in the political area, Senator McCarthy could
be the best of all possible agents—the bell-sheep for the
voting flock. Or, taking a further step which McCarthy
may have already taken in his mind but may never take
in actuality, he could move the nation into the logic
where the intentions of its power would change. I am
talking partly about the man but mostly about the
possible combination of groups that showed with his
candidacy.

To the Amphitheatre

If Convention Week was a national dream prophecy
—with wish and statement for the future, model and
metaphor of time to come—then the marches on Thursday night, the part of the dream that most forget or de-
emphasize, will point both toward, and away from
understanding.

If the march that tried to move out of Grant Park
yesterday had been obviously non-violent, the marches
on Thursday afternoon and night were glaringly passive.
The first march came early in the afternoon when some
30 members of the Wisconsin delegation had walked
down State Street leading a few hundred people, to see
if it were possible "to walk the streets of Chicago," in-
tending to walk to the Amphitheatre. They picked up a
goodly number of bystanders and demonstrators and
were stopped by the cops, who finally said, with what is

described as courtesy, that the Wisconsin delegates could walk to the Amphitheatre but those other people following them could not. The cops were authorized to interpret the law as they saw fit. That was that.

The first march that left from Grant Park on Thursday afternoon, with the voiced intention of marching to the Amphitheatre, was carefully controlled by the parade marshalls. A large proportion of the marchers were ex-McCarthy workers, with many students, while hippies were scarce. The march was negotiated with the police —that is, it was found by the parade marshalls after offering several alternatives that the police would accept people going in numbers no more than three abreast, virtually a part of normal sidewalk traffic, to 16th Street, and no further. It was intimated among the marchers and their leaders that somehow they would continue from 16th Street, somehow, to the Amphitheatre—how, was never said. It was almost as if this march were designed to be a baptismal for the McCarthy people, to ease them into involvement. Nobody could be sure what would happen at 16th Street, but anybody with experience in the days before knew that they were not going to be able to march to the Amphitheatre. Marching to the Amphitheatre was a mental posture for the marchers. If Lincoln Park had taught one thing, it was that people were the goal, not by symbolic action, but by direct involvement or by role-playing.

The marchers strolled along cheerfully on the sidewalk of Michigan Avenue toward 16th Street, giving the V sign exuberantly to black bystanders and car drivers and blacks leaning from windows. Black people answered the white marchers everywhere, from cars, from windows, from sidewalks, with laughter, with applause, with loud smiles, and with the V sign—the sign that had

now become, in feeling anyway, the salute of revolution. Behind a plate-glass window, a black woman in a
blue dress uniform—with a face so stern and bitter it
made you believe in the need for redemption—suddenly
broke into a smile at the sight of the demonstrators waving the V sign at her through the glass, and she signed
back, through the silence of glass. Blacks in cars were
honking their horns in sympathy and humor, as did
many whites on Michigan by the Hilton and on LaSalle
and Clark by Lincoln Park. There was wry astonish-
ment among the Negroes on the sidewalks.

But in one building all the workers, leaning out of
the windows, were white. They jeered and cursed the
demonstrators, gave them the up-the-ass finger, and
told them if they wanted to end the War to go to Vietnam and fight. The demonstrators, who were shouting,
"*Join* us! *Join* us!" changed to shouting up at the white
workers, "Jump, *jump!*" Even some of the white workers,
leaning out of the windows, laughed. But their disdain
of the middle-class protestors was intense, as if the mere
idea of peace-marching somehow demanded disdainful
declarations of manhood—just as the disdain of the cop
who wanted to club the man with the Seagram's manner
and silver hair, turned into sudden laughter when the
man complimented him.

The student-rebels were already talking, out of the
resonant depths of their romanticism, during Convention Week in Chicago of throwing away their love beads
and shaving off their beards and going to church and in
general going straight—to work among working-class
people to generate "class" awareness and yet another
form of political confrontation. That is all well and good.
Supposedly those American workers scratching around
the gates of the Dream have more potential for revolt

than the inheritors of its dust. But if the fences of the great "middle-class" go untended much longer, the students are liable to come back to find that most of the nation has become the fief and source of another power —and that their "historical" purpose has been merely to excite the growth of conditions that make the establishment of an American equivalent of a Roman emperor a necessity and an actuality, capable of responding quickly to social changes and demands with material sop, material permission, and/or material repression.

Military trucks, deuce-and-a-halfs, drove past the marchers, with the whine-grind of the military transmission toward 16th Street, where the Guardsmen would fix bayonets and face the marchers, but now the Guardsmen in the backs of the trucks, in significant numbers, were answering the marchers with the V sign. They didn't want to go to Vietnam, either. The marchers yelled, "Join us, join us," to the Guardsmen, to the Negroes, to everybody, even to the cops. "More pay for cops," they chanted. It was an enjoyable, nearly innocent stroll, and even the trucks carrying the Guardsmen did not hurry over much to get to 16th Street before the marchers got there.

Under the viaduct at 16th Street were lined up the Guardsmen with fixed bayonets, the cops, the jeeps with barbwire coverings, an armored personnel carrier with a machinegun on top of it that everybody called a tank, and other vehicles, completely blocking further passage. People were crammed into the street for two blocks north of the viaduct, *crammed into a trap,* with unbroken walls of buildings along the street, no exits, no alleys, no gangways. If the cops or the Guard charged, clubbed, or fired, there was no escape.

I looked at the machinegun on the personnel carrier

and at the street packed with people. It could have been
Chicago's own ravine at Babi Yar, where the Nazi Ger-
mans methodically shot down tens of thousands of Russian Jews. It could, more up to date and more possibly,
have been Chicago's own Plaza de Las Tres Culturas,
where the Mexican army, about a month after the Chicago Convention, marched upon a large student demonstration in a trapped situation, and fired upon it steadily
for two hours, killing between 200 and 400 students, according to witnesses who saw the bodies in the Plaza,
as reported in the March 1969 issue of *Evergreen Review*
and in an October 1968 edition of the *Los Angeles Free
Press*—a figure that differs from the 20 or 30 reported
killed in our "major" newspapers and magazines. Ironi-
cally, the Mexican students were demonstrating in the
Plaza because they had decided, out of fear, to accept
a government warning at its word and not march in
the streets.

"Always leave an exit," the kid told the cop back at
the Hilton. It is useful for the cops to leave an exit so
long as their aims are merely containment and dispersal.
Their aims may, however, change, and it is up to demonstration leaders never to enter or stay in a no-exit situation. Hardly anyone in this march knew who was actually leading it. Several demonstrators—students with
experience over the past few days in Lincoln Park—
were as alarmed as I was at the lack of exits, and they
were cruising nervously up and down looking for alleys
and gangways. There had to be flanks, there had to be
elbow room, there had to be the area where you could
move to, *fast*, and call it your own, such as the streets
around Lincoln Park. "Let's get out of here," the students were saying, and I was telling my wife and her
McCarthy friends the same thing. As if to prove our

fears, we looked back and saw cops lined up across the street north on Michigan Avenue. We were really trapped. If the Guard on one end and the cops on the other chose to do it, they had a couple of thousand people in a box, and they could really shake the box. Abbie Hoffman, skinny, wild-haired head—who had been at the head of the march among a group of Peace Corps drop-outs—was now actively leading the demonstrators down the street out of the trap. There was uneasiness as we approached the cop line, but they permitted the march to retreat along the sidewalks.

The marchers went back to Grant Park, followed by Guardsmen and cops all the way. "More pay for cops," they chanted again, and "Join us, join us." Many drivers dinned the air with their car horns when asked to honk by the demonstrators. But underneath the relief of getting out of the trap, the feeling among most of the demonstrators was depression, and something had to be done to keep all these people, with all their time and energy and eagerness, doing something, rather than milling about and then going home. Or stoning cops. Or storming the Hilton. Or. Or. They could not be left here to their own devices, disappointed, for some would go home ashamed to talk about their activity or to join another, while others would find plenty to keep the police busy in the immediate neighborhood of the Park and the Hotel. The problem required a clever man, and it found one in Dick Gregory, comedian-turned-pacifist-vegetarian-revolutionary, with an air always sly and proud, a man who walked light and bouncy on the earth.

The marchers streamed back into Grant Park, gaining energy and good humor at the sight of some kids trying to climb the John A. Logan equestrian statue again, and the marchers re-grouped on the smooth, green, rounded hill. They covered it so thoroughly, sitting and standing up, that it looked as if a *pointilliste* cape were thrown over the hill, with the Logan statue protruding at the top. The police moved up the hill, apparently to tell the kids climbing on the statue to get off or to pull them off. The cops were caught by their previous action on Monday, in that, to justify their violence in pulling kids off the statue then and breaking one boy's arm, they had to do the same thing today. So the cops went up the hill to the statue, and the people on the hill with a lot of laughter saw the opportunity, spoke it among themselves, and enclosed the cops. Among them was Deputy Superintendent Rochford. He seemed rather uncomfortable, a touch chagrined, when he realized that he was a hostage. People were talking, joking, about negotiating a march to the Amphitheatre with Rochford as the hostage in the bargaining. "Don't let him go," some were saying, though not a hand was put upon him. He simply couldn't move. Dick Gregory took the mike of the portable speaker at the foot of the hill and made a nice joke about setting the Deputy Superintendent free, and the people formed an aisle down the hill and let Rochford walk to freedom. No arrests were made this time for climbing on the statue. The Deputy Superintendent was glad for his skin—you could see it in his face. Gregory invited him to speak over the mike to the crowd. Rochford was greeted by many boos, and he was not understood clearly except that he said a march to the Amphitheatre would be stopped by the police. Now, was that news? He is reported to have also said, "Sometimes the law is not what I would like." That must have been his way of thanking the crowd for letting him go free. Once, in days past, Rochford was asked by newsmen if the police "would clear the Park by force tonight?" He answered, a touch cynical, "That remains to be seen."

Spokesmen, in a humdrum hortatory contest it seemed, passed the time while Gregory talked with Brigadier General Dunn of the National Guard. Dunn was more aware than Rochford of the real problem. Rochford said that no one would be arrested if they stayed in the Park and demonstrated there, failing to notice that there was no real permit for this either and that the "law" of which he was so protective, was therefore somewhat arbitrary, amounting to personal decision on somebody's part. But Dunn knew that to let the demonstrators stay in the Park would give them all the rest of the night to develop volatile feelings and attitudes. No, they must be occupied, usefully occupied, and so Dunn said that he could permit marchers to go as far as 18th Street—get that, two blocks farther south than 16th Street—and as far west as State Street, which was two blocks west of Michigan Avenue. The Secret Service, with whom Dunn apparently consulted constantly, advised that it would not be a good idea for the marchers to go farther south or west, clearly because the march would then enter deep ghetto where the Secret Service, Mayor Daley, and many concerned citizens thought a number of Negroes might find reason to answer the marchers' call of "Join us" and the activities in the streets could become livelier than anything seen yet. But to march to 18th Street was not emotionally equivalent to marching to the Amphitheatre, and it was then that Gregory became the man equal to the problem: the man to give promise of success to the posture of marching to the Amphitheatre.

Gregory explained to the demonstrators that they could march to 18th Street, no further. Then he said, "But there's nothing they can do if I invite you to my house." Gregory lives on 55th Street, way south. "Now, you're all my friends and I'm inviting you to my house, and we'll see if we have the constitutional right to walk on the sidewalks and come to a party at my house." His whole proposal was wonderfully put, in rhythm and intonation, sly, righteous, and very funny. He managed to intimate that once 18th Street was crossed people could head straight for the Amphitheatre. The marchers' energy, which had been dribbling down into depression since they let Rochford go free, climbed high again with Gregory's humor and his sly proposal. Most of the newcomer demonstrators obediently believed that police and Guard opposition must vanish before the wand of constitutional rights, and they thought that Gregory's idea must work, or that something must work because of it. It is amazing that most people really accepted this idea. No one seemed to know that Donald Peterson and the Wisconsin McCarthy delegates had tried earlier in the afternoon to see if the right to walk the streets of Chicago could be exercised, and they found that they had the privilege to walk to the Amphitheatre but the privilege did not extend to others with them. So, between Dunn and Gregory, the problem of occupying and directing everybody's time and energy was beginning to be solved. The initiation of the newcomers could continue. They would go toward Dick's house or know the reason why. The marchers, much larger in number now, went south on the sidewalks again, five abreast, in the rich August twilight. Medics were dressing themselves in white coats and organizing, and a few were intently coloring red crosses with crayons on their white armbands. The march moved slowly.

It was very dark by the time the march, massed on the east sidewalk of Michigan for several blocks, was stopped at 18th Street. It was a dead halt, gut-dull, gut-dreary with so much waiting that it seemed that some-one was really working to run the clock out. It is said that Gregory kept the march moving slowly to give time for a group of delegates to arrive and come to the head of the march. The parade marshalls controlled the march carefully, moving alongside it with the portable speaker, always admonitory, "Get up on the sidewalk! You are liable for arrest if you are in the street!" The McCarthy people were excited by the prospect of some statement through personal participation in whatever could happen, but moment by moment the march be-came dull, dreary, obedient, with all individual impulse excluded. "Here come the delegates!" someone shouted. As the delegates hiked by, near the curb, toward the head of the line, one kid said, "Thank you for coming!" The lead delegate turned and said, in a tone that could not help but be patronizing, "Thank *you!*"

Brigadier General Dunn had told Gregory that he hoped by the time the march reached 18th Street that it could be re-negotiated, but now Dunn told Gregory that re-negotiation was not possible. The Secret Service either did not agree with Dunn's paternalism or Dunn had been dissembling in the first place to gain time, but the General took the "advice" of the Secret Service as if it were orders, and now no one could go past 18th Street, not even to take a walk to Gregory's house. That did not end negotiations, however. The Guard officers and the leaders of the march and the police would now spend a good deal of time talking about arrest proce-dures and how many could be arrested. Everything was ceremonial. Marchers were sitting down on the curb and on the sidewalks. About a block away from 18th Street, I was conscious that I was not seeing anything. For the

first time during Convention Week, the mass of marchers
were out of touch with action, their will given up to
whatever happened at the head of the line. I left my
wife and her McCarthy friends, crossed the street, and
moved to the head of the event.

I was relieved to see that the area between the 16th
Street viaduct and 18th Street was more open than the
trapped area that afternoon. The Standard gas station
between 16th and 18th sold every last Coke, and the line
for its rest rooms was continuous. While the confrontation developed with a rending slowness, the more experienced students were checking out the area, finding
the alleys, the vacant lots, rocks, bottles, useful places
and items, entrances and exits. They also found that
cops waited at the end of most alleys going east and
west. The Guard was under the TV cameras for the nation to see, while the cops were waiting in the dark of
alleys to do their usual job. Parade marshalls admon-
ished demonstrators not to throw rocks, and sometimes
a student would say, "No, man, put that rock down," and
then a few minutes later the speaker himself would be
juggling a rock in his hands. They moved up close, sidled
back and forth, getting ready for the inevitable action
as soon as the negotiation game played itself out.

The corner at 18th and Michigan was jammed with
Guardsmen, demonstrators, a few cops, the delegates
and Dick Gregory and police and Guard officers. The
huge media trucks were parked in the middle of the
street with their lights blazing. The cameramen, with
their cameras on top of the trucks, were wearing helmets. Later, they would also be wearing gas masks. They
were well-prepared. The media's motorcycle messengers
moved in and out of the scene. Jeeps with the barbwire
frames were parked blocking the street, and there was

the armored personnel carrier with the machinegun, unmanned. Huge police vans could be seen on the other
side of the Guard lines, on 18th Street and south of 18th
Street on Michigan. It was the sight of the huge vans
that seemed to promise a more interesting turn to the
evening. People were jammed shoulder to shoulder,
front to back on the sidewalks, under the traffic light on
the west side of Michigan. A white kid had climbed on
top the traffic light, with his legs now wrapped around
it, thus securing for himself a fine view of whatever was
happening over there with the negotiations. The theater
of the week had regressed to quite stiff Ibsen. The traffic
light blinked faithfully over the massed heads throughout the proceedings: red-green-yellow, red-green-yellow,
click-clickety-click, doing its job, click-clickety-click, like
most everyone else.

Oh, those neighborhood blacks on the sidewalks
were wonderfully amused by all that white seriousness.
Some blacks faced the line of Guardsmen near the northwest corner of 18th and Michigan.

"Man, why are you *here?*" one black asked another.

"I like the smell of gas. I come out to smell it."

"But raggedy as I'm sure a lot of thems are," a black
woman was saying to a friend, as if trying to defend
the Guardsmen to a group of younger blacks who were
talking about the Vietnam War. The whole invasion of
white marchers generally well dressed—white soldiers,
white cops, white media-men on white trucks—was a
visitation from another world, seeking a toe-hold in a
new continent of the real, with one cocky Dick Gregory
walking around up front.

A black guy, about the same age as the Guardsmen in
the line, early 20's, stared for a minute or so across three
feet of air into the eyes of a Guardsman. "That's all right,"

he said, finally, "you don't look no worse than the rest of them out there." He got a smile from the Guardsman. Then a sergeant said something, and the line of weekend soldiers stiffened their faces.

The same black guy looked up and down the line and said, "Hard to know you all're in the same army. You all look awfully sloppy." The Guardsmen were, from a parade-ground point of view, a sorry looking bunch of soldiers, as if they had just drawn their fatigues from the supply room the day before and had not yet made the uniforms fit. Nothing was wrong with their discipline, as they had already proved and would further prove before this night was over, but everything about them had the feeling of rust from years ago, particularly their M-1s. I remember drill sergeants who would have screamed in personal agony at the sight of such weapons. It was strange, therefore, that the Guard would be the one to show the step of the future.

Comments came from above, too, where a young black guy had climbed up from the shoulders of a friend and balanced with his heels on the edge of a windowsill, with his arms spread out on the walls. He looked down and chided a Guardsman. "You know that's Mayor Daley's lamppost. Watch it. He might want to piss on it." And on and on went the banter, smooth in tone with sly edges, from the Negroes to the Guardsmen, from the neighborhood life to the invasion of the otherworldly.

There was the unmanned .30 caliber machinegun on the armored personnel carrier, behind the Guard lines on the south side of the intersection. This machinegun stirred up a particular indignation on the part of some of the largely white marchers at 18th Street, an indignation as innocently self-righteous as that of the newsmen who were beaten by the cops. The machineguns that showed up at points of confrontation in Chicago during Convention Week were unmanned and not even armed with ammunition.

In the riots in the black community in Miami during the Republican Convention in the first week of August, 3 blacks were reported killed, more were critically wounded, and over 150 were arrested. There was a lot of gunfire—meant to kill—in Miami between snipers and cops, and Florida National Guardsmen were standing by for action, too. Governor Kirk of Florida said that the insurrection would be put down with "Whatever force was necessary," echoing Governor Richard Hughes of New Jersey and Mayor Daley of Chicago. Yet the Miami Beach Republican Convention of 1968 was ineffective in making a deep impression on the public memory, though it nominated Richard M. Nixon who, because of what was now happening in Chicago, would be elected President in November.

During the April 1968 black insurrection in Chicago, one chill spring evening, I stood on the sidewalk in front of my home and listened to the rapid thunderclaps of a .50 caliber machinegun sounding off along with other gunfire a few blocks away in a ghetto area. The Illinois National Guard, commanded then too by Brigadier General Dunn, was attempting to "contain" that which would live and move and run its course, the April black insurrection. The "paternalistic attitude" that General Dunn insisted on showing during Convention Week seemed to depend on the color of the subject of his efforts. Blacks were shot to death by those machine guns that were used simply to threaten whites. No wonder the blacks met the Guardsmen with sly humor. No

wonder it was a white man's Convention, as if someone
tipped up our history at the beginning and let it slide
into our laps.

Now, at the barricade at 18th Street, Dick Gregory
talked again over the speaker, moving part way alongside the demonstrators on the east sidewalk. Finally, he
told them that after intensive negotiations with General
Dunn, "They ain't going to let you all come to my
house." He said that the General had said that anyone
who attempted to cross 18th Street by crossing the
Guard line would be arrested, so Gregory announced
that anyone who wanted to be arrested should move
forward, and that he wanted to keep the arrests non-
violent. It seemed that most of the marchers wanted to
be arrested: a few thousand. So now there was more
delay, more time run out on the clock, more waiting
stretched out, as the police sent for more of those huge
vans. "We'll walk to jail!" some of the demonstrators
shouted, and beneath the exuberance was a plea, a need
for validation. The demonstrators who wanted to be
arrested were left feeling that they *would* be arrested.

But the experienced students, moving around by the
narrow vacant lot near the corner on the west side of
the street, waited impatiently for the game that would
begin as soon as Gregory and the delegates were arrested
and gone. They constantly checked the alleys at the end
of the narrow lot, and once again picked up rocks and
pieces of board and put them down where they could be
found quickly when needed. A few were talking about
their fear that the Guard would make them sit there all
night long. It made provocation essential. I was certain
that my wife had moved forward to be arrested, and so
I crossed the street and moved north to look for her. I
could not find her or her friends, and I was angry. I

knew by now plenty of the stories of what happened
to the demonstrators and the Yippies when they were
arrested. As it turned out, when the call went out for
those who wanted to be arrested, she left her friends
because they were moving forward to answer the call.
She was weeping, pulled by the responsibility of our
children, as she went north on Michigan. Soon she would
be overtaken by the retreat of demonstrators fleeing
the gas.

Many people began queuing up to be arrested on the
east side of Michigan. In some places on this earth,
people stand in line to buy things. In the United States,
people stand in line to be arrested. That was a possible
comment. And most of the people standing on the sidewalk could buy a few things, if they wished, the things
that make for pleasant surroundings and pleasant things
to do in this nation. They had every reason to expect
that their arrest would be a pleasant experience, too—
a share in strong feeling, comradeship and honor, participation in an event that might make a worthy statement and give some relief from past failures and the
need for future succeesses. They could anticipate uneasily, but without conviction, a beating in a van, sadistic games in a police station, a club in the groin, and
perhaps these thoughts without conviction gave substance to the temptation. They are the eternally surprised of the earth; they make few connections in history
and they understand conspiracy only in melodramatic
terms; and so they give cover to the daily detail of real
conspiracy. "Oh!" says Alice, at every turn in Wonder-
land. That is one way of looking at them. Another is that
their duplicity is so profound and so exact that they see
and feel every personal commitment as something that
it is not. They feel themselves to be righteous innocents,

perhaps helpless, when in fact they are the vanguard or the outriders of the rationalizing force in our history that always, eventually, wins. We will get out of the Vietnam War. We will rebuild the ghettos and the educational system. We will have national health care and perhaps guaranteed incomes. We will have many, many things, if they win. They are the technocrat's Santa Claus, bringing moral gifts, public persuasion and justification for the technocrat's urgent ambition to order the society and its problems on a level as sophisticated as the technology, world-over. We will see. There are yet other ways of looking at these people who stand in line to be arrested. They have begun to walk on the water of history, where the current may have at last become strong enough to be irreversible, sharp turns ahead.

These are hard ways of looking at people. No one, surely, feels this way meeting another person. I am here. I feel comradely. We are looking at ourselves, blown up wildly in the mirrors of an event with incredible future implications. Where and *when*, oh Lord, will the implications of an event have human proportion and human perspective?

Out at the Amphitheatre, where the delegates were supposed to be going about the business of nominating a vice-presidential candidate, the Convention had split into two activities: one side yelling DOWN WITH DALEY and the other yelling WE LOVE MAYOR DALEY. WE LOVE MAYOR DALEY signs bloomed in the gallery, on the floor, and policemen on the streets around the Amphitheatre were seen tacking them to police barricades. Daley's helpers went into bars and gave men $10 to carry WE LOVE MAYOR DALEY signs; and many people who have no love for Mayor

Daley but were curious to see the Convention, took the chance. Daley was put into nomination for Vice-President. The mayor got the vote of Bull O'Connor, one time famous police chief of Birmingham, Alabama. Julian Bond was also nominated for the office. He got votes, until he withdrew his name, noting that even he could not step on history's accelerator to this extent because at 28 he was simply under-age.

The Democrats had shown a movie about Robert F. Kennedy, in memoriam, and the Convention was moved by what some reporters called its one moment of solemn, honest feeling. Many New Leftists, who mistrusted and begrudged McCarthy, supported Bobby Kennedy. When asked why, they gave as their sole and comprehensive reason: "his passion." These New Leftists, who generally prided themselves on their rigor in putting ideas before personality, allowed themselves this pleasant aberration; they had looked into his large, soft eyes and seen new worlds a-coming. Kennedy was probably killed because he did mean certain change, killed at the moment when it became certain that in winning the California primary he could win the Democratic nomination. What kind of change? That's where the New Left's aberration of feeling for him becomes important, in that they are apparently seeking a *patron*, baronial socialization, despite the thought and rhetoric where they say they put their feet. Delegates demonstrated for 18 minutes—who timed it? —after the movie, singing the "Battle Hymn of the Republic" and the California delegation unrolled a huge banner saying WE WILL ALWAYS REMEMBER YOU.

Senator Edmund S. Muskie of Maine was nominated for the vice-presidency; Richard Hughes sec-

onded the nomination; and Mayor Daley, pleased with
all the love around him, asked that Muskie be nominated
by acclamation.

In a TV interview held at the Amphitheatre around
midnight on Wednesday, Daley had told the world—
his remarks were quoted Thursday in Chicago papers—
that the reason for the police actions during Convention
Week was because of intelligence on his desk that assas-
sinations of Vice President Humphrey, Senators Mc-
Carthy and McGovern, and himself had been planned.
If some such information was typed on good paper and
put on the Mayor's desk, he would likely believe it. And
it probably meant that a plainclothesman—who, after
all, must justify his job—may have overheard a Yippie
saying in Lincoln Park, "I'd love to kill those bastards!"
If there were games of the Wars of Flowers, there were
also games of Wars of Information. And if the Mayor
feared assassination—as well he might in 1968—he
would have done well to look to the workings of his
own party, which is becoming more Roman by the day.

At 18th and Michigan, the "assassins" were lining up
to be arrested. On the northwest corner of the intersection, people were afraid that they would not know
the moment when Gregory was arrested on the other
side of the street. Then the kids standing on the first-
floor windowsills began to tell the people below what
was happening. Finally, *at last,* Gregory was arrested,
and all over the crowded intersection men held cameras
at arms' length above their heads, aiming at what they
hoped was the point of arrest, to take a picture of what
they could not see with their eyes. Gregory was guided
to a police van. Then a man in a wheelchair went
through the hole in the Guard line, and he was lifted

by the police, chair and all, into the van. The arrests continued until 79 delegates and notables were removed; then the arrests stopped. It is said that the arrests stopped because there was no more room in the vans. There were several of the huge vans, and one of them looked capable of containing 79 people by itself. The police were noted for packing paddy-wagons with arrested people, and there were other ways to continue the arrests all night long. But imagine what a statement it would be to the world if 3,000 or 4,000 people were arrested that night.

No, there was a more efficient and less visible way to handle the mass of the demonstrators once the notables were safely out of the way. Suddenly the Guardsmen facing us were wearing gas masks, and I whipped out my trusty wet handkerchief, tying it across my face, Lone Ranger style. The crowd rumbled back and forth nervously, but with readiness, and apparently the readiness impressed the Guard officers; they countermanded the order for gas. On the east side of the street, demonstrators who realized that they were not going to be honored with arrest and that they could not "walk to Dick's house"—as they put it—pressed sharply against the Guard line, trying to break through it. They were beaten back by clubbing with rifle butts. Then the mass of marchers, further north of the intersection, were caught by the ripple of awareness that the arrests had stopped, and they surged forward, crying "Take us, too!" Oh, pitiful plea! No, they would not be permitted such an easy exit and entrance to glory. The marchers were assassins in the imaginations of some and cattle to others, and we were going to get an inkling of what we would have to do to begin being human. The ex-McCarthy

workers—refugees from the 15th floor of the Hilton—
were confronted with a theater that was changing,
swiftly, toward educational cruelty.

War Games

The Guard was shifting. Energy everywhere was rising. "They're not going to make me wait here all night,"
a demonstrator said, and picked up a bottle to throw it
at the Guard. A fellow demonstrator grabbed his arm
from behind and stopped him. Demonstrators were
pushing at the Guardsmen and cursing them, in rage
and frustration.

Then the Guardsmen put on their gas masks again.
I looked across the street and saw that one Guardsman,
with the converted flamethrower tanks on his back, was
already hosing gas along the east sidewalk. The cameramen on top of the media trucks were now wearing gas
masks, bless them. But things were not moving fast
enough to suit the demonstrators on the west sidewalk
by the vacant lot. To my eye, the final order for gas on
this side coincided with the shower of rocks, pieces of
board, bottles, firecrackers that these students lofted
upon the Guard. The Guard was already gassing, the
students only made sure that the scale and intensity
would be sufficient for the game. The stubby tear-gas
guns went *pomp, pomp,* and the canisters sailed up
turning end over end in the air, falling among us, spewing out stuff that was the strongest tear-gas I'd yet encountered. Day by day it seemed to get stronger. The
Jiminy Crickets, with the converted flamethrowers,
poured gas into the street. The Guardsmen began moving forward in formation, bayonets on their rifles. The
hardest thing for some liberal minds to understand, at
their distance, is that provocation is a *human* necessity

in the face of the humiliation of being utterly blocked.
What were the demonstrators to do: *Sit there all night,
with no effect?* Bore the media? Bore everyone? Why,
the nation itself is at stake. Personal danger is much to
be preferred. A man without love of country is, as the
politicians observe, nothing. Ask not what you can do
for your country, but what you can make your country
do to you.

Once again The Walker Report, at a trigger point in
the action, behaves oddly: "A group of 100 came from
the west on 18th Street and began pushing the Guards,
who were ordered to push them west into an alley. Objects were being thrown from the rooftops and windows
of buildings. Bottles were thrown at the Guard lines by
demonstrators. Firecrackers were tossed. The glaring
lights of the TV vans heightened the tumult. Marchers
as far back as 14th Street were now in the street, trying
to find out what was happening ahead. The Guardsmen
put on gas masks and CS was hurled into the crowd."
The Walker Report description at this point is a mixture
of a few facts, a few fantasies on somebody's part, an
exaggeration and a misplacement of one small action in
both space and time, and the misplacement of another
action in time sequence, giving a totally false impression. I saw no objects thrown from windows and rooftops. When I first read The Walker Report, I was pretty
sure that the group of 100 coming from the west on
18th Street was a considerable exaggeration of the brief
shower of missiles that came from the narrow lot just
north of 18th Street. Then, in the *Chicago Journalism
Review*, Christopher Chandler, reporter on the *Chicago
Sun-Times*, says the following about The Walker Report
and this incident: "The Report, for instance, talks about
a 'flank attack' from the west by some 100 demonstrators

just before the gassing at 18th Street and Michigan
Thursday night, when in fact, the only people who could
possibly have come from that direction [and this reporter saw no one] would have been reporters using a
telephone in a bar on the southwest corner. But the reports of the bottles which were said to—but did not—
rain from the roofs helped in retrospect to explain the
official action—tear gassing of the demonstrators—and
therefore were judged as accurate. Similar 'explanations'
dot the report, often attributed in a confusing manner."
Chandler also says: "In some ways The Walker Report
provides the most amazing example of dodging the
major issues that has been produced in the long history
of middle-of-the-road committee studies."

Also, I can add that the Guardsmen had already put
on their masks and were gassing by the time the "provocation" occurred. The mis-reporting of objects "being
thrown from windows and rooftops" implies that neighborhood people were involved and would seem to justify
not permitting the march to go past 18th Street into
the deep ghetto. The Task Force that assembled the
information and wrote The Walker Report was composed
largely of businessmen and lawyers, who were very concerned with the implications of "blame" and at the same
time trying to give City and Police Administrations a
chance to re-shape their strategy in dealing with civil
disturbance.

The Guard vehicles, the jeeps with the barbwire
frames and that armored personnel carrier that people
persisted in calling a tank, moved down the street too,
backing up the formation of foot soldiers. At the sight
of the ARMY IN MOTION, the thousands of demonstrators, so many of them new to the game, were hit in
the gut with panic, hit in the eyes and lungs with gas,

and they started running north on Michigan. Tear-gas canisters fell generously among them, puffing here, there, everywhere. I yelled out—and I may have been the first—"Walk, don't run!" Others cried it, too, but it slowed only those near enough to feel the command of the cry, and most of the marchers slipped more and more into panic. Several students, either in a martyr-ready rage or to make sure the Guard kept coming, rushed the advancing soldiers with rocks, boards, bottles, firecrackers, cherry bombs. Others called them off, waving wide and hard, "Back! Back!" Now several people were vigorously and methodically shouting, "Walk, don't run! Walk, don't run!" People did slip and fall, and those coming up from behind stumbled over them. *"Walk, don't run!"* The crowd fear kept jerking out of control: the people were near to trampling each other.

Overhead, a helicopter yammered up and down the length of Michigan Avenue from the Hilton to 18th Street, playing its searchlight on the crowd rushing north and on the alleys. Perhaps the helicopter was radioing information to the Guard and the cops, but mainly it was there to frighten, to intimidate. Everyone in the crowd knew that in Vietnam a machine gun could be working away behind the searchlight. The searchlight played around the 16th Street viaduct and the lots nearby—I was reminded of the telephone directory advertisement, "Let Your Fingers Do the Walking"—and then it shifted and stopped on me on the corner north of the Standard station. I stared up into the Pig's eye, and it shivered round and round, boring at me. I was the only one in the center of the spread of the light on the ground. I raised my fist and shook it at the light, and then it turned into a staring game, who would move first, me or the searchlight. Not me. I kept on shaking

my fist and cursing loud enough that they might actually
be able to hear me. They kept the light on me longer
than usual, and I can imagine the fellow behind the
light, curling his lip at my affront, fingering a trigger
and saying, "Oh, what I could do, buddy boy, oh, yes,
what I could do." It was what he was doing and what
he could do that made me so angry. The nation had
finally found a level where everybody could get their
kicks. He shifted the light away from me, then shifted
it back again briefly, as if taunting me, then away. No
doubt it was because I was dressed in suit and tie, hand-
kerchief-masked face, that his anger was touched when
I shook my fist.

Just north of the 16th Street viaduct, the running
mass of people was getting far ahead of the Guard, and
the more experienced students in the rear raised their
arms. "Stop! Come back! Come back! Keep contact!
Make them drop the gas all the way down the street!"
The signal of the raised arms was compelling for those
near enough to see it and hear their voices. The strung-
out panicked mass stretched—then broke in two. A few
hundred of the people stayed to keep contact with the
Guard, while the main mass farthest down the street
proceeded briskly toward the Hilton. The media trucks
were trying to keep up with the action, staying behind
the Guard. The students gathered themselves, faced the
Guard, walked backwards, and gave the Guard a shower
of rocks and firecrackers. Now that is audacious—taunting an army with firecrackers! The Guard answered duti-
fully by lobbing a shower of tear-gas canisters. Some of
these soldiers, now in gas masks, had answered the demonstrators with the peace sign a few hours before. The
canisters were shot high through the air, and I was
afraid of them hitting someone or myself on the head,

so I kept looking to see where they would fall and calling out. "That's it," the marchers yelled among themselves, "make them drop it all the way down the street
in front of the Hilton!" Drop it in front of the delegates
and the cameras! This was the 6th time that week that
I had been in gas. I had got to the point where, by
forcing my eyes to stay open and watering, with a wet
handkerchief around my head as a mask, I could dance
on the edge of a tear-gas cloud, before it began to disperse widely, and not get a bad dose. These students
also knew how to stay on the edge of a tear-gas cloud,
and people began to take pride in such skills. In a lot
near 16th Street, a tear-gas canister was crawling around
on the ground in that way of tear-gas canisters, as if in
a death agony, and a kid, with an oven glove on his
right hand, leaped and danced around it, picked it up
and turned to throw it back at the Guard. When he saw
that the Guardsmen were wearing gas masks, he threw
the spewing canister down in disgust and walked away
down the street. The skill of these demonstrators in
street action was wonderful, and it gave a warm, good,
confident feeling to see it. They had no gas masks, only
their wits, and they stayed in action right in front of
the Guard all the way.

The Guard was throwing CS gas, gas with a nausea
agent added to it, and it was strong stuff. Some demonstrators—usually well-dressed and inexperienced in confrontation tactics—were doubled up on the sidewalks,
retching and weeping. MCHR medics and doctors were
positioned and moving along the length of the retreat,
with bottles of water, cans of water and most clever of
all, plastic ketchup squirt bottles with water. People
knelt and turned up their agonized faces, and water was
poured or squirted into their eyes. A black minister stood

at one point on the street with a five-gallon can of water, splashing it on the eyes of those kneeling before him. One medic ran and jumped with glee in the street, singing out, as if he were a vendor, "Water makes gas *feel* better! Water makes gas *feel* better!"

Out in the street, the portable speaker was balanced on the head of one fellow, his face smooth of expression the way the face beneath the speaker was always smooth, and the man behind him using the mike exhorted the crowd, "Keep contact! Make 'em shoot the stuff all the way down the street! Make 'em drop the gas right in front of the Hilton!" A fellow set fire to the paper in a large wire trash basket and rolled it toward the advancing Guardsmen, who merely kicked it aside. The cry was relayed down the street, "Keep contact, make 'em drop it in front of the Hilton!" The Guard obediently poured out the gas.

Here was the image of time to come, kicks for everyone: these Guardsmen moving in a march-time ballet, gas masks, helmets, fatigue uniforms, M-1s with bayonets, with no impulsive movements, no individual actions, keeping pressure on the demonstrators, who mirrored the ballet, but not so precisely. The police waited in the alleys for those who preferred individual treatment. The War of Flowers: game confrontations with rules and blood. The one rule that seemed to be accepted by both sides during Convention Week, albeit grudgingly and tenuously, was that there would be no killing of people, no shooting or knifing. As for the Guardsmen, I would have found them more believable if I had been told that they were metallic Martian insects who had to spray this cloud before them so they could live and move on earth. Yet I meet them anywhere in Chicago, in different dress, some of them students, too, some of them part of the pot culture and against the Vietnam War for very personal reasons.

With the enthusiasm of the demonstrators who were leading the Guard to drop the gas in front of the Hilton, the medic who had been singing out "Water makes gas *feel* better!" leaped into the street with another cry, waving his plastic ketchup squirt bottle, "Want so many people irate in this town about Daley, they *do* something!" (Chicagoans in general were irate, all right, so irate they gave the Mayor's slate of candidates in the November election—the Mayor himself was not up for re-election that year—the largest majority that it had enjoyed in several years, Nixon winning Illinois notwithstanding.) The medic, along with his fellows in the street, was quite angry about the last chance for a major march to the Amphitheatre to protest the Democratic Party's betrayal being turned back at 18th Street. He was also expressing a general thought of those in the streets. Provoke repressive action and thereby create a revolutionary reaction. Convention Week itself had demonstrated the half-truth of the idea, but it was naive and borrowed, in the way that the cries of the women in *The Battle of Algiers* and the mannerisms of other revolutions were borrowed—brought gaping out of context from Ché Guevara and the Viet Cong, from the Cuban, the Algerian and the Chinese revolutions. The demonstrators were romancing with this borrowing, in the streets and among the buildings and the machines and the general apparatus of the super-industrial state of the world.

Yet the borrowing, too, fed into the theater events, giving sense of role and validation of feeling. What if Convention Week was a gigantic acting-out on the part of everyone, a giant, screaming, wild blast from the safety valve of the society?—releasing the pressure, re-organizing and opening the structure while keeping it whole, a sort of game kamikaze attack on the Democratic Party, swan song of the first phase of the currents of rebellion that issued from the late Fifties. What if, because the revolt—all those determined to make money as free as the cancer-inciting air that we breathe—was not strong enough for actual power at this point, it made sure that the other alternative of unabashed totalitarianism would not be permitted, that the society out of which the revolution must be born would continue, technocrat style, until such time as the revolution was strong enough to impel its own birth? Then we are at one and the same time making the monster and setting ourselves free, with our bodies, our blood, the wishes of our soul and the strength of our mind. What if, out of the least touched depths of the nation's consciousness, that is what we gave ourselves? Then the games are dynamic, our Wars of Flowers; the end was the beginning, and a confession of strength is in order. In one sense, the revolt won a great victory in Chicago. In another sense, the ground was cut from under it. In the latter sense, it was faced suddenly with the demands of revolution and it withdrew into the patterns of dissent. We are not ready —the spectrum of the American revolt is not ready for any agreed-upon action.

Broad actions that can encompass many different styles and concerns and degrees of risk, yet have a basic purpose, must be developed, embodying the life to come. That is why we do the things that we must do, because we are not yet ready, and the haunted frontier appears and disappears, changes and stays the same under our feet as we go, tempted into the future by material and spiritual promises beyond mention.

South of the Hilton another line of Guardsmen was ranged across Michigan Avenue from Grant Park to the west side of the street, making the demonstrators bound like rabbits into the "liberated area" of the Park in front of the Hilton, hastened by the motion of rifle butts. I stopped in a doorway at the base of the Guard line on the west side of the street. The nearest weekend soldier looked out of his gas mask at me and motioned with his rifle butt for me to keep moving. I looked at his eyes shifting behind the eye-pieces and I did not move. I had had enough. The sweeping line of Guardsmen, walking fast and driving demonstrators before it, now approached. I stared at the soldier on the very end of that line too, and he bumped his rifle butt at me to keep me moving. I did not move, and he, as if embarrassed, stepped in a stammer to the side and went around me, leaving me behind him and behind the Guard line, where the gas was thick—rolling clouds of it. I cut west on a street toward Wabash, thrashing my head in agony and fury, unable to open my eyes. I encountered a group of medics, who tried to tell me what I already knew: "Get your eyes open." The fury of burning seemed to be pulling my eyes back into my head, and I could not get them to open so the medics could pour water in them. I pushed away from them. With my eyes closed beyond my control, I plunged straight down that street. On Wabash, tears began working, my eyes started opening, blinking, washing the gas away. I decided to take another look at the "liberated area," anyway.

I came around the Hilton, east on Balbo, across Michigan, around the Guard line and into Grant Park, where gas drifted through the trees and in the depressions like mist in a Japanese painting, but the feeling was that of a desert where everything barely survived the heat of the day. There was the portable speaker talking to the Hilton, to the Guard, to the bystanders on the sidewalk in front of the hotel. Somewhere people were moaning in a chant, "The whole world is watching." Furious demonstrators were screaming and throwing a thing or two at the Guardsmen, and the Guard stolidly answered with more gas.

On the sidewalks around the Hilton, men who called themselves World War II vets—bless them for their honorable war—were seeking out demonstrators to quarrel with them and find honorable excuse to beat them up. The scene was ritualized. Everybody had learned unspoken lessons, accepted implicit rules, and the great spontaneous actions of the days previous could not be duplicated. I had been on the streets, day and night, for ten days, and I turned around and headed for home, tired in a way that hummed in the bones, empty of feeling but looking forward to waking up in the morning and seeing my son and daughter, who will be a part of the most crucial generation of all in this country. I found myself looking at a light truck with WE LIGHT THE WAY painted on its side.

I drove north and cruised deliberately down Stockton Drive through Lincoln Park. All was quiet and empty, with the puzzlement of something gone in the dark under the trees.

Wednesday August 28. Grant Park. Photo by Fred Schnell.

friday

McCarthy Headquarters Attacked

I did go back to the Hilton late Friday morning, to find that in the dawn hours, the police had invaded the McCarthy headquarters on the 15th floor, ostensibly because McCarthy people were dropping smoked fish, mind you, and other objects on the Guard and the cops in front of the Hilton. Perhaps they were. Guardsmen, cops, and hotel employees say they watched the windows through binoculars and rifle scopes and pin-pointed one suite as the source of the objects. But that was not the only room that the police invaded. They also went into rooms where everyone was asleep. One young McCarthy worker told me he'd been pulled out of his bed by a cop and shoved onto the floor, and, though more asleep than awake, he knew exactly what was required of him, and mumbled, "All right, all right, I'm going, just let me get my bag." So it happened with others, too. Out in the lobby, still dazed, he saw a cop literally break his club in two over the head of a McCarthy worker:

this remarkable climax to Convention Week is also docu-
mented by sources other than my informant, such as
The Walker Report and Chicago newspapers. The Mc-
Carthy people were cursing the cops in high rage and
shoving back at them, the girls screaming and weeping,
as they all refused to let the police get away with it.
They had moved rapidly from electoral dissent, to demonstration dissent, to hitting back. That's a lot of education to have to stomach in a short while. The police were
trying to clear the floor, get the McCarthy people out
of the Hotel and out of town, but then things were
cooled when the Senator himself arrived to give comfort and assurance and to face once again the potential
of his responsibility. He stayed in Chicago while his
personal plane flew back and forth from Chicago and
other points in the nation, taking his workers home.

Some aides who had been with the Senator since New
Hampshire had a different feeling about them in the
way that disaster brings people warmly together. I remember the great river floods in the Ozarks in my boyhood and the warm communal effort to defend against
it and the virtual dissolution of antagonism between
men. The well-schooled coolness and arrogance of the
McCarthy kids was gone. When asked what they were
going to do now, their most common answer was either
that they no longer believed that the "system" could be
made to work and they had to think about what they
were going to do, or simply that they had to take some
time to think about it. I've never heard people speak
with such conviction about thinking about something.
"I am not quite ready to join SDS," said a girl who'd
worked as a press coordinator, "but that is all I see."
The fact that their candidate was clearly the popular
choice shoved them hard to the Left. "He could beat

Nixon, and Humphrey can't." They were saying that on Friday, too. They seemed to see the Democratic Party committing suicide simply to spite them.

On the sidewalk on Balbo I saw Stephen Mitchell, McCarthy's campaign manager and formerly manager for Adlai Stevenson's presidential campaigns, walking as if his brain were removed from behind his eyes, and answering questions with barely a shrug. He was supposed to have lost some years ago to Mayor Daley in a power struggle in the Democratic Party in Illinois, and it was said that he had no little motive of revenge in becoming McCarthy's campaign manager. In addition, Daley's—the City's and the cops'—general rage must have been further fired when McCarthy crossed the lines and spoke to the demonstrators, with all its implications. The cops, I repeat again, were slashing the tires on cars with McCarthy stickers in Lincoln Park and arresting kids passing out McCarthy literature. Convention Week gave impetus to the politicalization of the police, too, a nation-wide impetus, in which they, or those who control them, with their general apparatus and much expanded "intelligence" departments, could bring unexpected arm-twisting to bear upon public figures who displease them. Political polarization is dizzying with its promises of shoot-outs at every old corral. The police did not need much excuse to make the Friday morning raid on McCarthy's headquarters.

But during the day on Friday there was a cleansed and easy feeling among the McCarthy workers and the demonstrators who moseyed about the Hotel and the sidewalks.

The day was clear, mild and exhilarating.

Thursday August 29. South Michigan Avenue near 16th Street. Photo by Bill Hood.

in the months afterward

When the Game Changes

On Saturday the overt danger from the cops was gone, and the certainty, the exhilarated Us or Them feeling, went with it. Let's tell the story backwards. No one was killed during Convention Week itself. The cops expressed themselves freely with their clubs, their Mace, their gas, but they apparently had orders to shoot only in the air to scare, unless they had to shoot to save their own lives. They showed the quality of their discipline by doing almost exactly that.

Jimmy Breslin said, in his article "Police Riot," in *New York* magazine, "So these pigs in police uniforms punched and gassed and clubbed and I still don't know why they didn't shoot. Certainly, they wanted to. They were beside themselves." Yet, if we re-live any of the street confrontations and let ourselves stand in the middle of the raging energy while reflecting upon it, it becomes a remarkable point for study: no one was killed. Despite the extent of the violence through the streets and parks of the City, despite the fact that the confrontations continued for five days and nights—from Sunday afternoon to Friday morning, involving thousands of people: no one was killed. If we consider the hundreds of cracked skulls and wounds from other kinds of violence over the 5 days of action, it is nearly a miracle that not only did the cops not shoot to kill, but that not once did a cop in utter rage club a demonstrator to death, though one came close to doing it with the seminary student by the barricade in Lincoln Park Monday night. It is almost as wonderful that a demonstrator did not in some way kill a cop. Apparently the opponents knew each other subtly well. Apparently rules were present and emerging in everybody's actions, though no one knew for sure if the rules would hold from second to second, a fear that upheld the action with terrific suspense every day of the week. Anyone severely hit on the head during Convention Week will at this point say, with a tone of rectitude, that we are generalizing in the abstract. But listen to the casualty lists of black riots/insurrections: 11 killed, hundreds wounded; 43 killed, hundreds wounded; 23 killed, hundreds wounded; etcetera. And wounded here means, more than not, gunshot wounded.

A few days after Convention Week, I was sitting at a table in a Lincoln Park bar with a couple of fellows who were discussing Chicago's most compelling topic, when suddenly one of them realized that *no one had been killed;* he was shaking in the face and shifting his eyes down as he said hastily, "I bet if you checked out all the hospitals and injuries you'd find people who died." It was as if he would lose all historical validity, all honor, if no one had been killed. Perhaps there is more cohesion, more agreement, more rules concerning estimations

of one another throughout white America than anyone
would have supposed. May we expect game confrontations, with rules, with blood, with satisfaction, with perhaps even sacrificial killing and martyred mournings—
for what purpose, now and in the future?

A couple of months after Convention Week a cop shot
to death a 14 year old black boy, while the boy was
burglarizing a house supposedly, a few blocks from my
home. The boy threatened the cop with a butcher knife
and the cop shot him, that's the way it was reported.
Another report is that the cop ran out of his squad car,
down the gangway between houses, and, without a moment's hesitation, started shooting. There were other reports that the boy, mortally wounded, tried to crawl
back up the steps into the house while the cop simply
watched, watched the boy die. There is no way of knowing with these reports what actually happened. The
point is, whether the boy attacked the cop with a
butcher knife or the cop shot the boy immediately on
sight, or whether it was a personal vendetta, there were
no barriers, no limitations, no family restraint. On Thursday of the week before the Convention, Dean Johnson,
American Indian, hippie, was shot to death in Old Town
by police, and even his friends, as reported in the *Ramparts Wallposter*, say that when the cops asked to see
what he was carrying in his bag he pulled out a gun.
The black boy and the Indian. That is one thing that
the two incidents have in common. If the reports are
correct, both the Indian and the black pulled a weapon.
That is another thing that the two incidents may share.
But yet another thing that they share is that the black
boy and the Indian boy acted *individually*, out of fear,
anger or hatred, but they either gave or became individual targets for the cops. I remember the red-faced

cops, with guns extended, screaming at the corner of Eugenie and LaSalle, "Give us a target!" The demonstrators and hippies during Convention Week acted in common, and forced the cops to act in common too.

It was the kids who drew the cops into the game, the War of Flowers, modern American style. It was the kids, who in their wonderful and perverse sense for the American future, and for the satisfactions of now, forced the police, the City, and the Federal agencies, to play a most important, most delicate, most intricate, most dangerous game, the game of confrontation. In these confrontations, the black kids were treated as the other kids so long as they were involved in common with the larger number of whites. When the black kids were caught alone, in the alleys of Old Town, or in a melée, the cops beat them as blacks. It was because the cops understood the game too well that they raged so hard, though one must give them credit for intense enjoyment, on occasion, of their work. But it was because the cops and kids were mostly white that both accepted the rules, knew each other the way I knew the National Guard Corporal and Private, virtually beyond their personal power of deciding whether they would accept or not, and with extraordinary skirting of ultimate intentions, ended up with no one killed.

Right at this moment the Vietnam War is forcing such a realization onto the United States Government. The rules change with escalation, but from the inside, from the outside, the game will win. There is more love in it than one might think.

In the confusion after Convention Week, the cops became remarkably courteous for a while, at least to certain definable groups of whites, though they busted hippies hard as ever and were unchanged toward blacks and Puerto Ricans. The Chicago police had shown a pattern of action, quite visible by now, and that was that they are violently repressive one time, and then beautifully restrained the next time, the test time. Many months later, however, it seemed that every time in white peace-marching Chicago had become the test time due to the impact and repercussions of the tremendous publicity about Convention Week events, and the fact, made evident by Humphrey himself, that the national Democratic Party could hardly be expected to look kindly on Mayor Daley for its defeat in November.

Convention Week had acted as a powerful conversion ritual for most of the direct participants. Indeed, that week may have been the most vital current that ever hit white liberal Chicago. In their confusion and bitter uncertainty after the Convention, many Chicagoans who thought that specific group feeling should be upheld and immediate group action taken against the Mayor and the City, discovered finally that the important thing that had happened was to themselves, to their own consciousness. They then went out to create new things: newspapers such as the *Chicago Journalism Review* and *World War III;* electoral reform organizations such as the Independent Precinct Organization and others; film groups, theater groups and town meetings cropped up fast. For the first time in many years, serious challenges by liberal (Adlai Stevenson wing) Democrats were made in the early spring of 1969 aldermanic elections, with the Daley machine, which seemed to win so well in November 1968, taking a few novel defeats.

Peace and protest marches swelled hugely in number. On September 28—one month after the Balbo-Michigan "massacre"—the largest protest march in Chicago history up to that time took place, going down Michigan Avenue to Grant Park, past the place where the demonstrators had massed opposite the Hilton and where now the beaten ground was stripped and there were piles of new sod for laying. The purpose of the march as given, was to re-assert the right of demonstration, assembly, dissent. The march had a permit. It was a huge march— estimates vary from 15,000 participants to 45,000, and the police say 10,000: You speak whatever figure supports your position.* The march was most peaceable, and the police, in some cases, guided it in good humor, though not without a mocking tone. At one corner on Michigan Avenue, a group of bystanders was watching a football game on one TV set and a baseball game on the other, both in the same store window, with their backs to the march; they hardly looked over their shoulders at the march going by for a long time in the street. A helicopter pounded along the air above the march, from the Hilton to Randolph Street, back and forth, back and forth, and every time it turned near the Public Library at Randolph and Michigan, a great flock of pigeons lifted and swirled above the silence of the

* The Peace March held on April 5, 1969—which was much larger than the September march—was initially headlined in Chicago papers as having 10,000 participants; but this figure was so ridiculous—since the march reached the Coliseum before its last group was stepping off back at State and Wacker Drive some 5 miles away—that the newspapers were laughed into revising the figure on their front pages up to 20,000 which means that between 30,000 to 50,000 might be more accurate, since no newspaper would like to admit that it was that susceptible to either error or bias. Why didn't someone take aerial photographs of the whole extent and time of the march and mark it off in a grid and count heads per square, if numbers were that important? The march was *big*.

marchers. The huge mechanical street-sweepers grumbled along behind the march, wiping out every last sign of its occurrence. South of the Logan statue in Grant Park, the marchers massed to hear speeches, wearisome peace-rally speeches; but the marchers were mainly listening to each other and feeling very good because their numbers were great.

Both the Protest March in September and the Peace March the following April were unattended by police attack. Both marches gained front-page headlines, affirmed the restraining power of publicity, but they didn't re-assert any right or liberty whatsoever. They simply made clear the general strategy of the administrators of repressive forces—to keep people off-balance, and to keep their personal commitment in a never-never land so that resistance does not become clear and strong. Constant, general repressive measures might excite revolutionary political response. The objective of control is more efficiently achieved by occupying people's time and energy in swings between fear and assurance, certainty and uncertainty. Among blacks and Puerto Ricans the police may have even sharpened their punitive attacks, with shootings happening frequently. If strong publicity were given to these actions, it might again act as a restraint.

Long-term indignation over specific incidents is channeled into the courts, into wearing litigation, where likely the police and the City do not much care what happens in most individual cases. They had figured in the first place that a club on the head was more effective for handling protestors and the general public than a $50 misdemeanor fine, so they did not arrest the thousands they might have arrested if they were employing different tactics. Six hundred and sixty eight persons were arrested during Convention Week. That the lesson under the club would go in the direction of further entrenchment and widening of the revolt was something the City did not anticipate. The police and the City care mainly that the cops retain their liberty to act in the streets in a flexible way, being restrained with some and ruthless with others, in direct proportion to the subject's ability to bring down adverse publicity upon the heads of those superior City and police officials whose orders are the reason for the cops' action. When a case reaches the court, conviction is sought earnestly, and everyone is invited to join in the general sluggish hypocrisy of guilty pleas. The judges—most of whom tend to be failed politicians—are steeped in the desires of other politicians. Political appointment is how they got there in the first place.

Judges also often depart from their judicial functions to indulge in lecturing on what is acceptable dissent. One afternoon in late October, I saw one magistrate at the Criminal Courts Building lecture a young man who had been arrested in Lincoln Park for "disorderly conduct" during Convention Week. The young man had chosen to plead guilty and so made life easier for everyone. Apparently the magistrate felt he would not necessarily continue to be so easy-going. Acceptable dissent for the magistrate was "voting" and "writing to your Congressman." The young man took it with his own kind of smile, then paid his fine and walked out of the courtroom still smiling and catching the knowing glances of a great many people in the courtroom.

The September 28, 1968 march and the April 5, 1969 march in Chicago showed that more people than ever before in the City thought there was more reason than ever before to make a simple statement. White liberal

Chicago was, finally, galvanized by the actions of Convention Week and the repercussions. They came out to protect themselves, giving the impression of power that might be able to hold the "threat" accountable and in abeyance.

In December 1968, it was rumored that the Federal Grand Jury, which had been convened to hear testimony on Convention Week cases, would soon return indictments against several demonstration "leaders" and several cops. Then, through January and February 1969, the Grand Jury appeared to vacillate; it was even rumored that it would not return any indictments because the "evidence," gained supposedly through wiretapping, would endanger our relationships with certain —never named—foreign powers. And the implication was that since the evidence was gained by wire-tapping it could not be used in prosecuting the "leaders." (The *Chicago Sun-Times* commented in a brief, sharp editorial that if this were a way of covering up the fact that there was no real evidence against the demonstrators, then the attempts at indictment should be dismissed.) The vacillation of the United States District Attorney's Office and the Grand Jury must have reflected the pulse of the Nixon Administration as it tried to decide its stance toward civil rebellion. (Truly, President Nixon might feel a secret generosity toward the "leaders" of the action in the streets and parks of Chicago during the Democratic National Convention, which, sent by the media into every home in America, provided the stigma, the confusion and the guilt among Democratic voters that Humphrey could not overcome fast enough to beat Nixon in November.) The U.S. District Attorney's office may have set up the cover of "wire-tapping" as a way out of bringing indictments. And what happened when Mayor Daley heard that the Federal Grand Jury might not return indictments? Did he, in the desperation of throwing his weakening weight around, demand that the indictments at least be brought, whether the demonstrators were finally imprisoned or not, and that the concept of a "riot" fomented by conspiracy of outside agitators be affirmed in a large sector of the public mind? After all, the Mayor was in mighty need of justification in Chicago and in the national Democratic Party, which blamed him for its November defeat.

In March 1969, eight demonstration "leaders"—Rennie Davis, David Dellinger, Tom Hayden, Abbie Hoffman, Jerry Rubin, Lee Weiner, John Froines and Bobby Seale—were indicted by the Federal Grand Jury for crossing state lines to incite to riot and to resist and obstruct policemen—an indictment made under a provision attached to the Civil Rights Act of 1964. At the same time, eight cops were indicted—seven "for depriving civilians of their civil rights by assaulting them," and one for perjury in denying before the Grand Jury that he had struck demonstrators. *Eight* cops. Five of these cops were indicted specifically for hitting newsmen; and three of them for beating John Linstead of the *Chicago Daily News* on Monday night, August 26, 1968 in a much publicized incident. (These three policemen were found not guilty in June, 1969, and one is made wary about the thinking that went into the making of these indictments of policemen in the first place.)

All sixteen of these men—demonstrators and cops— are scapegoats, pounds of flesh, and their indictments are both appeasements for one area of power or another and threats toward others. But a number of Americans feel such equality—eight of there'n and eight of our'n—

is only fair, scapegoats being better than no goats at all, blood always being thicker than water. No doubt many Chicago citizens also feel that eight good cops—and they must be good or they wouldn't be indicted for their aggressiveness—were a plenty big sacrifice to balance and justify the harassment and possible elimination by imprisonment of the demonstration "leaders." In addition, the cops are being asked to take the rap for their superiors and for the City Administration:* namely,

* Not only were white liberal Chicagoans galvanized by the impact of Convention Week, not only did the liberal political and artistic people create new organizations and publications, but tremendous, actively expressed disaffection occurred among rank-and-file policemen, too, because they had to take the "heat" for what happened in the streets. The Confederation of Patrolmen (C.O.P.) took up the cause of the cop in the street, organizing legal defense funds, lobbying activities, and what it calls "living, working benefits," helping meet the general needs of policemen and their families. In April 1969, the *C.O.P. Newsletter* states: "A recent audit of C.O.P. membership records indicates that we are now within the proverbial 'stone's throw' of our goal. Achieving what no organization, in the history of the Chicago Police Department, has been able to accomplish. An actual 50% membership of working Chicago policemen. One out of every two patrolmen is a dues-paying member of C.O.P. 65% of our organization is under 30 years of age. Clearly, the handwriting is on the wall." They are concerned about implementing a "uniform level of professionalism for all law enforcement agencies." They expect 75% of working Chicago policemen to be members of C.O.P. by the end of 1969. They seem to imply that their organization is not entirely welcomed by the higher ranking police department officials. In their newsletter, they say: "We were assured after the last printing of the inter-department phone directory, that the name of our organization was omitted in error. We had applied for the listing SIX MONTHS IN ADVANCE. We recently learned that through an OVERSIGHT, we are going to be omitted once more. Put C.O.P. Box 45431 Phones 666-9188 and 478-5008 in the phone book. This will correct the "OVERSIGHT."

Mayor Daley. One can contemplate the police anger, and look to police revolts, police coups and police juntas in our cities. Such revenge must be a police fantasy, anyway.

But what really tickles one's sense of the desperately absurd is the idea that these demonstration "leaders" had anything to do with leading, inciting, or helping to happen in any way the revelations of Convention Week. The Mayor's Office and the Corporation Counsel's Office of the City of Chicago and the U.S. District Attorney's Office do not find it useful to understand publicly that there was an extreme division among the demonstrators —with the stay-cool, stay-clean "leaders" of traditional demonstration tactics on one side, and the very young,

---

C.O.P. regards the work of the police Internal Investigation Department and the suspensions of policemen that have resulted because of Convention Week, without trial or conviction in the courts, as an unjust way of proceeding. *C.O.P. Newsletter* says in an article entitled *Inquisition Ended??*: "We were truly disappointed with the TOTAL investigations. We knew in advance that our Chicago Patrolmen would take the heat, as they always have. Traditionally, we don't pass the heat up in the ranks. However the men WERE given DIRECT ORDERS in regard to the name tags and stars . . . Further, they were GUARANTEED that NO MAN would be SUSPENDED for any action taken at the time of the riots. We are greatly disappointed that NONE of the men who gave the orders, on those nights of trouble, stepped forward to defend the patrolmen WHO ARE NOW PROTECTING THEM. We are proud of these stand-up patrolmen. At the same time, we are sorely disappointed in the capons who permitted this injustice to occur. These suspensions are damn poor pay, for services rendered." These organized patrolmen also complain of being regarded by higher-ups as "second-class citizens," who are guilty until proven innocent and punished without trial.

Here is the advice in C.O.P. Newsletter (April 1969) of the President of Confederation of Patrolmen to the working police of Chicago: "It seems there are people, within the de-

generally inexperienced "catalytic" persons on the other. This division occurred every day and night of Convention Week. The Federal Government could not let itself appear as a bumbling bully. It was the mass-media concentration on such men as Jerry Rubin, Abbie Hoffman and Tom Hayden, over months and even years prior to the Democratic Convention, that made them worthy targets for Federal indictment and plausible agents of the devil in the public mind. But members of the Federal Grand Jury—Judge William Campbell presiding, and U.S. Attorney Thomas A. Foran prosecuting—were apparently not unaware of their dilemma, in that they

---

partment, who are bent on the destruction of our morale and unity. Recent directives and suspensions have created turmoil and anger from the men. Now it has become necessary to let the Mayor know of the unrest within the police department. Our advice to you regarding future incidents and/or riots as follows:

"1. Don't believe ANY oral guarantee, that there will not be diciplinary (sic) measures taken against you.
 2. Do believe that there will be, if you are so much as one inch out of line.
 3. Don't get involved in any emotional appeals from anyone up high.
 4. Don't believe that you can feed your family on 'lip service' or the good intentions of the people.
 5. You only have one duty, TAKE CARE OF NUMBER ONE and think of your family first.
 6. Obey orders when given to you but know WHO gave the order.
 7. Do act in a professional manner at all times, NO MATTER THE SITUATION.
 8. THINK . . . before you act.
 9. ACT prudently and cautiously and remember that you're on 'CANDID CAMERA.'
10. It is strongly suggested that patrolmen keep accurate notes of 'Controversial' orders, such as date, time and content. Just in case you are suspended or indicted, you will be able to refresh your memory."

knew they could not give credit for any event in the streets and parks during Convention Week to these "leaders." And so they strained and came up with indictments on other counts:

First: that Dellinger, Hayden, Davis, Hoffman and Rubin conspired *before* the Convention to "encourage people to come to Chicago to participate in massive demonstrations during Convention Week." The plain truth is that when Sunday came at the beginning of Convention Week, all eight of these leaders were failures because everything that they planned, hoped for, and visualized *failed* to happen. In many cases, they were actually discredited for "obeying the law and playing the Pig's game" in the eyes of many of the young people who, in spontaneous response in mass situations, freed from the traditional structures of demonstrations, took over the "leadership." Let us tease the thought that the real reason the Grand Jury brought forth these indictments was in the hope that they would, through the massive publicity the court cases promise, restore these eight good men to positions of control, so that future demonstrations will be more peaceable, with honor for everyone, unlike Convention Week where men lost their honor and knew it and raged against it. "I accept, I accept, I accept," Jerry Rubin is quoted as shouting with joyous irony in response to news of his indictment: "This is the greatest honor of my life. It is with sincere humility that I accept this Federal indictment." It must have been doubly humiliating, and therefore doubly joyous and ironical to these "leaders" to be indicted for something that they were unable to do—they were unable to attract great numbers of demonstrators and hippies to Chicago. As for Bobby Seale, Black Panther National Chairman, he was in Chicago for only a short time,

and spoke in Lincoln Park and Grant Park, saying nothing that was not already being said by the kids in the
Park. Seale was indicted simply because of his position
in the Panther Party.

Second: the first five men, along with John R. Froines,
an Assistant Professor of Chemistry at the University
of Oregon, were indicted under provisions of the same
attachment to the Civil Rights Act of 1964, for con-
ducting self-defense training sessions in Lincoln Park
for Mobe parade marshalls; for training them "in techniques of resisting and obstructing police action, including karate, Japanese snake dancing, methods of freeing
persons being arrested and counterkicks to knee and
groin." I have already described the self-defense training of the parade marshalls on the baseball diamond in
Lincoln Park in the week before the Convention. It was
training in simple defensive tactics: how to deflect a
club, how to use a rolled-up magazine, how to kick a
man in the groin if he will stand still long enough for
you to do it, etcetera. For the most part, it was a charade
for TV, and a charade to lift the mental outlook of the
marchers, to put-on the City and maybe give confidence
to the marchers. The marshalls were supposed to be
trained in a few short training-sessions in a few days to
use these tactics for self-defense *and* then turn around
and magically train all marchers in parades to use them,
too. Absurd. Hardly any of that training was ever used:
it went up for grabs, except for the first-aid training, as
did all the plans. In any case, the current of Convention
Week took such a sharp turn that all of that training
became irrelevant.

The real genius of these "leaders" was in their ability to stage a seeming event, with the posture, the

symbol, the gesture that would keep reverberating and reflecting crazily in the funny-house of the media and the public mind. They did it pretty much as Abbie Hoffman suggested—in a July issue of *The Realist*—that they would do it; but the Mayor's Office was not smart enough to read or take seriously Hoffman's article. If you feed an image into the media—that of lowly long-haired demonstrators training themselves to kick cops in the groin—you are guaranteed strong and contradictory emotional responses from all sides. Once the image is let loose in the media, it gets a life of its own by feeding itself on everybody's responses and growing bigger and bigger. So you get two lean, hard-muscled black guys, for example, to stand before the flabby white demonstrators and show off some rather startling karate tactics. The black guys are well-trained, they yell and leap dramatically, they look good, and they give a vivid image for the screen in everybody's living room. Such an image—two skilled *black* guys training *war protestors* in exotic deadly *karate*—excites strong feelings of fear and excitement for viewers in the living room. But the image of the pale, flabby, unathletic marshalls wobbling as they try to balance on one foot, falling over, sweating, panting, etcetera, is not so satisfying because it allows for the safe feeling of ridicule and boredom and is therefore not guaranteed to fascinate an audience. No fascinated audience, no sponsor. The Walker Report gives the picture of the two black guys doing some startling karate on the baseball diamond in Lincoln Park without saying that they were trainers and were the only two men in the park so capable, barring perhaps a couple of plainclothesmen. Many white middle-class viewers spilled their seed extravagantly before these

images, and made up their minds to act as stupidly as
possible, and then they got hit on the head by the action
of the cops.

The root revelation of Convention Week was that our
ancient spirit—always naked, though covered, some
millions of years old—is, when freed of the structures
that hide and re-direct it, immensely trustworthy, imaginative, quick, cooperative and individual at once, and
capable of developing awesome group energy when the
needs of the urgent moment are confronted and the dy-
namics of the "hunt" begin. Yet it seems that the re-
surgence of this full and quick awareness, with all its
social and individual radiance, requires the immediate
focus of the Beast out there around us—the Beast that
gave us both food and danger of the chase and danger
of attack for a couple of million years. The fact that the
Federal Grand Jury indictments have only an arbitrarily
conceived relationship to the reality of what happened
during Convention Week, and that no indictments have
been returned against those who decided to block all
aspirations of the dissenters in the streets, means the indictments are levelled against this very body and soul
of humankind.

The general revolt in America is growing fast, but its
strength, once confessed, is not to be measured only in
the rapidly increasing numbers of its activists, but in the
breadth and depth of sympathy and tolerance for it in
certain areas of American life—the communications
area, for instance. The Federal indictments point to the
growth of a certain strategy of repression, which may
be able to divide and drain this sympathy which has
given breathing time and latitude for the rebels. The
strategy: indict a few, kill a few, imprison a few, club
some more, expel others, take candy in the form of schol-

arship support out of the mouths of yet others, jail a
few, suspend a few from their schools, fine a few, exhaust a few supposed principals in endless litigation,
perhaps put others in detention camps—but the more
arbitrary and sometimes the less institutionalized the
action, the better. Add to this the mass infiltration of
student movements by provocateurs who are there to
report, to finger, to disrupt, to take over, and the worst
thing that can happen to a revolutionary group is to have
its daring and its common sense usurped by infiltrators
and provocateurs. That's the wisdom of arbitrary repression. You try to break up unity by letting most participants go free and unharmed, and then co-opt and at
least partly satisfy the issues that made them take risks
in the first place. You might compare this type of repression to Janowitz' tactical concept of "selective response"
in his essay on *Social Control of Escalated Riots*. Mass
repression, differing from "arbitrary" repression, could
turn whole areas of the country into Lincoln Park.

Convention Week was a fruition, swan song, end in
beginnings, coming together of the streams of rebellion
that sprang forth separately in the Fifties. Sunday,
Monday, Tuesday in Lincoln Park a few thousand Americans shook off old skins that divide one kind of consciousness from another, and came out acting, with their
whole minds, spirit and body, in images that made a
great many connections at once. They made actions that
were living metaphors throwing light in all directions,
beacons and signals in a code for awakened eyes to see.

The American question—such as the Czechs asking
the Russians "Why are you here?"—is not yet found.
But the answer is in the power of the ancient movement
of response that upheld and carried these Americans as
they stormed the ramparts of paradise, in memory of the

Eden that pulses in the fingertips of every man and
woman. They gained a foothold, a heady glimpse of the
Time To Come. They fell away. But they bore the
glimpse as a touchstone for all that they then went
forth to do.

Postscript

I had spent about two weeks, day and night, awake
and asleep, in a burning dry clarity of mind and feeling.
It would not go away. Toward mid-November, I succumbed to the urgings of friends and my fears that what
I'd seen might be lost, and talked with a Walker Report
investigator. In December, when the Report was published, I found that the writers had done exactly what I
had feared they would do—winnowed out all the terrible
dignity of human motive and decision. I consider it a
prize worth winning that I once again learned the lesson
that you keep alive by staying in relatively frequent contact with the enemy.

I was ready, in that clear dry fury of Convention
Week, to refuse any cliff-hanging Federal, state, city or
foundation financial support for Story Workshop programs, since such support seemed imminent. About
three years before, I had originated in great excitement a wholly new way of teaching writing: by personal discovery in a group situation, called Story Workshop—a flexible, always-developing method with an
arsenal of verbal and perceptual word, telling, reading
and writing exercises of increasing demand. By the time
of Convention Week, the Story Workshop method, being
used now by several directors who had worked with me,
had effected an impressive array of "miracles" in educational situations—in adult and college workshops, in
Freshman English workshops, in workshops for drop-

outs from the public-school system, and in many other situations, both inside and outside the established institutions. The method is flexible for each director and each workshop. The wonderful book-magazine f^1 came out of the Story Workshops. The beauty and downright revelatory excitement that happened in these workshops made me know again and again that the revolution of consciousness is process, in which people move in ways both sudden and slow. Convention Week had awakened in me the old romantic necessity for a continuous, apocalyptic front-line of revolt, or lines drawn as the cops drew the lines. I came out of my anger seeing that the front-line is consciousness growing and defended from wherever it is sparked, in situations at once material and spiritual. The enemy is everywhere, within and without ourselves, and we fight him and submit to him, become part of him and disengage ourselves, every day. This is the way that we stay alive and set ourselves free and set free people and things connected with him.

The mind of the revolt is always in danger of succumbing to the burning comfort of being smothered by its "authentic" clichés. It can lobotomize itself with the rhetoric of issues that may themselves be only in part true. It can organize activities that seem impressive, only to be hit by the truth of the story about the seed that fell on the thin soil on rocks, which grew suddenly because of the heat in the rocks and wilted suddenly because there was nothing to sustain it. The revolution of consciousness is process, profoundly accepting of need and demand. Trotsky said somewhere in his book *My Life* that a revolutionary movement must constantly seek into the nature and origin of human beings, and compare and change revolutionary thought and intentions and issues, according to what it finds out about human nature. It was the way the kids acted in the streets that was far more revealing than the issue of the streets belonging to people.

I remember telling one New Left intellectual of some renown that most Americans, in their manipulative attitudes about imagination and perception and about the very body of life itself, no matter if their politics are right, left, or center, suffer from the same dread disease: manipulative lunacy. He said with a shrug, "Well, we all come out of the same culture," as if, for that reason, it deserved no further examination. His attitude seemed to suggest that a revolution now would be a palace-coup of a small area of the mind, out of which we could only hope that a disengagement from imperialistic postures and a re-distribution of wealth would make the unleashing of the Multiple and Social Oneness of body and mind and spirit imperative. It is the basic cultural revolution, the revolution of imagination and perception, of consciousness of human wholeness, of self and sex and fellows, that will be long and labyrinthine, with many masks and diversions, because it is real, because it is lasting, because it alone is capable of containing and supporting all that is necessary. There I find myself.

afterword

The "Before and After Marker of Your Life,"
or Notes to Young Writers

Up to 1968 I had published a few nonfiction stories without even thinking of them as participant-observer journalism. I had been mainly a fiction writer and originator of the Story Workshop method of teaching writing in which there is a strong emphasis upon seeing and telling events, imaginative and otherwise, with audience in mind and the storyteller aware of his or her tendencies to withhold and distort perception and feeling. Then, in April of 1968, on the night after Martin Luther King Jr.'s "sojourn on earth went blank" in Memphis (Taylor Branch, *At Canaan's Edge*), I stood on the sidewalk outside our apartment on Mohawk Street in Lincoln Park and listened to the bamety-bam-bam sounds of a machine gun twelve to fifteen blocks south of us in the Cabrini Green housing area where a good deal of violent African American response to King's assassination, includ-

Thanks to Dean Blobaum and Maggie Hivnor, for their encouragement and helpful suggestions.

301

ing sniper fire, occurred. I had crawled under machine gun fire in basic training and heard machine guns elsewhere in the Army. When you asked National Guard and city officials, they denied that any such weaponry was used. It sounded as if they did not wish to admit that for one night—and one week—they had effectively put the city of Chicago onto a war footing against a large percentage of its African American population, 80 percent of whose registered voters had voted for the mayor and made his victories possible, with small reward to them. This discrepancy between my perception and official and mainstream journalism assertions about the riots in which eleven were killed, hundreds injured, and block upon block of buildings burned lent force to my sense of vital stories developing in our country that weren't being told. By July, I was certain that such events were coming to Chicago with the Democratic convention. I called my editor, Fred Jordan, at Grove Press and Evergreen Review and asked for press credentials to go to work on this story.

The point was to bring the reader into the moment of story. Readers have said that the dialogue in *No One Was Killed* and in *The Chicago Conspiracy Trial* feels "novelistic," sometimes indicating they thought I had made it up. Not so. Every line was spoken, either directly reproduced, or pared carefully out of recorded speech in notes or transcripts, with an eye and ear to making sure the resulting exchange stayed "true" to the original in its dramatic context as I noted or remembered it. I would try to take into account my own biases without eliminating my—or anyone else's—feelings, and without trying to simplify or turn away from ambiguities.

Besieged by protest within and without, and ripped apart along the political divisions in the party and in the country, the Democratic National Convention of 1968—DemCon, as it was called in thousands of pages of intelligence documents that I have since reviewed—is one of the least understood of American political events. David Halberstam, author of *The Best and the Brightest*, called it "the central moment of the sixties," the climax of a period that saw rapid change in American life and institutions. Gloria Steinem, then a journalist traveling with the McCarthy campaign, called the DNC of 1968 "the before and after marker of your life." Don Rose, Democratic political strategist and press secretary of the National Mobilization to End the War in Vietnam, said "the convention of 68 totally transformed the Democratic Party." Democrats across the spectrum of the party have told me the same. The DNC of 1968 was the only event of the sixties to bring into one arena most players, aspects, and issues of American political life in a drama that shaped the 1968 election and reshaped the Democratic and Republican parties and American politics for years to come.

All of this called for different techniques and protocols. If, as a writer, you did not see and sense the subjective force in such events—or any newsworthy events, for that matter—and tell them so the reader could see them, you were in imminent danger of having your audience fill in your words with a kind of stereotyped imagery as a substitute for what you did not provide. Looking back, this was a fairly remarkable presumption, but the air was charged with permission to do things different—in the rubric of the times to "tell it like it is." Describe, organize, and interpret events so that we both, the storyteller and you the reader, can, if we are lucky, see and feel and evaluate them, too.

The idea was to do a better job with fact. Hemingway said that to get to the truth of what happened—truth as he understood it was important to him—you had to pay attention to the sequence of motion and feeling. Henry Adams cautioned that the writer who "cares for his truths is certain to falsify his facts." These two admonitions go hand in hand in the process of witness/participant storytelling.

Often the accounts of events that were presented in the pages of newspapers and magazines had little to do with actual events, particularly those that had to do with social protest and the reaction of authorities. Such journalism—and the history developed from it—falsified the sequence of events, added "facts" and played facts up and down to suit the writer and the publishers' political agenda and frequently contradicted the original accounts delivered by reporters. This was done almost ritually in national news media when, as in the case of the DNC of 1968, the authorities and powerful figures in government and the political parties were in danger of being held responsible.

The tweaking and resequencing of facts often took place in the up-front paragraphs, in a way that created a sort of look-alike scene, but with entirely different implications of motivation and responsibility. You could, with frustrated wonderment, read or view or listen to accounts of events in which you had participated or that you had observed and burst out impulsively in the very act of reading or viewing, "That's not what happened at all!"

For instance, if the first lines of reports about a confrontation between police and protestors state that protestors threw missiles at the police, or that the day of trial was disrupted by defendant demonstrations, without giving the sequence of events that led up to, or motivated, these actions, the reader will become predisposed to reject more complete reports telling what the writer saw happen.

Many of the basic principles of witness/participant storytelling and commentary are, in theory at least, basic principles of the rules of evidence. What did you see? What did you hear? And as the rules allow, What did you understand?

Protest events became matters fought over in the courts. Whose "facts" could be made to stick persuasively in jurors' minds? Which came first, the beer can thrown or the police club administered? For many Americans, this was—and still is—an issue of fairness, crucial to public understanding and the forming of policy. That readers may find the political understanding of the resequenced reports, which point toward blame, easiest to assimilate does not mean readers are incapable of absorbing a more true, more complex drama that could lead to a new understanding and, possibly, new policies. This was demonstrated during many of the 1970s trials of activists, when juries, enabled by their situation to hear strong presentations of fact, decided to acquit defendants who had effectively been convicted by most of the news media. Very few of those many trials resulted in convictions.

I went into the moments of story with adrenalin-driven clarity of sight, hearing, and feeling, looking to all sides at what people were doing, reacting intuitively while trying to comprehend an overall movement, with dread in the belly that shooting to kill was about to happen, with sudden rage, but determined to follow the story wherever it was going, and no one was going to knock me out of it.

As a participant/witness on the streets of Chicago I heard people again and again ask police why they were doing what they were doing, and heard the cops say again and again: "I've got my orders, buddy!" NBC reporter, Tom Brokaw, stepped out of his hotel and saw a cop deal with a U.S. Postal Service mailman who was intent on carrying out the postal service's charge to deliver the mail no matter what, which meant entering the hotel. The cop threw the mailman face down to the sidewalk and cuffed his hands behind him. When Brokaw asked the cop why he did that, the cop gave exactly the same phrasing: "I've got my orders!" And,

306 NO ONE WAS KILLED

because I saw the police move on orders, I didn't have to accept Rights in Conflict's (the Walker Report) concept of "a police riot" in which the authorities were decidedly exempted from responsibility. I had been interviewed by a Walker Report investigator and, to my mind, the Report writers did, indeed, draw upon and scramble the sequence of accounts taken from my Evergreen Review story and my testimony. Many protesters and journalists and political people felt "the police riot" was at least "half a loaf." The "police riot" became a preferred solution and sidetracked further examination. The very term "police riot" suggested that the cops were somehow disengaged from local and federal authorities and were even disobeying their own commanders for five days and nights—a version of events insulting to the cops. (See the footnote on page 290.)

From the beginning and, increasingly, day by day, night by night, the DNC of 1968 became in the streets and parks of Chicago, in hotel hallways, and in the aisles and halls of the Amphitheatre, a vast demonstration of Antonin Artaud's concept of theater in which the distance between audience and stage, audience and story, dissolves and the spectators are "engulfed" by events and the blood streaking down faces is real. How else can we understand events driven by a powerful sense of inevitability, with the charged feelings of a national drama engaged, yet with the participants exercising their choice to be there and acting and reacting to the demands they felt in the moment?

It is likely the DNC of 1968 cannot be repeated, no matter how much the authorities and the establishment of society and political parties may fear it and take extreme measures to prevent what their worst fears conceive, or how much protest movements may, if frustrated and backed into a corner, wish to promote it. A few months after the August convention the *New York Times* editorialized that the country had come to "the brink of civil war." It was as if the blind powers of history declared those five days and nights in the city of Chicago, in the heart of the country, to be a new kind of theater for civil war.

John Schultz
Chicago, August 28, 2008

acknowledgements

The material of this book results from what I saw and thought about Convention Week in Chicago. For that, I am responsible. But I am happy to acknowledge the help of several people for their responsiveness in all my various activities that finally resulted in this book: to Dennis Cunningham, Paul Sills, Reverend Herb Davis, Reverend Bruce Young and Reverend James A. Shiflett, fellow Lincoln Park residents; to Tom Erhardt, who said in a Lincoln Park bar, "Why don't we get history out of jail?"; to the members of the "Monday night" group that I directed in a loose workshop in which a few participants in Convention Week confrontations tried to reconstruct what had happened to them and to understand the experience, especially to Al Melton, Howard and Jean Alan, and Elizabeth Eddy; and to Betty Shiflett, Mona Cunningham, and Al Melton for incidents they told about that I have re-told in the "Sunday" section; and to Reverend Bruce Young for his information about "Monday" and "Tuesday"; to Herman Kogan; to Jon Wagner; to Nick Zdunich; to the Lo Guidice Gallery for its help in finding photographs; to Pat Meehan; to my wife, Anne Schultz; to *Evergreen Review*, in which some portions of the book first appeared in different form (November 1968 issue), and particularly, to Fred Jordan, Managing Editor of *Evergreen Review*; and finally to my editor, Paul Carroll.